Subject and Predicate

Pack It Up!

The LaRose family is taking a trip through the United States, starting from their home in Seattle, Washington. Today, Mom, Dad, Judi, and Peter are packing up their minivan, the Blue Torpedo.

A sentence is a group of words that tells a complete thought. A sentence has a **subject** and a **predicate**. The subject names someone or something. The predicate tells what the subject does.
This is a sentence: *Dogs bark.*

If a group of words lacks either a subject or a predicate, it is not a sentence.
Chases the squirrels has no subject. It is not a sentence.

Read the groups of words.
Write **sentence** or **not a sentence** after each item.

1. Our tent is blue and red. _sentence_

2. My toothpaste and washcloth. _not a sentence_

3. We need bathing suits and sandals. _sentence_

4. Peter has his camera. _not a sentence_

5. Mom's sunglasses. _not a sentence_

6. Putting gas in the minivan. _not a sentence_

7. Have to get up early in the morning. _not a sentence_

8. The juice and crackers are in the cooler. _not a sentence_

9. Judi packs her suitcase. _sentence_

10. In the back with the sleeping bags. _not a sentence_

1

Buoyancy and Density

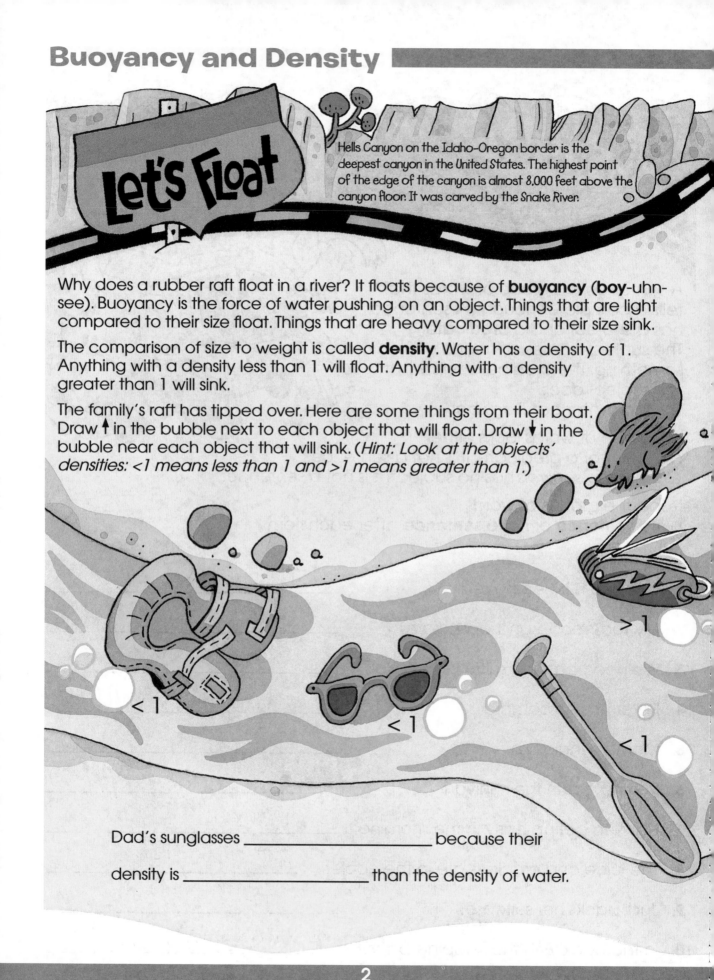

Let's Float

Hells Canyon on the Idaho-Oregon border is the deepest canyon in the United States. The highest point of the edge of the canyon is almost 8,000 feet above the canyon floor. It was carved by the Snake River.

Why does a rubber raft float in a river? It floats because of **buoyancy** (**boy**-uhn-see). Buoyancy is the force of water pushing on an object. Things that are light compared to their size float. Things that are heavy compared to their size sink.

The comparison of size to weight is called **density**. Water has a density of 1. Anything with a density less than 1 will float. Anything with a density greater than 1 will sink.

The family's raft has tipped over. Here are some things from their boat. Draw ↑ in the bubble next to each object that will float. Draw ↓ in the bubble near each object that will sink. (*Hint: Look at the objects' densities: <1 means less than 1 and >1 means greater than 1.*)

>1

<1

<1

<1

Dad's sunglasses _____ because their

density is _____ than the density of water.

> 1

< 1

< 1

< 1

Go For It

Plan a rafting trip. Draw a map of a river and show your route. Put in people, animals, trees, and other things you might see.

Know What?

Daredevil rider Evel Knievel tried to jump the Snake River Canyon on a rocket-powered motorcycle in 1974. He did not make it to the other side. His parachute opened too early, and he floated safely to the ground.

©School Zone Publishing Company 06320

Buoyancy and Density

Compare Numbers/Operational Symbols

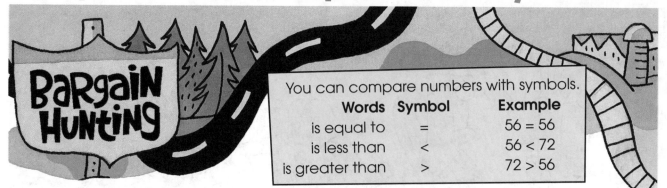

You can compare numbers with symbols.

Words	Symbol	Example
is equal to	=	56 = 56
is less than	<	56 < 72
is greater than	>	72 > 56

To compare whole numbers, look at the same-place digits in each number, starting on the left.

Example: 56   72   50 is less than 70.
                            56 is less than 72.
          more tens   56 < 72

The LaRose family forgot to pack some things for the trip. They are shopping for those things in Spokane. Look at the ads for the two stores. Compare the prices.

Write the prices on the lines. Write <, =, or > in the circles.

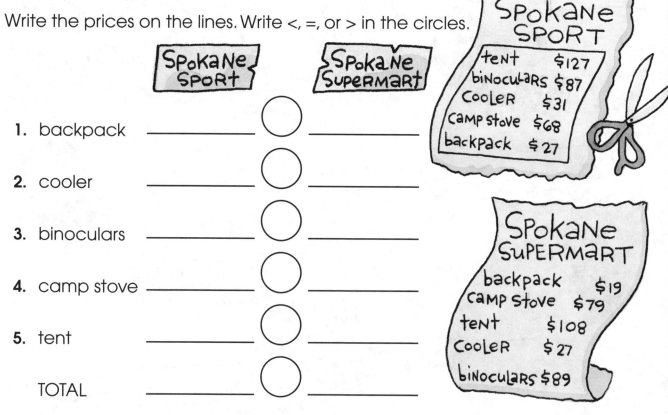

1. backpack

2. cooler

3. binoculars

4. camp stove

5. tent

TOTAL

Spokane SPORT
tent $127
binoculars $87
cooler $31
camp stove $68
backpack $27

Spokane SUPERMART
backpack $19
camp stove $79
tent $108
cooler $27
binoculars $89

6. The LaRose family wants to go to only one store. Which one should they choose to save money?

_____

7. How much will they save? _____

Compare Numbers/Operational Symbols   ©School Zone Publishing Company 06320

Descriptive and Persuasive Sentences

Natural Treasures

Yellowstone National Park in Wyoming is the world's first national park. It is most famous for its **geysers**, spouts of hot water. Old Faithful shoots boiling water over 100 feet into the air about 20 times a day.

Many national parks are beautiful wilderness areas. Others are important historical places. National parks are protected from farming, mining, and other activities that might damage them.

Think about a place you would like to protect. It can be any place that's important to you—a park, a patch of woods, a building, or even a vacant lot.

What and where is your place? _____

_____

Describe it. _____

_____

_____

_____

_____

Why do you want to protect the place? Give at least three reasons.

_____

_____

_____

_____

_____

_____

5

Dakota Addition

In South Dakota, farms and ranches cover much of the land. There are lots of corn, soybean, and wheat fields and huge herds of cattle.

The LaRose family is visiting South Dakota's best-known attraction.

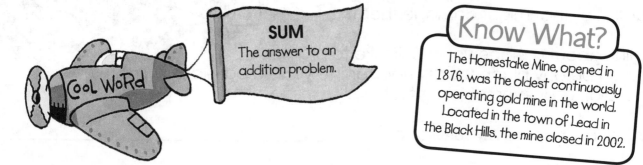

Cool Word

SUM
The answer to an addition problem.

Know What?
The Homestake Mine, opened in 1876, was the oldest continuously operating gold mine in the world. Located in the town of Lead in the Black Hills, the mine closed in 2002.

Write the sums. Then write the letter next to each sum to decode the message.

```
   33        25        99        49        10
 +  4      + 16         2         5        15
                      +  3      + 60      + 11
   O         U         T         S         R


   34        72        10        12
   28         9         0        25
 + 17       + 8       +  7      + 29
   E         N         H         M
```

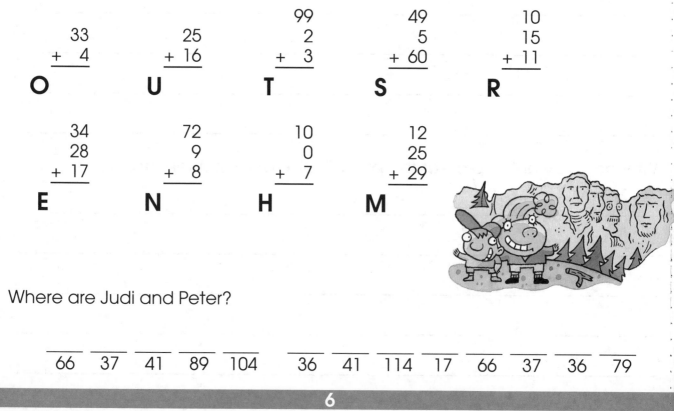

Where are Judi and Peter?

| 66 | 37 | 41 | 89 | 104 | | 36 | 41 | 114 | 17 | 66 | 37 | 36 | 79 |

Parts of Speech

The Mall of America in Bloomington, Minnesota, is one of the biggest shopping malls in the world. It has more than 500 stores, an indoor amusement park, and an aquarium complete with sharks.

Parts of speech are words that do jobs in sentences. Nouns name people, places, or things. Verbs tell what nouns do. Adjectives tell more about nouns, and adverbs describe verbs and adjectives. Adverbs often end in *-ly*.

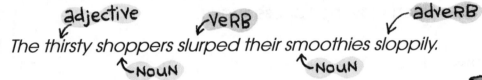

The thirsty shoppers slurped their smoothies sloppily.

adjective — VERB — adverb
NOUN — NOUN

Read the paragraph. Identify the part of speech for each underlined word. Write the verbs in Mom's shopping bag, the adjectives in Dad's, the adverbs in Judi's, and the nouns in Peter's.

Nickelodeon Universe in the Mall of America is a <u>big</u> theme <u>park</u>. Though it is indoors, the park looks like it is outdoors. The <u>sun</u> <u>shines</u> <u>brightly</u> through skylights. Many <u>tall</u> <u>trees</u> and plants <u>grow</u> in the park. Sometimes, insects <u>attack</u> these plants. So gardeners have let <u>ladybugs</u> loose in the park. The hungry ladybugs <u>quickly</u> <u>gobble</u> up the <u>harmful</u> insects.

Verbs

Nouns

Adjectives

Adverbs

Subtraction Facts

Lake Superior is the world's largest freshwater lake in terms of surface area. It is the largest, deepest, and cleanest of the five Great Lakes that share part of the border between the United States and Canada.

The LaRose family is traveling around Lake Superior. Find each difference, and write it in the blank. Then write the differences next to the cities near Lake Superior. You will see which way the LaRoses went.

1. 27 – 18 = _____ Ironwood

2. 136 – 119 = _____ Ashland

3. 285 – 283 = _____ Sault Ste. Marie (U.S.)

4. 276 – 190 = _____ Thunder Bay

5. 179 – 21 = _____ Nipigon

6. 158 – 39 = _____ Sault Ste. Marie (Canada)

7. 81 – 27 = _____ Superior

8. 91 – 83 = _____ Copper Harbor

9. 52 – 49 = _____ Marquette

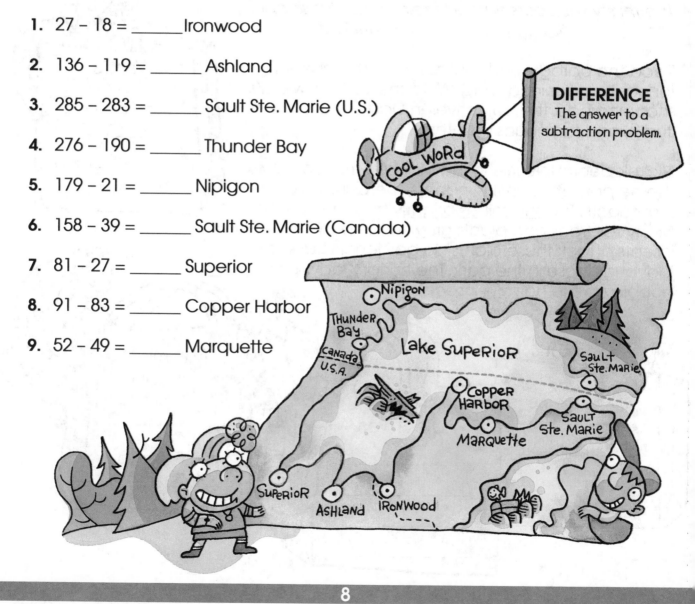

DIFFERENCE
The answer to a subtraction problem.

Cool Word

8

Food Groups

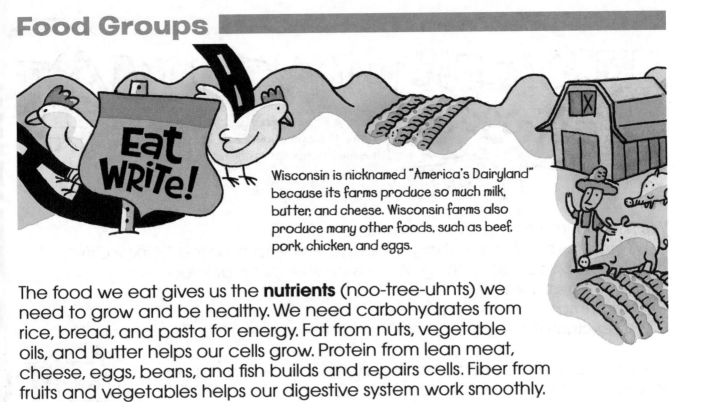

Eat WRiTe!

Wisconsin is nicknamed "America's Dairyland" because its farms produce so much milk, butter, and cheese. Wisconsin farms also produce many other foods, such as beef, pork, chicken, and eggs.

The food we eat gives us the **nutrients** (noo-tree-uhnts) we need to grow and be healthy. We need carbohydrates from rice, bread, and pasta for energy. Fat from nuts, vegetable oils, and butter helps our cells grow. Protein from lean meat, cheese, eggs, beans, and fish builds and repairs cells. Fiber from fruits and vegetables helps our digestive system work smoothly.

Sit down to a yummy picnic of healthful foods from a Wisconsin farm. For each of the foods pictured, write whether it contains mainly carbohydrates, fat, protein, or fiber.

1. _____ 2. _____ 3. _____

4. _____ 5. _____ 6. _____

Types of Sentences

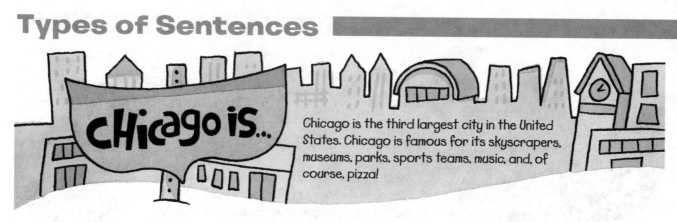

Chicago is the third largest city in the United States. Chicago is famous for its skyscrapers, museums, parks, sports teams, music, and, of course, pizza!

We use four main types of sentences.

A **statement** tells something. *Chicago's nickname is the "Windy City."*

A **question** asks something. *What is on the menu at your favorite restaurant?*

A **command** gives an order. *Don't forget to buy tickets.*

An **exclamation** expresses a strong feeling. *Everything is expensive!*

Identify the sentences in the picture. Write **s** in the box if the sentence is a statement. Write **q** if the sentence is a question. Write **c** if the sentence is a command. Write **e** if the sentence is an exclamation.

Types of Sentences

Common and Proper Nouns

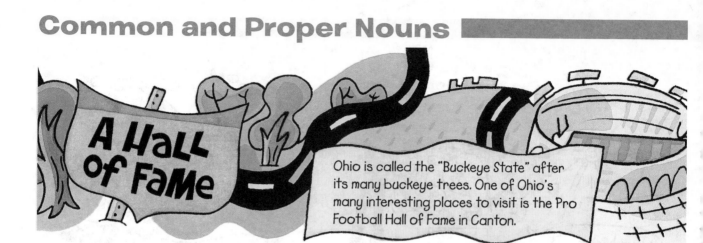

A **common noun** names any person, place, or thing. A **proper noun** names a particular person, place, or thing. Proper nouns begin with capital letters.

Common Nouns	Proper Nouns
person	Judi
month	April
place	Beech Street
state	Ohio

The paragraph below has several mistakes. Draw this mark ≡ under letters that should be capitalized. Draw this mark ╱ through letters that should not be capitalized. *Hint: remember that sentences begin with capital letters.*

Example: judi and Peter went to the football Game.

The Stars of football shine at the Pro Football

Hall of Fame in canton, ohio. the Hall of Fame

opened on september 7, 1963. Every year,

the league names a few of its Best players

to the Hall of Fame. there, visitors can See

pictures of these players, their Uniforms,

and their equipment.

Map and Map Key

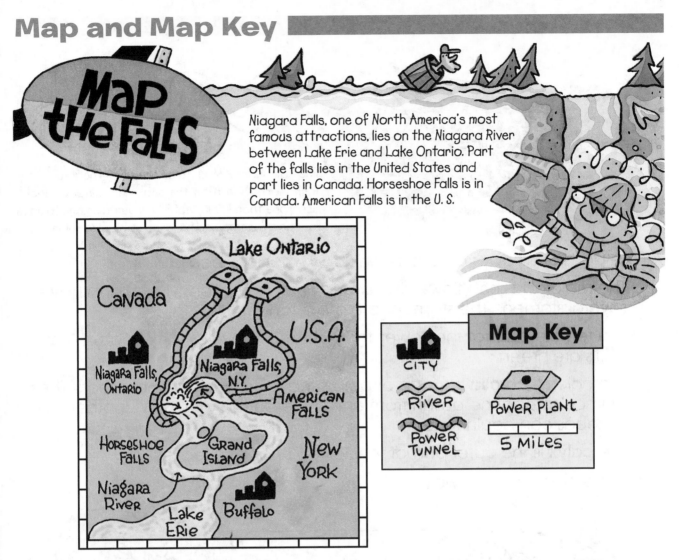

Map the Falls

Niagara Falls, one of North America's most famous attractions, lies on the Niagara River between Lake Erie and Lake Ontario. Part of the falls lies in the United States and part lies in Canada. Horseshoe Falls is in Canada. American Falls is in the U.S.

Map Key
- CITY
- RIVER
- POWER TUNNEL
- POWER PLANT
- 5 MILES

A map is a special kind of picture. Maps give information about an area using lines, colors, shapes, and other symbols. These symbols show where roads, cities, rivers, lakes, and many other things are located. The part of a map that tells what the symbols mean is called the **key** or **legend**.

Use the map and key to answer the questions.

1. How many power plants are shown on the map? _____

2. What is the name of the big island? _____

3. About how many miles wide is it? _____

4. What does this symbol mean? _____

5. How many lakes are shown on the map? _____

6. What are their names? _____

©School Zone Publishing Company 06320

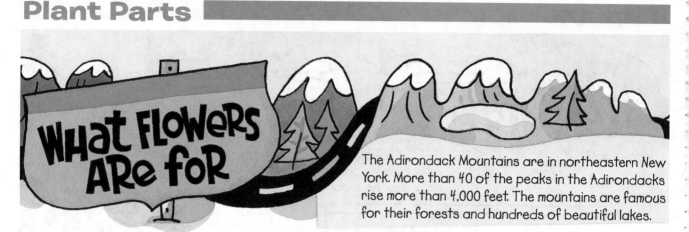

The Adirondack Mountains are in northeastern New York. More than 40 of the peaks in the Adirondacks rise more than 4,000 feet. The mountains are famous for their forests and hundreds of beautiful lakes.

All the parts of a flower do a different job in making seeds.

- The male parts of a flower, the **stamens**, make pollen. Most plants have several stamens. The stamens are often tan.

- The female parts of the flower, the **pistil**, make ovules (**ohv**-yools). Most pistils are green.

- The colorful **corolla** is made of petals that attract birds and insects. These animals spread the pollen from one flower to the ovules of another flower so seeds can begin to form.

- The **calyx** is the outer part of the flower. It has little leaves.

Label the parts of the flower.

Why do most plants need seeds?

_____

_____

Timeline

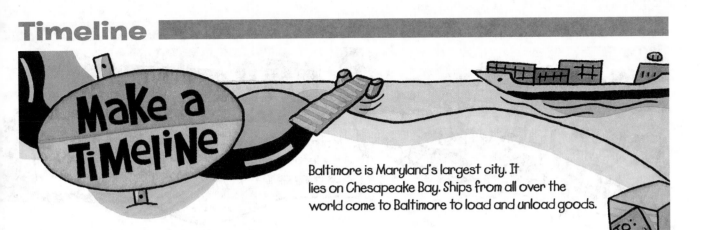

Baltimore is Maryland's largest city. It lies on Chesapeake Bay. Ships from all over the world come to Baltimore to load and unload goods.

A timeline is one good way to show the order of events.

Use the information in the paragraph below to fill in the blanks in this timeline.

The Port of Baltimore was founded in 1706. In 1729, Baltimore Town was founded. Eighty-five years later, Francis Scott Key wrote "The Star-Spangled Banner" after he watched the British attack the city. Most of the downtown area of Baltimore burned to the ground in the Great Baltimore Fire of 1904. Eighty-eight years after that, the Baltimore Orioles baseball team got a new stadium.

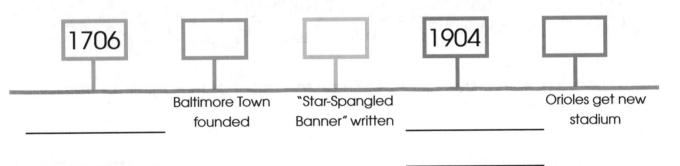

| 1706 | | | 1904 | |

| _____ | Baltimore Town founded | "Star-Spangled Banner" written | _____ | Orioles get new stadium |

Comparative Relationships

New York, New York

More than 8,000,000 people live in New York City, the largest city in the United States. That's twice as many as in the next largest city!

There are many tall buildings in New York City.

Number the buildings from 1 to 4 to show the order of the buildings from tallest to shortest. (1 = tallest)

_____ Chrysler Building, 1,046 feet

_____ Citigroup Center, 915 feet

_____ Empire State Building, 1,250 feet

_____ GE Building, 850 feet

How much taller is the tallest building than the shortest building?

_____

_____

New York City is made up of five parts called **boroughs**: the Bronx, Brooklyn, Manhattan, Queens, and Staten Island. Many bridges and tunnels connect the boroughs.

Bridge	Connects
Brooklyn	Manhattan and Brooklyn
George Washington	Manhattan and New Jersey
Queensboro	Manhattan and Queens
Verrazano-Narrows	Staten Island and Brooklyn
Williamsburg	Manhattan and Brooklyn

Write the name or names of the bridge or bridges.

1. Which bridges connect Brooklyn and Manhattan?

   _____

2. Which bridge connects Staten Island and Brooklyn?

   _____

3. Which bridge connects Queens and Manhattan?

   _____

4. Which bridge connects Manhattan and New Jersey?

   _____

17

Comparative Relationships

Antonyms, Synonyms, and Homophones

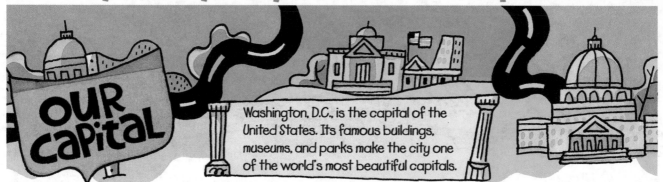

Washington, D.C., is the capital of the United States. Its famous buildings, museums, and parks make the city one of the world's most beautiful capitals.

Words that have opposite meanings are called **antonyms**. Words that have about the same meaning are called **synonyms**. Words that sound alike but have different spellings and meanings are called **homophones**.

Look at the words in the picture. On the line near each word pair, write *antonyms*, *synonyms*, or *homophones*.

1. _____

2. _____

3. _____

4. _____

Antonyms, Synonyms, and Homophones   ©School Zone Publishing Company 06320

5. _____

6. _____

7. _____

8. _____

9. _____

10. _____

Antonyms, Synonyms, and Homophones

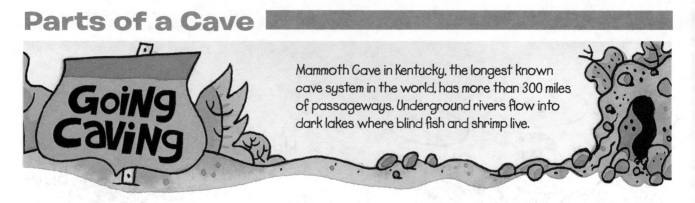

GOING CAVING

Mammoth Cave in Kentucky, the longest known cave system in the world, has more than 300 miles of passageways. Underground rivers flow into dark lakes where blind fish and shrimp live.

Caves are formed when water drips through the earth and eats away a hollow in the rock underground. When the water flows away, a cave remains. Here are some parts of a cave:

- **chamber**—a large "room" in a cave
- **stalagmite**—a pointy pillar that rises from the cave's floor
- **stalactite**—a pointy "icicle" that hangs from the cave's ceiling
- **column**—a pillar formed when a stalactite and stalagmite join

Write the names of the cave parts on the lines.

Go For It

Use modeling clay of various colors and a cardboard box to build a model of a cave. Make chambers, stalagmites, stalactites, and sinkholes.

Ordered Pairs

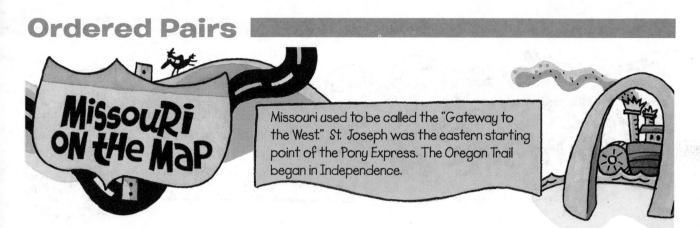

Missouri used to be called the "Gateway to the West." St. Joseph was the eastern starting point of the Pony Express. The Oregon Trail began in Independence.

Judi and Peter are using ordered pairs to find Springfield on the map. First they find the 4, and then they go up to B. Springfield is at (4,B).

Write the city for each ordered pair.

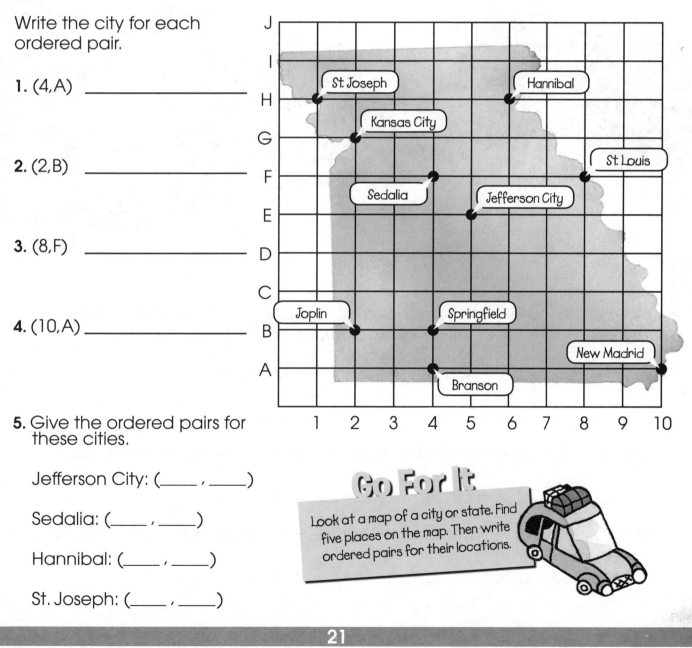

1. (4,A) _____

2. (2,B) _____

3. (8,F) _____

4. (10,A) _____

5. Give the ordered pairs for these cities.

Jefferson City: (_____ , _____)

Sedalia: (_____ , _____)

Hannibal: (_____ , _____)

St. Joseph: (_____ , _____)

Go For It

Look at a map of a city or state. Find five places on the map. Then write ordered pairs for their locations.

Ordered Pairs

Equations

The Great Smoky Mountains National Park covers more than 520,000 acres and is about evenly divided between Tennessee and North Carolina.

The LaRoses are planning a route from Memphis to the Great Smoky Mountains National Park. The park has entrances at Gatlinburg, Tennessee and Cherokee, North Carolina.

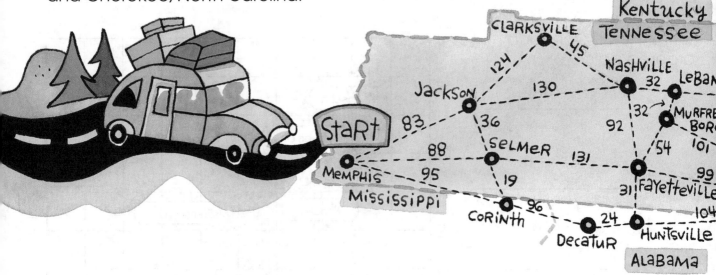

Follow each route from Memphis to the park. Write the number of miles between each pair of cities. Then calculate the total number of miles.

Memphis → Jackson → Nashville → Lebanon → Knoxville → Gatlinburg

_____ + _____ + _____ + _____ + _____ = _____

Memphis → Selmer → Fayetteville → Chattanooga → Cleveland → Cherokee

_____ + _____ + _____ + _____ + _____ = _____

Memphis → Selmer → Fayetteville → Nashville → Lebanon → Knoxville → Gatlinburg

_____ + _____ + _____ + _____ + _____ + _____ = _____

22

Find one way to get from Memphis to the park going through Murfreesboro and traveling only in Tennessee. Name the cities through which you would travel, and calculate the total number of miles.

_____

_____

Find a way to get from Memphis to the park traveling through more than two states. Name the cities through which you would travel, and calculate the total number of miles.

_____

_____

Who's there?
Shelby.
Shelby who?
Shelby comin' around the mountain when she comes...

Equations

Irregular Verbs

Go For It

You can play Go Fish with irregular verbs. Use index cards to make your own deck. Write 26 irregular verbs and their past tense forms on separate cards. Match each verb with its past tense form to play.

Dahlonega, Georgia, is located on top of the largest gold deposits found east of the Mississippi River. Visitors can tour old gold mines and rent equipment to search for gold. They get to keep all the gold they find!

The past tense of most verbs is made by adding the letters -ed to the present tense of the verb. But irregular verbs break that rule. How do you learn irregular verbs? You memorize them.

The LaRose family is panning for gold. On each nugget, write the past tense of the verb.

Dad

Peter

FIND

LOOK

THINK

DRINK

SWING

BRING

PECK

ROW

BITE

RUN

WIN

COME

Mom

Judi

Now that you have written all the past tenses, color the nuggets with irregular verbs yellow.

Which person has the most gold? _____

Irregular Verbs

©School Zone Publishing Company 06320

Space Exploration Vocabulary

EXPLORING Space

At the Kennedy Space Center in Florida, you can learn all about the space program. You can go on a simulated ride into space, look at rockets, see movies on a screen that's five stories tall, and even watch a real space shuttle launch.

Scientists learn about space by sending space probes to fly through space or land on planets. Space probes send information back to Earth. Rovers ride around on the surface of a planet. Satellites travel around and around, or **orbit**, Earth. They are used for communication, navigation, weather forecasting, scientific research, and even spying. People ride into space on a space shuttle, where they do experiments. A space station **orbits** Earth. Astronauts may live on a space station for months at a time.

Fill in the blanks with space terms. Then write the numbered letters in the correct boxes below to discover the mystery word.

1. A space ____ ____ ____ ____ ____ may land on a planet.
                1

2. A ____ ____ ____ ____ ____ ____ ____ ____ ____ travels around Earth.
                    2

3. Astronauts can live on a space ____ ____ ____ ____ ____ ____ ____ .
                                     3   4

4. Astronauts ride into space and back on a

    space ____ ____ ____ ____ ____ ____ .
              5

5. To ____ ____ ____ ____ ____ means to travel around a planet.
                       6

6. A ____ ____ ____ ____ ____ can ride around on a planet's surface.
             7   8

  5   4   6   7   8   1   3   2

25

Logical Reasoning

Tourists love to visit Florida's many animal parks, including SeaWorld, Discovery Cove, Disney's Animal Kingdom, Busch Gardens, Lion Country Safari, and Jungle Island.

Use logic to solve these word problems about animals the LaRoses see in Florida. Read the clues. Then fill in the chart to solve the problems. Here is an example.

Peter, Judi, and Dad are watching **different** animals. Who is watching each animal?

Dad is not watching the panther.

	panther	pelican	deer
Judi			
Peter			
Dad	No		

Judi is not watching the panther either.

Peter must be watching the panther.

	panther	pelican	deer
Judi	No		
Peter	Yes		
Dad	No		

Dad is not watching the pelican.
Dad must be watching the deer.
Judi must be watching the pelican.

	panther	pelican	deer
Judi	No	Yes	No
Peter	Yes	No	No
Dad	No	No	Yes

1. Write the animal each person is watching.

Judi _____   Peter _____   Dad _____

Go For It

Make up a logic problem. Challenge a friend to solve your logic problem.

Know What?

Marineland of Florida is known as the world's first oceanarium. It was built in 1937 on Florida's Atlantic coast south of St. Augustine.

Dad, Mom, Judi, and Peter each have a **different** favorite Florida animal. Which animal is each person's favorite? Fill in the chart completely to find out.

Judi's favorite animal is not the alligator.

Judi's favorite animal is not the manatee.

Dad's favorite animal is not the alligator or the anhinga.

Judi's favorite animal is not the anhinga.

Peter's favorite animal is not the anhinga.

	turtle	alligator	manatee	anhinga
Judi				
Dad				
Peter				
Mom				

2. Write each person's favorite animal.

Judi _____   Dad _____

Peter _____   Mom _____

Logical Reasoning

Definite and Indefinite Articles

A-Mazing Everglades

The Everglades are wetlands located at the southern tip of Florida. The area is home to unusual plants, such as a kind of tall grass called sawgrass, and animals, including panthers, manatees, alligators, and anhingas.

The words *a, an,* and *the* are special adjectives called **articles**. *A* and *an* are used before nouns that aren't specific. For example, **a** book. It could be any book. *A* comes before nouns that begin with a consonant sound. *An* is used before nouns that begin with a vowel sound. *The* refers to a specific object and is used both before nouns that name one and nouns that name more than one. For example, **the** book. It refers to a specific book.

Help Judi and Peter find their way out of the Everglades maze. If you run into a picture that shows a noun that goes with *an*, your path is blocked. But if you run into a picture of a noun that goes with *a*, you can continue.

Definite and Indefinite Articles

Who's there?
Everglade.
Everglade who?
Am I Everglade to see you!

CiViL RiGHTS

Montgomery, the capital of Alabama, was the birthplace of the African-American Civil Rights Movement. Martin Luther King, Jr., a leader of the movement, was the minister of Montgomery's Dexter Avenue Baptist Church.

The right of all Americans to be treated equally and fairly is protected by the United States Constitution. This right is one of what we call **civil rights**. However, African Americans have not always enjoyed the same civil rights as white Americans. For example, in the past, some cities and states did not allow African Americans to sit in the front rows of buses. In 1955, Rosa Parks, a black woman in Montgomery, refused to give up her seat on a bus to make room for a white passenger. She was arrested, and many black people protested by boycotting (refusing to use) the city's bus system. Martin Luther King, Jr., led the boycott. After a year, the United States Supreme Court declared Montgomery's law to be unconstitutional because it did not support African Americans' civil rights.

Answer the questions.

1. What is the name given to rights protected by law?

   _____

2. How did Rosa Parks start the Montgomery bus boycott?

   _____

   _____

3. What is the word that means "refuse to use"?

   _____

4. Imagine riding on the bus with Rosa Parks that day in 1955.

   Describe your thoughts and feelings.

   _____

   _____

Punctuation: Comma

New Orleans is an old city near the mouth of the Mississippi River. People visit New Orleans to enjoy its charming architecture, jazz music, delicious food, and Mardi Gras celebrations.

Commas separate the parts of a sentence and help make the meaning clear. Commas are used in the following ways:

- to separate three or more items in a list: *We ate gumbo, shrimp, and hush puppies.*
- between the day and the year in a date: *February 16, 2016*
- between the city and state or city and country: *New Orleans, Louisiana, is on the Mississippi.*
- when connecting two complete sentences into one sentence using *and, or, for, nor, but, so,* or *yet*: We went to the parade, and we saw colorful dancers.

Add commas where they belong in the sentences.

1. Mardi Gras is an ancient festival but people still enjoy it.

2. New Orleans Louisiana has a big Mardi Gras celebration.

3. People celebrate with food music parties and parades.

4. Musicians play and colorful floats roll down the street.

5. Riders on the floats throw coins necklaces and toys.

6. The LaRose family met some people from Berlin Germany at Mardi Gras.

7. The people from Berlin spoke English so the two families enjoyed the parade together.

8. Then they went to a restaurant where they ate crayfish gumbo and jambalaya.

31

Context Clues

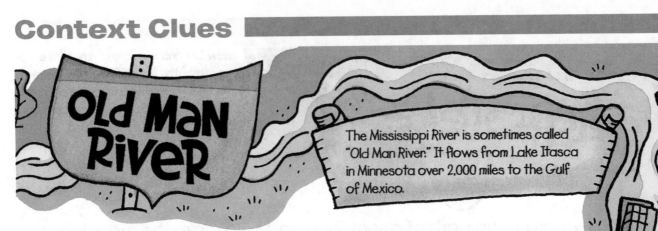

OLD MAN RIVER

The Mississippi River is sometimes called "Old Man River." It flows from Lake Itasca in Minnesota over 2,000 miles to the Gulf of Mexico.

What should you do when you're reading and come across words you don't understand? One thing you can do is keep reading. The words around the unknown word, or the **context**, can help you. You can also get meaning clues from illustrations.

Read the paragraph and figure out what the underlined words mean. Then draw a line to match each word to its meaning.

The Mississippi River grows as it travels south! <u>Tributaries</u>, such as the Arkansas River, just keep adding to its amount of water. There, the river twists and winds around in loops, forming <u>oxbow lakes</u>. The river also <u>deposits</u> soil on the shore to create natural <u>levees</u>. The southern Mississippi River is especially important for shipping <u>cargo</u>. <u>Agricultural</u> products, such as corn and wheat, travel on <u>barges</u> pushed by tugboats.

1. tributary   goods moved by boat, airplane, or vehicle

2. oxbow lake   to dump or place

3. deposit   a high mound along the bank of a river

4. levee   a horseshoe-shaped body of water

5. cargo   a large, flat boat

6. agricultural   a smaller river that flows into a larger one

7. barge   made or grown on a farm

Elapsed Time

Texas Time

El Paso is in the far western part of Texas. It's so far west that it's in a different time zone from most other Texas cities!

To find what time it will be in the future, add hours or minutes.

The time is 7:25.

In 2 hours, it will be 9:25.

In 10 minutes it will be 9:35.

What time will it be in 3 hours?

1. _____   2. _____   3. _____

What time will it be in 20 minutes?

4. _____   5. _____   6. _____

What time will it be

in 4 hours?   in 25 minutes?   in 40 minutes?

7. _____   8. _____   9. _____

Elapsed Time

Possessive Nouns

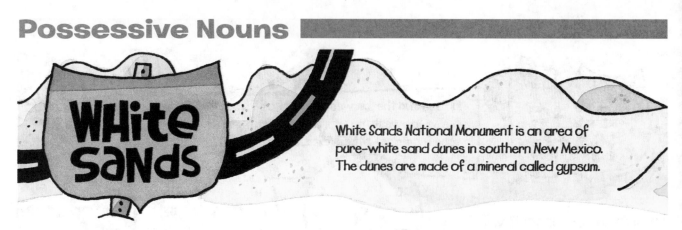

White Sands National Monument is an area of pure-white sand dunes in southern New Mexico. The dunes are made of a mineral called gypsum.

A possessive noun shows that a person or thing owns something. Add *'s* to most singular nouns to show possession: *dog's bowl, Judi's hat.* Add *'* to most plural nouns to show possession: *parents' maps, dunes' shapes.*

Write a sentence to describe each scene from the LaRose family's day at White Sands. Use the possessive form of a noun in each sentence.

1.

2.

3.

4.

Shapes and Symmetry

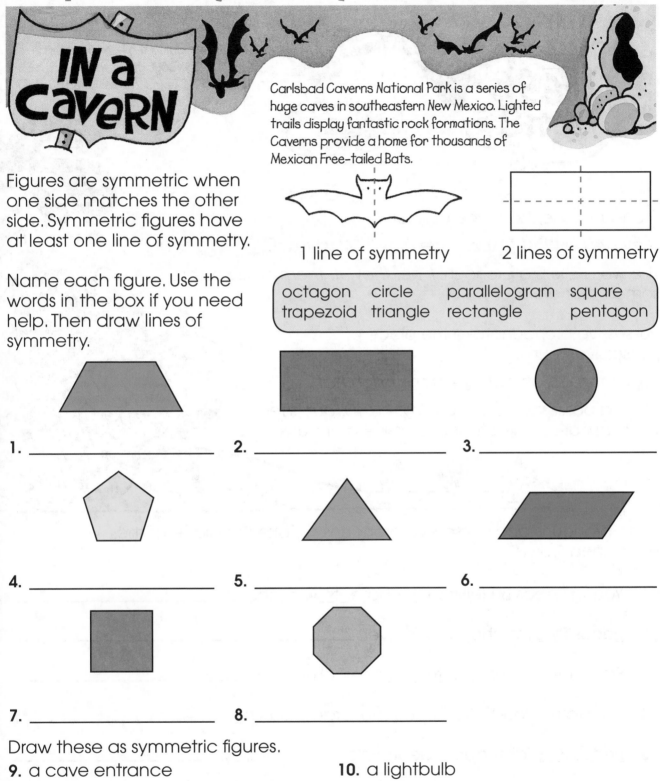

IN a CAVERN

Carlsbad Caverns National Park is a series of huge caves in southeastern New Mexico. Lighted trails display fantastic rock formations. The Caverns provide a home for thousands of Mexican Free-tailed Bats.

Figures are symmetric when one side matches the other side. Symmetric figures have at least one line of symmetry.

1 line of symmetry   2 lines of symmetry

Name each figure. Use the words in the box if you need help. Then draw lines of symmetry.

| octagon | circle | parallelogram | square |
| trapezoid | triangle | rectangle | pentagon |

1. _____

2. _____

3. _____

4. _____

5. _____

6. _____

7. _____

8. _____

Draw these as symmetric figures.

9. a cave entrance

10. a lightbulb

Pronouns and Possessive Pronouns

West Texas is a region of dry, treeless plains and rugged mountains. It is one of the most important oil-drilling areas in the U. S. Cowboys drove their herds of cattle from Texas to be shipped by rail to markets in the East.

Pronouns take the place of nouns.

Suzy lives in West Texas.   *She* lives in West Texas.

The word *she* is a pronoun. *I, he, they, it, them*, and *you* are some other pronouns.

Possessive pronouns take the place of possessive nouns.

Suzy's ten-gallon hat   *her* ten-gallon hat

Her is a possessive pronoun. *My, his, its, our, their,* and *your* are some other possessive pronouns.

Write pronouns and possessive pronouns to take the place of the underlined words.

1. Young Pecos Bill fell from <u>his parents'</u> wagon. _____

2. <u>Pecos Bill's</u> life changed forever. _____

3. From then on, he was <u>the coyotes'</u> child. _____

4. The storm cloud's flood dug <u>the Grand Canyon</u>. _____

5. <u>Pecos Bill's</u> fall made a dent called Death Valley. _____

6. <u>Pecos Bill's sweetheart</u> was Slue-Foot Sue. _____

7. <u>Sue's</u> adventures were astonishing, too. _____

8. <u>Mary's</u> favorite stories are tall tales. _____

Fact and Opinion

San Francisco's many attractions include Golden Gate Park, Chinatown, and Fisherman's Wharf. Visitors enjoy views of twinkling ocean waters from atop tall hills. They love the cable cars that chug up and down steep, narrow streets.

When we read, we often come across statements that are facts. Facts can be proved: *San Francisco is in California*.

We also read opinions: *San Francisco is the most beautiful city in California*. Opinions can't be proved.

Tour the city with the LaRose family. They'll hear some information from the tour guide. Write *f* under those that are facts. Write *o* under the statements that are opinions. Write *f + o* under those that contain facts and opinions.

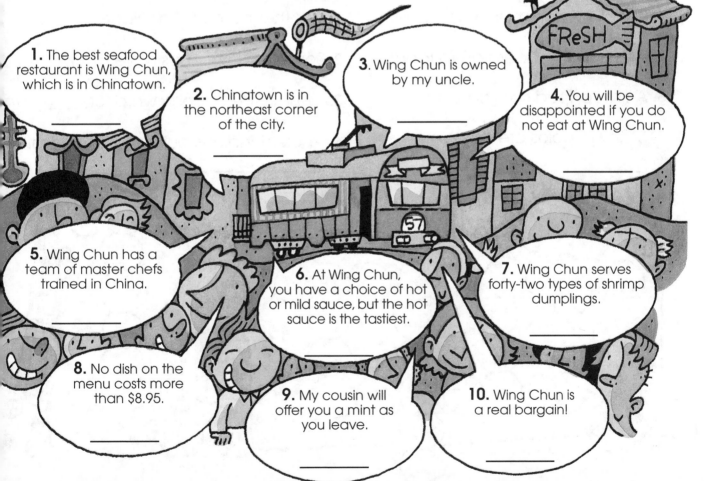

1. The best seafood restaurant is Wing Chun, which is in Chinatown.

_____

2. Chinatown is in the northeast corner of the city.

_____

3. Wing Chun is owned by my uncle.

_____

4. You will be disappointed if you do not eat at Wing Chun.

_____

5. Wing Chun has a team of master chefs trained in China.

_____

6. At Wing Chun, you have a choice of hot or mild sauce, but the hot sauce is the tastiest.

_____

7. Wing Chun serves forty-two types of shrimp dumplings.

_____

8. No dish on the menu costs more than $8.95.

_____

9. My cousin will offer you a mint as you leave.

_____

10. Wing Chun is a real bargain!

_____

Fact and Opinion

Pueblo Indians

PUEBLO INDIANS

You can see ruins of cliff dwellings in Mesa Verde National Park in southern Colorado. Ancient Indians built these dwellings on ledges of high cliffs. Over 600 different dwellings have been documented. Some are like apartment buildings with many different rooms.

Some Pueblo Indians live in villages called **pueblos** (**pweb**-lohz) in New Mexico and Arizona. Many of their houses are similar to the cliff dwellings at Mesa Verde. Many pueblo dwellers follow their old ways of life and religion. They hold religious ceremonies in underground rooms called **kivas** (**kee**-vuhz). The Pueblo people make beautiful pottery and baskets.

Know What?

Mesa means "**table**" in Spanish, and verde means "**green**." Spanish-speaking people named the flat-topped hills of the Southwestern United States *mesas* because they look like giant tables. Why do you think they called the hills *verde*?

Use the clues to fill in the words in the puzzle.

Across

1. Pueblo Indians make beautiful ____.

4. A ____ is an underground room.

5. A flat-topped hill is called a ____.

7. Many Pueblos are in New ____.

Down

1. Another name for a village is ____.

2. Some cliff dwellings have many ____.

3. *Mesa* is the Spanish word for ____.

6. Ancient Indians built ____ dwellings.

Desert Animals

DESERT CRAWLERS

In southern Utah, winds and rains have carved sandstone into wondrous towers, arches, canyons, and bluffs. The water in the Great Salt Lake in northern Utah is saltier than the ocean.

The desert is a harsh place, but many insects and spiders are right at home there.

- The thistledown velvet ant is actually a wingless wasp that lives in the sand. Its body is covered with hairs, so it looks like a cotton ball. It feeds on nectar.
- Wind scorpions are yellowish-brown and about an inch long. They catch insects, lizards, and other small animals with their large pincers.
- The trapdoor spider digs a burrow with a trap door made of dirt, vegetation, and silk. It lies in wait in its burrow and grabs passing insects.
- The black cactus longhorn beetle is shiny and black with long feelers. It eats cactus.

Below are drawings of parts of the creatures described. Figure out which bug each part belongs to. Write the names of the creatures on the lines.

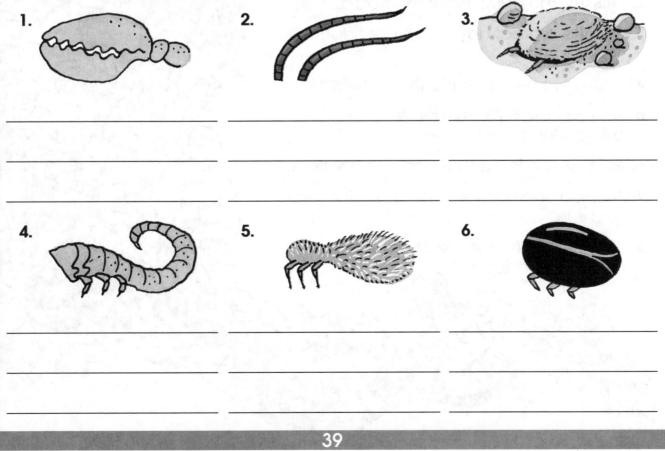

1. _____

_____

_____

2. _____

_____

_____

3. _____

_____

_____

4. _____

_____

_____

5. _____

_____

_____

6. _____

_____

_____

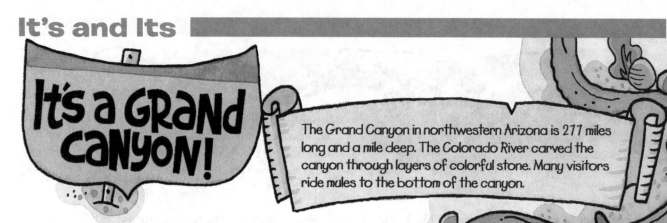

It's a GRAND CANYON!

The Grand Canyon in northwestern Arizona is 277 miles long and a mile deep. The Colorado River carved the canyon through layers of colorful stone. Many visitors ride mules to the bottom of the canyon.

The words *it's* and *its* look similar, but they have very different meanings. *Its* is a possessive pronoun. *Its* takes the place of a noun that names an object or an animal: *Its hair grew six inches last summer.*

It's is a contraction for the words *it is*: *It's not my fault!* A contraction is a short form of two words. A letter or letters are left out and an apostrophe takes their place.

Circle the correct word to complete each sentence.

1. Dad said, "**It's   Its** time to get up."

2. "**It's   Its** too early," Peter mumbled.

3. "**It's   Its** a great day for a mule ride!" Dad replied.

4. Judi gave her mule **it's   its** breakfast.

5. "Do you think **it's   its** going to rain?" asked Mom.

6. Peter saw a lizard that had lost **it's   its** tail.

7. "Look at the squirrel with **it's   its** furry ears," said Judi.

8. "**It's   Its** a different color from squirrels at home," she added.

Thermometer

Death Valley is a desert trough in east-central California. The lowest part, 282 feet below sea level, is near the city of Badwater. The highest temperature ever recorded in the United States, 134°F, was reported there in 1913.

You can use a Fahrenheit thermometer to measure the temperature. The one at the right shows some temperatures to remember.

Write the temperatures in degrees Fahrenheit.

1. _____ 2. _____ 3. _____ 4. _____

Look at the temperatures. Which is the most reasonable for each picture? Write the temperature under each picture.

18° F	59° F
80° F	101° F

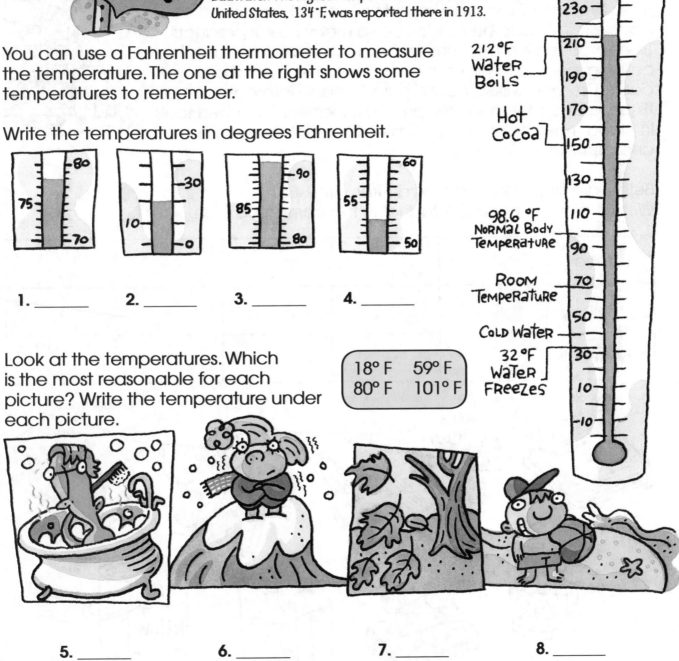

5. _____   6. _____   7. _____   8. _____

©School Zone Publishing Company 06320

Thermometer

Products from Trees

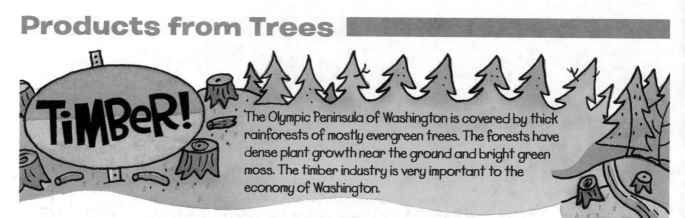

TiMBeR!

The Olympic Peninsula of Washington is covered by thick rainforests of mostly evergreen trees. The forests have dense plant growth near the ground and bright green moss. The timber industry is very important to the economy of Washington.

Trees are one of the most important natural resources because they can be made into so many useful products. Trees produce lumber. Lumber products include boards for building, pencils, furniture, musical instruments, baskets, and doors. Crushed wood, called pulp, is made into cardboard, tissue, and paper for books and newspapers. The chemicals in wood make cellophane, plastic, ink, paint, dye, cloth, and cement.

Below are some products made from trees.
Write the name of each product in the correct column.

Lumber				
Pulp				
Chemicals				

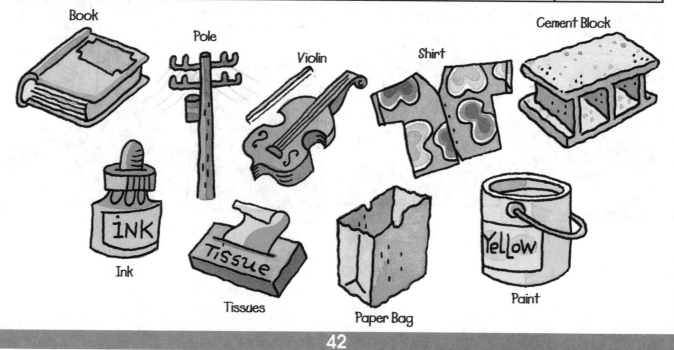

Book

Pole

Violin

Shirt

Cement Block

Ink

Tissues

Paper Bag

Paint

Parts of a Paragraph

Write on Home

The LaRose family is finally back at home in Seattle after their vacation. Have you learned a lot and enjoyed the trip as much as they have?

A paragraph is a group of sentences about one idea. Often, the first sentence is a topic sentence that tells what the paragraph is about. The first sentence is indented. Supporting sentences give more information, or support, the topic sentence. Often, a conclusion sums up the paragraph.

Write a paragraph about home. It can be about your town, your house, your family, or a place you would like to live. Make sure the paragraph has the three parts described above.

_____

_____

_____

_____

_____

_____

_____

_____

_____

_____

_____

_____

_____

43

Words with c, ck, ch

The **k** sound may be spelled **c**, **ck**, or **ch**.

Write the correct word to finish each sentence.
Then circle the word in the puzzle.

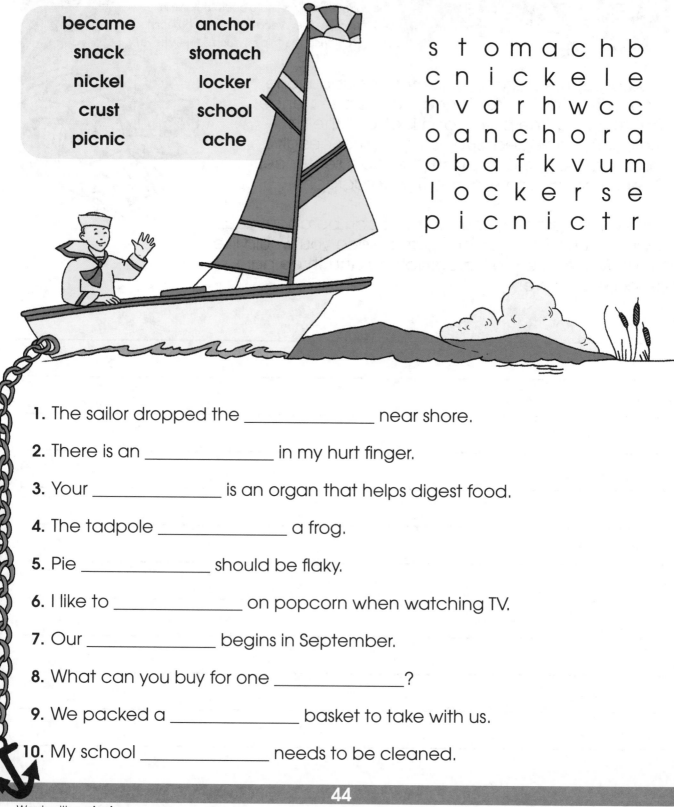

became	anchor
snack	stomach
nickel	locker
crust	school
picnic	ache

```
s t o m a c h b
c n i c k e l e
h v a r h w c c
o a n c h o r a
o b a f k v u m
l o c k e r s e
p i c n i c t r
```

1. The sailor dropped the _____ near shore.

2. There is an _____ in my hurt finger.

3. Your _____ is an organ that helps digest food.

4. The tadpole _____ a frog.

5. Pie _____ should be flaky.

6. I like to _____ on popcorn when watching TV.

7. Our _____ begins in September.

8. What can you buy for one _____?

9. We packed a _____ basket to take with us.

10. My school _____ needs to be cleaned.

Words with Long a

Long **a** words may be spelled **a_e**, **ai**, or **ay**.

Write the correct words in the puzzle.

stray	brain
spray	trail
place	snake
plain	locate
paint	decay
mistake	whale

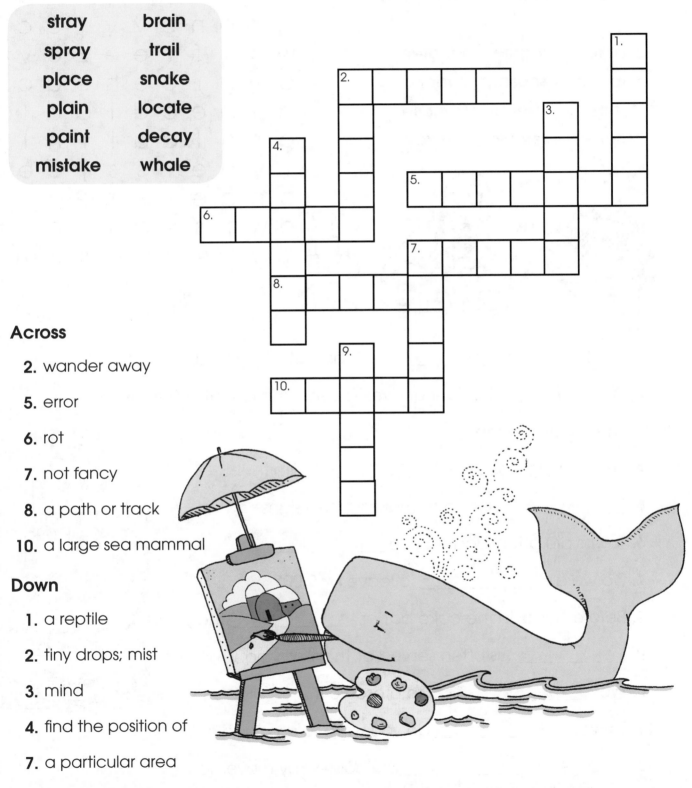

Across

2. wander away

5. error

6. rot

7. not fancy

8. a path or track

10. a large sea mammal

Down

1. a reptile

2. tiny drops; mist

3. mind

4. find the position of

7. a particular area

9. a liquid form for coloring

Words with Long e

Long **e** words may be spelled **e**, **ee**, **ea**, or **ey**.

Write the correct word to finish each sentence.
Then circle the word in the puzzle.

valley	agree	degree
speed	season	freeze
east	Neon	grease
money	female	Turkey

```
g m o n e y v f q c
w g g f r e e z e v
d e g r e e h e a a
a s p e e d l a b l
g r h i a a l r n l
r v o e m s s j e e
e n g e l s t e o y
e w f s e a s o n e
t u r k e y e s k m
```

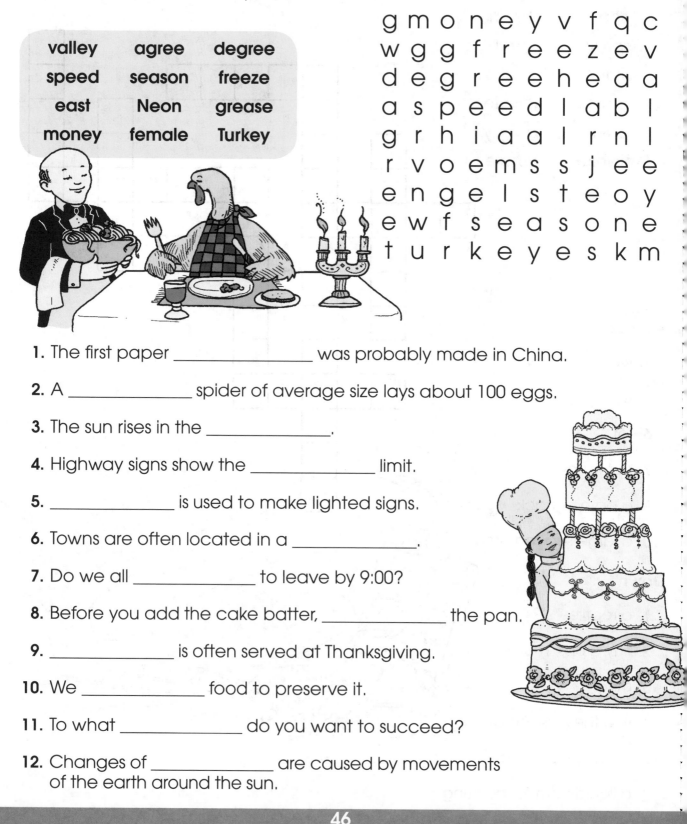

1. The first paper _____ was probably made in China.

2. A _____ spider of average size lays about 100 eggs.

3. The sun rises in the _____.

4. Highway signs show the _____ limit.

5. _____ is used to make lighted signs.

6. Towns are often located in a _____.

7. Do we all _____ to leave by 9:00?

8. Before you add the cake batter, _____ the pan.

9. _____ is often served at Thanksgiving.

10. We _____ food to preserve it.

11. To what _____ do you want to succeed?

12. Changes of _____ are caused by movements of the earth around the sun.

Words with Long **e**

Words with Long i

Long **i** words may be spelled **i**, **i_e**, or **y**.

Write the correct words in the puzzle.

beside	shy
deny	child
silent	icy
mild	invite
Divide	kindly
rhyme	lilac
pilot	sign

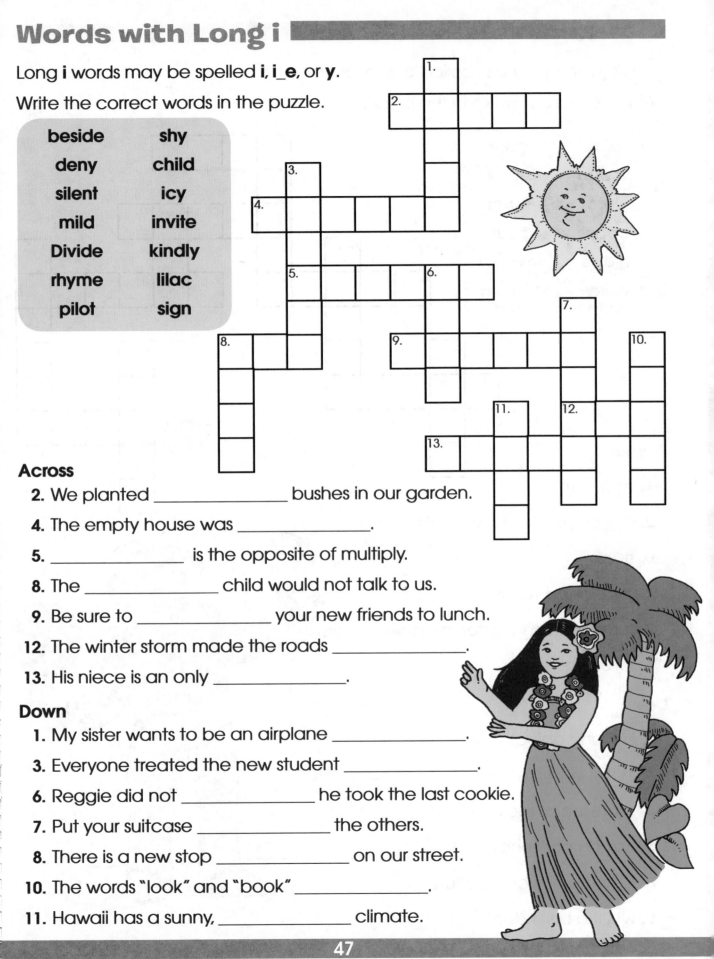

Across

2. We planted _____ bushes in our garden.

4. The empty house was _____.

5. _____ is the opposite of multiply.

8. The _____ child would not talk to us.

9. Be sure to _____ your new friends to lunch.

12. The winter storm made the roads _____.

13. His niece is an only _____.

Down

1. My sister wants to be an airplane _____.

3. Everyone treated the new student _____.

6. Reggie did not _____ he took the last cookie.

7. Put your suitcase _____ the others.

8. There is a new stop _____ on our street.

10. The words "look" and "book" _____.

11. Hawaii has a sunny, _____ climate.

Words with Long **i**

Long **o** words may be spelled **o**, **o_e**, or **oa**.

Write the correct words in the puzzle.

ago	goal
ocean	slope
vote	robot
coast	float
globe	lonely
obey	tomato

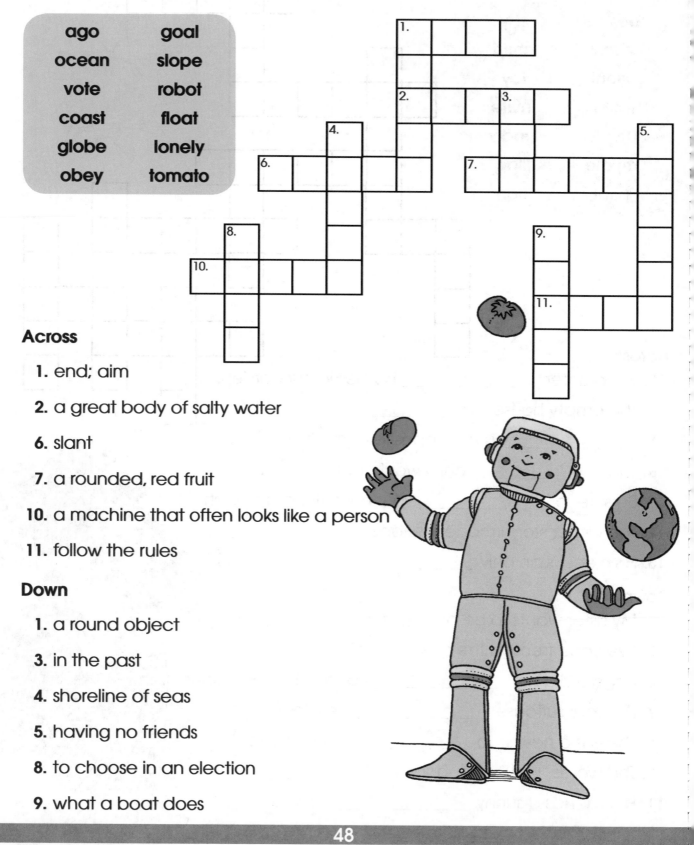

Across

1. end; aim

2. a great body of salty water

6. slant

7. a rounded, red fruit

10. a machine that often looks like a person

11. follow the rules

Down

1. a round object

3. in the past

4. shoreline of seas

5. having no friends

8. to choose in an election

9. what a boat does

Words with Long u

Long **u** words may be spelled **u**, **u_e**, or **ue**.

Write the correct word to finish each sentence.
Then circle the word in the puzzle.

pupil	value
human	useful
fuel	future
amuse	usual
perfume	units
regular	refuse

```
v r p u p i l r s
a u e p u n i t s
l s r e g u l a r
u e f u e l h m e
e f u s u a l u f
h u m a n c b s u
d l e y s m n e s
r s c f u t u r e
```

1. Mr. Hanns has room for one more _____ in his class.

2. This baseball card has little _____.

3. We gave Mom _____ for Mother's Day.

4. Grandmother brought a new toy to _____ the baby.

5. A dictionary is a _____ source of information.

6. The jet needs _____ before it can leave.

7. Students need to plan for their _____.

8. The _____ voice is feared by wild animals.

9. After the storm, we had school as _____.

10. Six o'clock is our _____ dinner hour.

11. The offer of extra credit was too good to _____.

12. The book was divided into 12 _____ of study.

Words with Long **u**

Words with c, ss, sc

The **s** sound may be spelled **c**, **ss**, or **sc**.

Write the correct word to finish each sentence.
Then circle the word in the puzzle.

press	scent
scene	scissors
center	address
lesson	dance
ounces	pencil

```
k r c e n t e r s
t p a p r e s s o
f e r d a n c e u
z n l p d b l v n
s c e n t r r m c
g i r m s c e n e
d l e s s o n s s
r s c i s s o r s
```

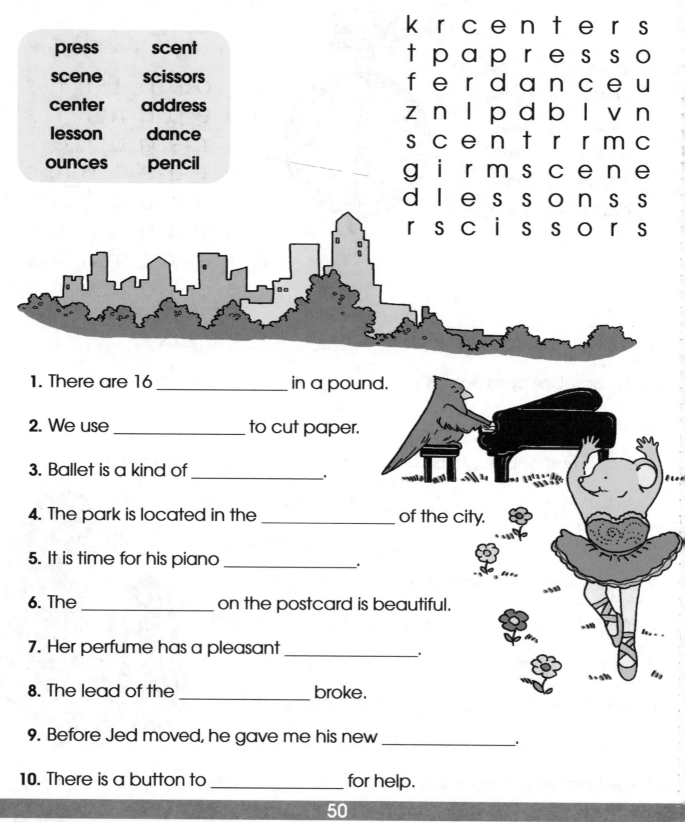

1. There are 16 _____ in a pound.

2. We use _____ to cut paper.

3. Ballet is a kind of _____.

4. The park is located in the _____ of the city.

5. It is time for his piano _____.

6. The _____ on the postcard is beautiful.

7. Her perfume has a pleasant _____.

8. The lead of the _____ broke.

9. Before Jed moved, he gave me his new _____.

10. There is a button to _____ for help.

Words with j, g, dge

The **j** sound may be spelled **j**, **g**, or **dge**.

Write the correct word to finish each sentence.
Then write the word in the puzzle.

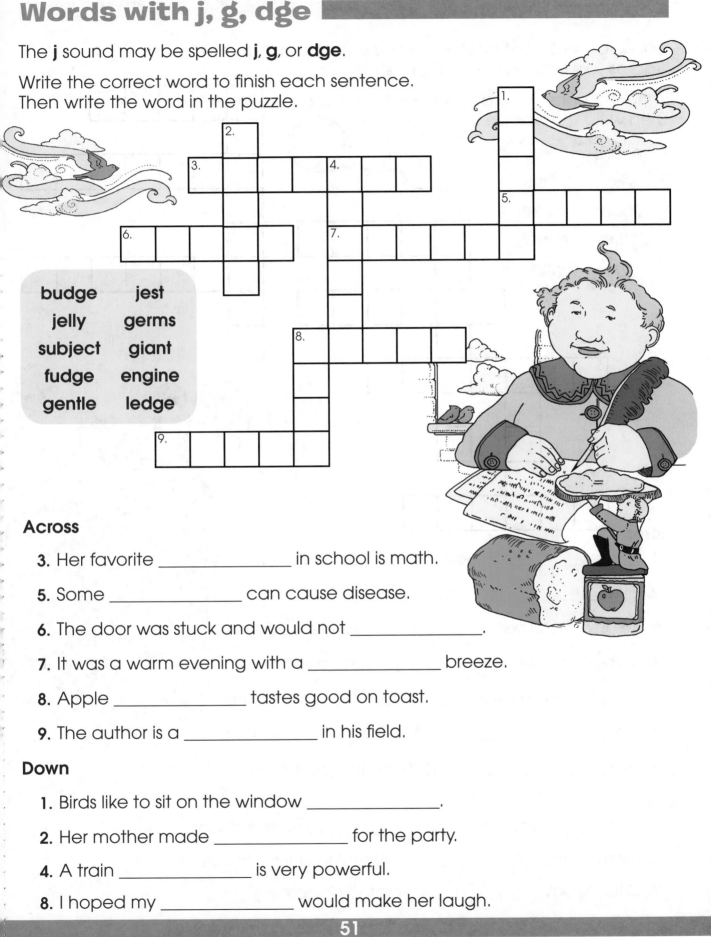

budge   jest
jelly   germs
subject   giant
fudge   engine
gentle   ledge

Across

3. Her favorite _____ in school is math.

5. Some _____ can cause disease.

6. The door was stuck and would not _____.

7. It was a warm evening with a _____ breeze.

8. Apple _____ tastes good on toast.

9. The author is a _____ in his field.

Down

1. Birds like to sit on the window _____.

2. Her mother made _____ for the party.

4. A train _____ is very powerful.

8. I hoped my _____ would make her laugh.

Adding s and es

Add **s** to the end of most words to name more than one.
Add **es** to words ending in **ch**, **ss**, **sh**, or **x**.

Write the correct word to finish each sentence.
Then write the word in the puzzle.

match	tax
wish	Fox
finish	nickel
friend	hunch
flash	pass

Across

1. _____ are related to dogs and wolves.

2. Five _____ equal one quarter.

3. We invited all our _____ to the party.

4. Sometimes our _____ can help us.

5. We all received free _____ to the game.

6. The _____ fell in the water and became wet.

8. Jed _____ he had met the performer.

Down

1. He may go when he _____ doing the dishes.

3. There were _____ of lightning during the storm.

7. Citizens pay _____ on their income.

Words with f, ph, ff, gh

The **f** sound may be spelled **f**, **ph**, **ff**, or **gh**.

Write the correct word to finish each sentence.
Then circle the word in the puzzle.

~~laugh~~	telephone
(coffee)	trophy
rough	alphabet
forest	enough
office	finger

```
k r b g z n y d s t
t d f o r e s t e t
f e r o u g h b o r
i e l p v b a v f o
n n z e t h r m f p
g o r m p j y b i h
e u p l x h l k c y
r g a h f r o r e q
g h l a u g h n s h
t c o f f e e c e y
```

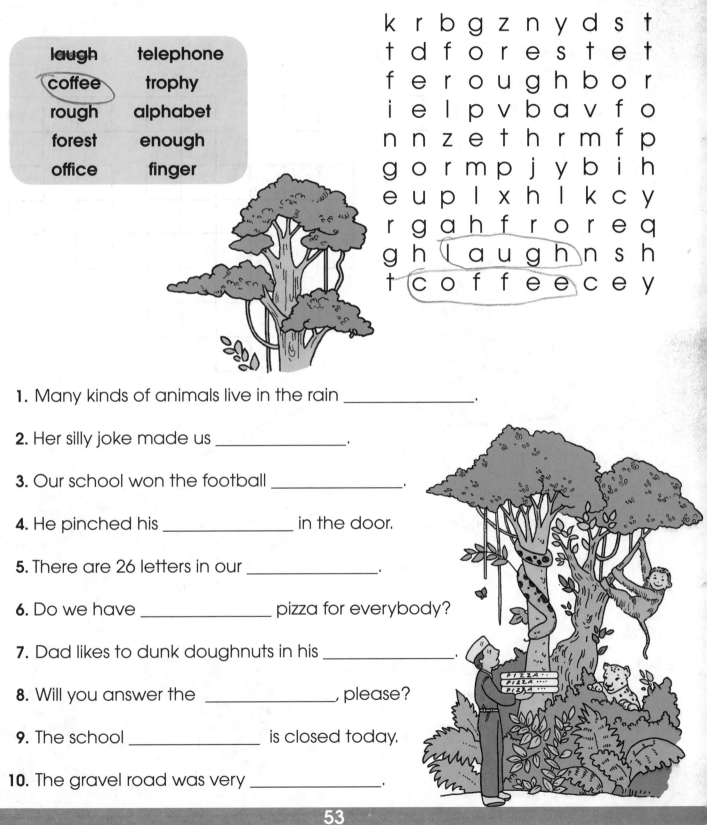

1. Many kinds of animals live in the rain _____.

2. Her silly joke made us _____.

3. Our school won the football _____.

4. He pinched his _____ in the door.

5. There are 26 letters in our _____.

6. Do we have _____ pizza for everybody?

7. Dad likes to dunk doughnuts in his _____.

8. Will you answer the _____, please?

9. The school _____ is closed today.

10. The gravel road was very _____.

©School Zone Publishing Company 06320

Words with **f, ph, ff, gh**

Consonant Digraphs: ch, sh, th, wh

A consonant digraph is two consonants written together to spell one sound, such as **ch**, **sh**, **th**, or **wh**.

Write the correct words in the puzzle.

chest	cloth
thick	choose
author	share
leash	whim
wheat	both

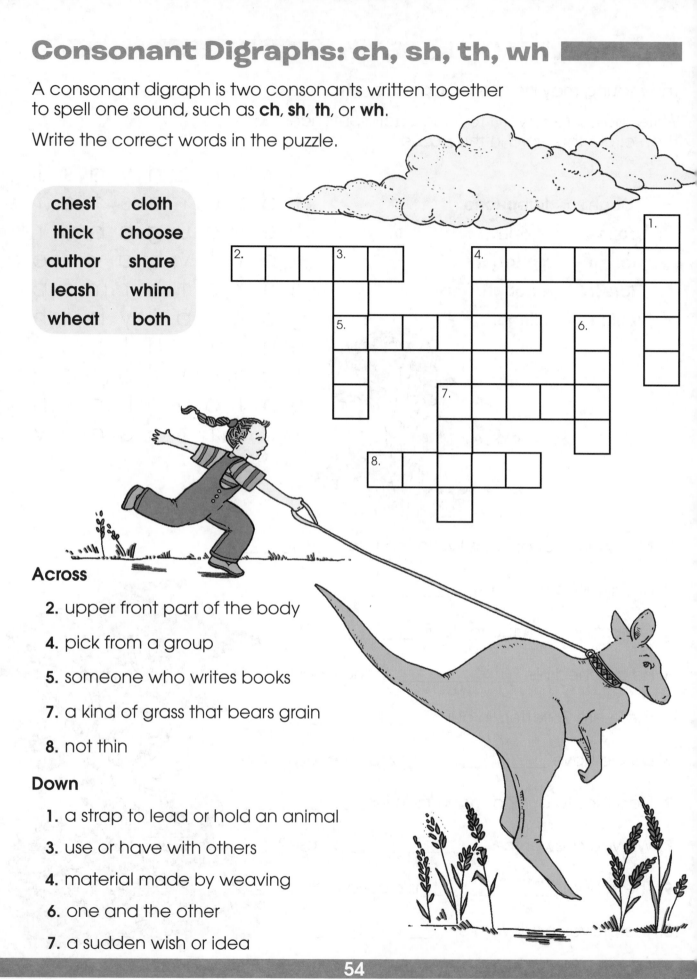

Across

2. upper front part of the body

4. pick from a group

5. someone who writes books

7. a kind of grass that bears grain

8. not thin

Down

1. a strap to lead or hold an animal

3. use or have with others

4. material made by weaving

6. one and the other

7. a sudden wish or idea

Consonant Digraphs: **ch, sh, th, wh**　　　　　　　©School Zone Publishing Company 06320

Vowel Sounds with r

The vowel sound with **r** has the same sound in the words **her**, **turn**, and **bird**. This vowel sound with **r** may be spelled **er**, **ur**, or **ir**.

Write the correct word to finish each sentence.
Then circle the word in the puzzle.

thirsty	serve
shirt	dirty
every	further
curve	verb
surprise	burned

```
k r b u r n e d s
t f v e r b e b u
h c u r v e v c r
i s e r v e e o p
r d i r t y r m r
s t r l t h y b i
t r o t e w e c s
y r s h i r t r e
```

1. A _____ is often an action word.

2. The pitcher threw a _____ ball.

3. His pants got _____ when he fell.

4. The robber was caught by _____.

5. The old factory _____ to the ground.

6. We will not discuss it _____.

7. Eating peanuts makes me _____.

8. He spent _____ dime he had.

9. What shall we _____ for dinner?

10. Matt tore his _____ on the fence.

©School Zone Publishing Company 06320

Vowel Sounds with **r**

Vowel Sounds with r

The vowel sound with **r** in **star** is spelled **ar**.
The vowel sound with **r** in **horn** is spelled **or**.

Write the correct word to finish each sentence.

market	morning
sport	smart
labor	thorns
apart	orange
garden	start

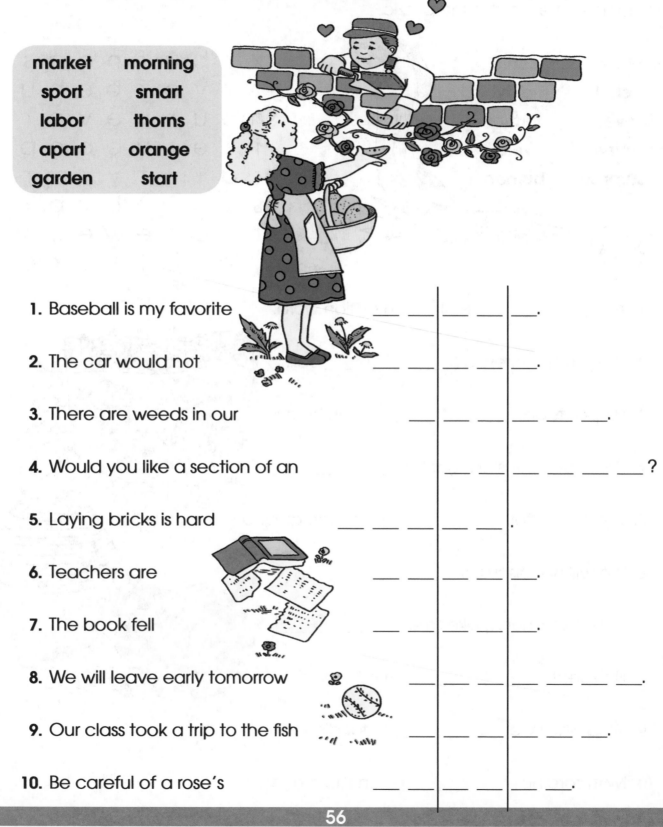

1. Baseball is my favorite ___ ___ ___ .

2. The car would not ___ ___ ___ .

3. There are weeds in our ___ ___ ___ ___ ___ .

4. Would you like a section of an ___ ___ ___ ___ ___ ___ ?

5. Laying bricks is hard ___ ___ ___ .

6. Teachers are ___ ___ ___ .

7. The book fell ___ ___ ___ .

8. We will leave early tomorrow ___ ___ ___ ___ ___ ___ .

9. Our class took a trip to the fish ___ ___ ___ ___ ___ .

10. Be careful of a rose's ___ ___ ___ ___ ___ .

Words with ou and ow

These words have the vowel sound in **out**.
This vowel sound may be spelled **ou** or **ow**.

Write the correct word to finish each sentence.

cloud	frown
aloud	flowers
shout	crowd
proud	about
fowl	power

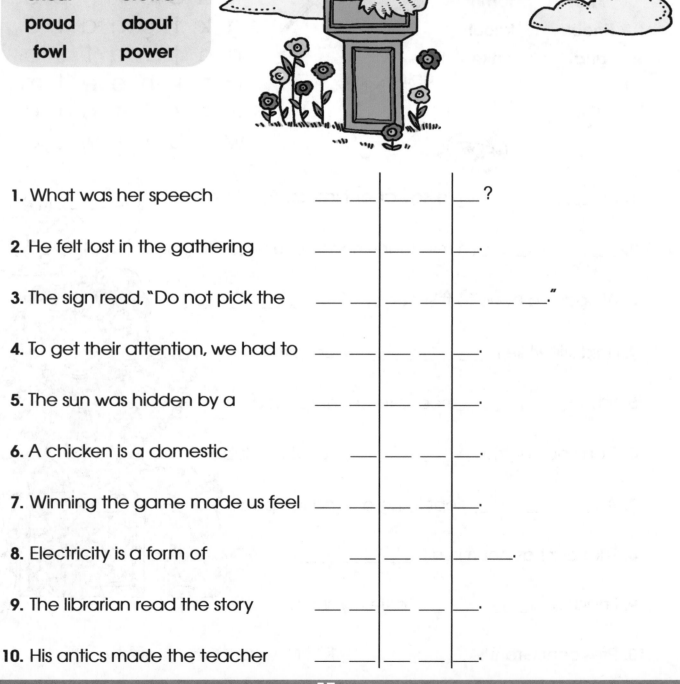

1. What was her speech __ __ __ __ __ ?

2. He felt lost in the gathering __ __ __ __ __ .

3. The sign read, "Do not pick the __ __ __ __ __ __ __ ."

4. To get their attention, we had to __ __ __ __ __ .

5. The sun was hidden by a __ __ __ __ __ .

6. A chicken is a domestic __ __ __ __ .

7. Winning the game made us feel __ __ __ __ __ .

8. Electricity is a form of __ __ __ __ __ .

9. The librarian read the story __ __ __ __ __ .

10. His antics made the teacher __ __ __ __ __ .

57

Silent Consonants

When the consonants **gn**, **kn**, **mb**, and **wr** are written together in a single syllable, the letters **g**, **k**, **b**, and **w** are silent.

Write the correct word to finish each sentence.
Then circle the word in the puzzle.

wrote	gnaw
wreck	comb
knot	tomb
Knock	kneel
gnat	knife

```
k r w r e c k r
k n o c k h p b
g k i g n a t c
n n j f q l s o
a o k n e e l m
w t r l t o m b
w r o t e w f c
```

1. I _____ an essay about insects for class.

2. _____ on my door when you're ready to go.

3. We gave a bone to the puppy to _____.

4. Hold still while I _____ your hair!

5. This _____ needs to be sharpened.

6. Can you get the _____ out of this ribbon?

7. A _____ kept flying around the pear.

8. That car has been in a _____.

9. I had to _____ to tie my shoe.

10. President Grant's _____ is in New York City.

©School Zone Publishing Company 06320

Words with Long a and e

The long **a** sound may be spelled **eigh**.
The long **e** sound may be spell **ei** or **ie**.

Write the correct word to finish each sentence.
Then write the word in the puzzle.

weigh	niece
believe	ceiling
receive	deceive
sleigh	relief
field	eight

Across

2. It was a _____ to get out of the cold.

4. His _____ arrived by plane.

7. How much does an elephant _____?

9. Camouflage helps _____ enemies.

10. I _____ he told the truth.

Down

1. The snowy night was perfect for a _____ ride.

3. Did you _____ the tickets for the play?

5. Four plus four equals _____.

6. The football _____ is muddy today.

8. The kitchen _____ needs to be painted.

59

Adding ed and ing

When verbs have a consonant-**y** ending,
change the **y** to **i** and add **ed** (hurry → hurried).

Write the correct spelling of the words to finish
each sentence.

carry	copy	try
deny	bury	marry

1. He _____ the suitcase upstairs.

2. She _____ to fix the broken doll.

3. Sam _____ breaking the dish.

4. She was _____ last June.

5. When their pet turtle died, they _____ it.

6. He _____ his name by tracing it.

When verbs have a silent **e** ending, drop the
letter **e** and add **ing** (make → making).

smile	rise	drive
vote	write	excite

1. We will be _____ to Yellowstone Park.

2. The sun will be _____ in the east.

3. The tennis match was _____.

4. Mom is _____ a letter to my sister.

5. Which candidate are you _____ for?

6. We took a picture of her _____.

Words with Long o

The long **o** sound may be spelled **o**, **o_e**, **oa**, or **ow**.

Write the correct words in the puzzle.

borrow	protect
growth	hollow
cocoa	most
broke	global
pillow	roast

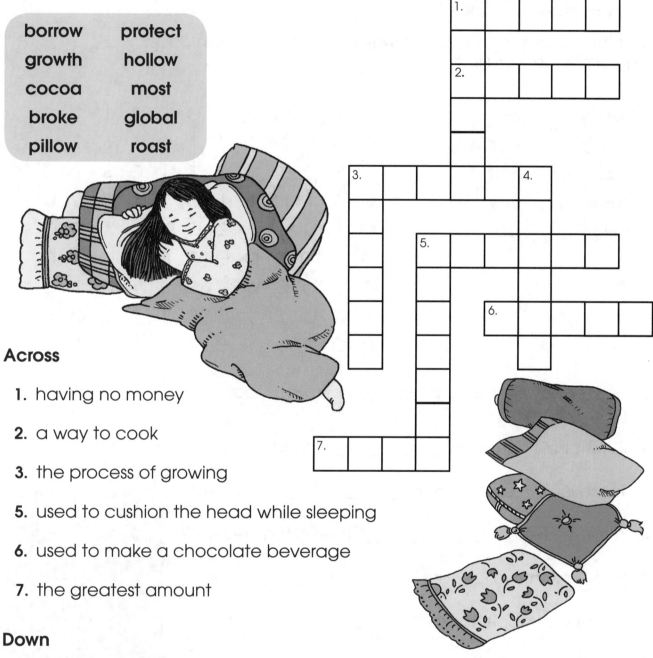

Across

1. having no money

2. a way to cook

3. the process of growing

5. used to cushion the head while sleeping

6. used to make a chocolate beverage

7. the greatest amount

Down

1. to use something temporarily that belongs to someone else with his or her permission

3. worldwide

4. an unfilled space inside something

5. guard

©School Zone Publishing Company 06320

Words with Long **o**

Comparisons

To compare two people or things, add **er** to the ending of a word.
To compare more than two people or things, add **est**. Change the **y** to **i**
before adding **er** or **est** to words that have a consonant-**y** ending
(tricky → trickier → trickiest).

Add the correct ending to the words to finish each sentence.
Then circle the word in the puzzle.

happy	fast
pretty	clean
soft	short
sweet	noisy
rough	busy

```
h r f a s t e s t l t s
c a s h o r t e r s t r
l s p r e t t i e s t o
e h f p r f d t l h s u
a f u j i z e m f l o g
n u m h p e q n c b f h
e l p d w y s s m n t e
r b u s i e s t t f e r
n o i s i e r c t y r s
```

1. He is happy at Thanksgiving and Halloween, but _____ at Christmas.

2. Is this pillow harder or _____ than yours?

3. Those lovely flowers are the _____ I've seen.

4. A five-year-old is _____ than a ten-year-old.

5. People with two jobs are the _____ of all.

6. This kind of apple tastes the _____ of all.

7. Traveling by jet is the _____ way to go.

8. The floor is _____ since we mopped it.

9. You can hear that traffic is _____ during the day than at night.

10. The brick road is bumpier, or _____ , than the highway.

62

Prefixes

The letter groups **un, re, in,** and **dis** are prefixes. When added to the beginning of a word, they change the meaning of the word.

Write the correct words in the puzzle.

un means **not**
re means **again**
in means **into** and sometimes **not**
dis means **lack of**

untied	rewrite
unhappy	dislike
incorrect	renew
disagree	rebuild
indirect	unjust

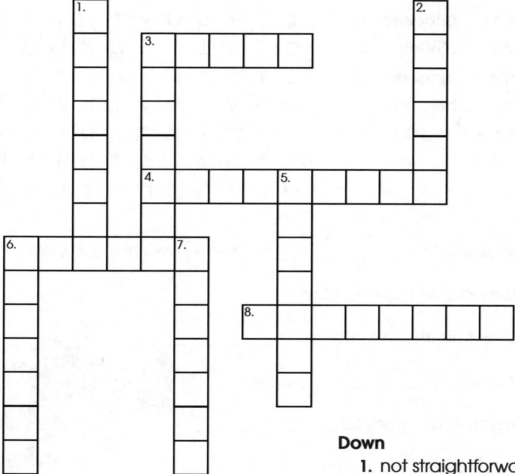

Across

3. make or become new again

4. not correct; wrong

6. not tied

8. differ; argue

Down

1. not straightforward

2. not just; unfair

3. write again

5. build again

6. not happy; sad

7. not like; hate

Suffixes

The letter groups **ful**, **less**, and **ly** are suffixes. When added to the end of a word, they change the meaning of the word.

Write the correct word to finish each sentence.
Then circle the word in the puzzle.

ful means **full of**
ly means **how**
less means **not having**

thankful	priceless
helpful	loudly
neatly	endless
softly	beautiful
homeless	safely

```
b a p r i c e l e s s l w
y e s r n j h l g f e o h
t s a r e g l c n v n u o
x o f u a v r w r f d d m
c f e z t w g x b d l l e
s t l c l i h r t s e y l
d l y t y y f k q y s q e
c y p j k m g u k c s x s
s t h e l p f u l f h r s
d c t h a n k f u l t k t
```

1. Snowflakes fell _____ , covering everything in white.

2. The tornado left many families _____.

3. The view from the mountain was _____.

4. She called _____ for help.

5. The suitcase was packed _____.

6. The highway appeared to be _____.

7. His art is _____.

8. The pilot landed the plane _____.

9. The pilgrims were _____ for their blessings.

10. My mother found the store clerk very _____.

Antonyms

Antonyms are words with opposite meanings (big, little).

Write the antonym for the bold word in each sentence.
Then circle the word in the puzzle.

laugh	sour
short	easy
light	start
big	lose
dirty	slow

```
l a u g h p q s
o l b i g v h l
s o u r n o l o
e h n c r e i w
c t p t k a g x
s t a r t s h r
d i r t y y t k
```

1. My father is a **tall** man. _____

2. Did you **find** your money? _____

3. It is time to **stop** the game. _____

4. The lemonade is too **sweet**. _____

5. The story made him **cry**. _____

6. I thought the test was **hard**. _____

7. The horse was **fast**. _____

8. Is your shirt **clean**? _____

9. The package was **heavy**. _____

10. Her dog is **small**. _____

Synonyms

Synonyms are words with almost the same meaning (look, see).

Write the synonym for the bold word in each sentence.
Then write the word in the puzzle.

noisy	harm
solid	weak
roast	speak
quiet	select
welcome	jolly

Across

4. The crowd became very **loud**. _____

5. It is time to **bake** the turkey. _____

7. Which dress did you **choose**? _____

8. She went to the door to **greet** him. _____

9. His sickness made him **feeble**. _____

Down

1. Everyone was in a **merry** mood. _____

2. It was a **still** summer evening. _____

3. The fall did not **hurt** her. _____

6. The peach felt **firm**. _____

7. Did Mr. James **talk** to your class? _____

Homonyms

Homonyms are words pronounced alike, but with different spellings and meanings (to, too, two).

Write the correct homonym to finish each sentence.
Then circle the word in the puzzle.

peace	Write
piece	weak
there	week
their	hear
right	here

```
s r g f h e a r h
p i t t w h t b w
e g t h e h r q r
a h n c e l s p i
c t p i k r x m t
e h r k j h e r e
p i e c e w e a k
```

1. After the quarrel, there was _____ and quiet.

2. Would you like a _____ of pie?

3. They lost _____ tickets to the game.

4. How do you get _____ ?

5. _____ a letter to tell me about your trip.

6. How many answers did you get _____ ?

7. His vacation begins next _____ .

8. The flu left her feeling _____ .

9. I could not _____ what she said.

10. Did you get _____ on time?

67

Adding es

To spell the plural of a word ending in **f** or **fe**, change the **f** to **v** and add **es**.

Write the correct spelling to finish each sentence.
Then write the word in the puzzle.

knife   life
Calf   Leaf
elf   wife
half   shelf

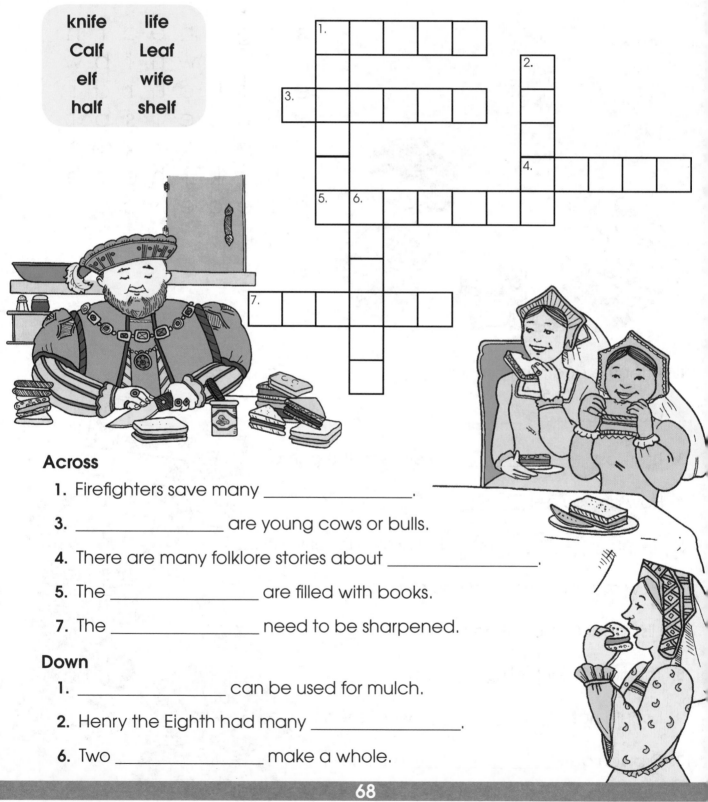

Across

1. Firefighters save many _____.

3. _____ are young cows or bulls.

4. There are many folklore stories about _____.

5. The _____ are filled with books.

7. The _____ need to be sharpened.

Down

1. _____ can be used for mulch.

2. Henry the Eighth had many _____.

6. Two _____ make a whole.

Verb Endings

Most verbs are not changed when **ed** or **ing** is added.
Double the final consonant before adding **ed** or **ing** to one-syllable verbs
that have a vowel-consonant ending (flip → flipping).

Write the correct word to finish each sentence.
Then circle the word in the puzzle.

melt	slam
walk	carry
slip	reach
point	trot
drip	step

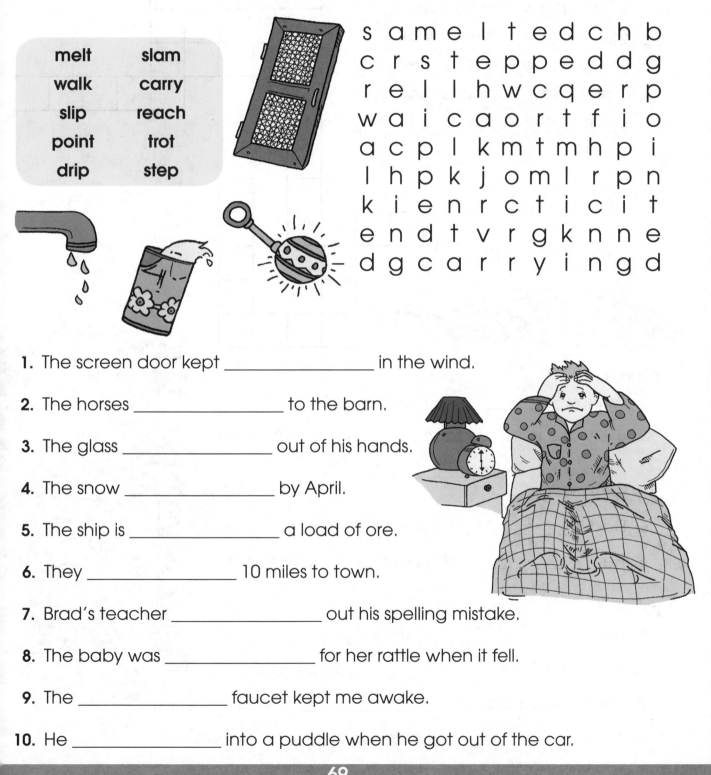

```
s a m e l t e d c h b
c r s t e p p e d d g
r e l l h w c q e r p
w a i c a o r t f i o
a c p l k m t m h p i
l h p k j o m l r p n
k i e n r c t i c i t
e n d t v r g k n n e
d g c a r r y i n g d
```

1. The screen door kept _____ in the wind.

2. The horses _____ to the barn.

3. The glass _____ out of his hands.

4. The snow _____ by April.

5. The ship is _____ a load of ore.

6. They _____ 10 miles to town.

7. Brad's teacher _____ out his spelling mistake.

8. The baby was _____ for her rattle when it fell.

9. The _____ faucet kept me awake.

10. He _____ into a puddle when he got out of the car.

69

Irregular Verbs

Some verbs do not spell the past tense by adding **ed**.

Write the correct word to finish each sentence.
Then write the word in the puzzle.

> grow - grew   swing - swung
>
> fight - fought   write - wrote
>
> freeze - froze   drive - drove
>
> feel - felt   leave - left
>
> tear - tore

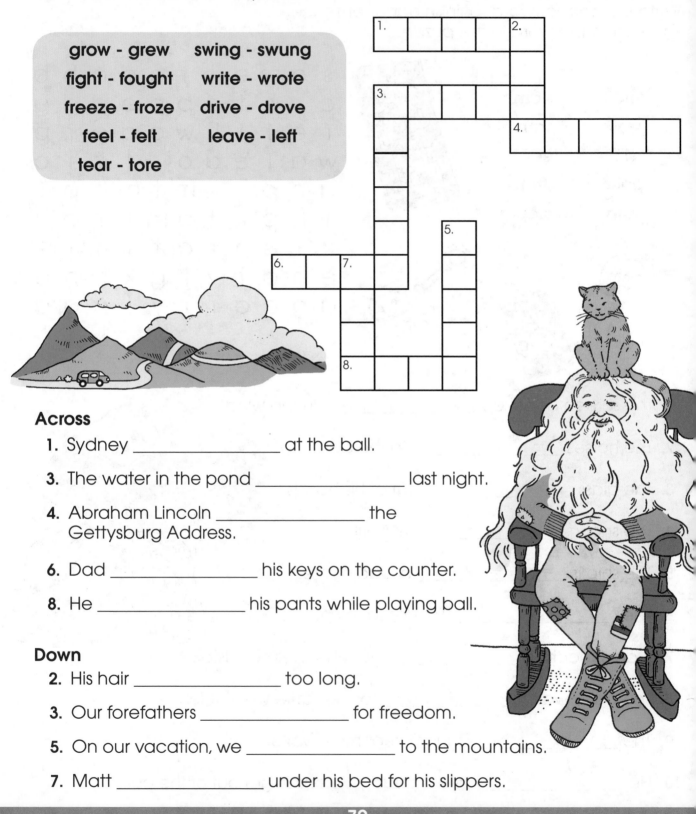

Across

1. Sydney _____ at the ball.

3. The water in the pond _____ last night.

4. Abraham Lincoln _____ the Gettysburg Address.

6. Dad _____ his keys on the counter.

8. He _____ his pants while playing ball.

Down

2. His hair _____ too long.

3. Our forefathers _____ for freedom.

5. On our vacation, we _____ to the mountains.

7. Matt _____ under his bed for his slippers.

Idioms

Idioms are expressions or phrases that do not mean what they seem to say.
("You crack me up!" means "you make me laugh.")

Draw a line to match each idiom with its meaning.

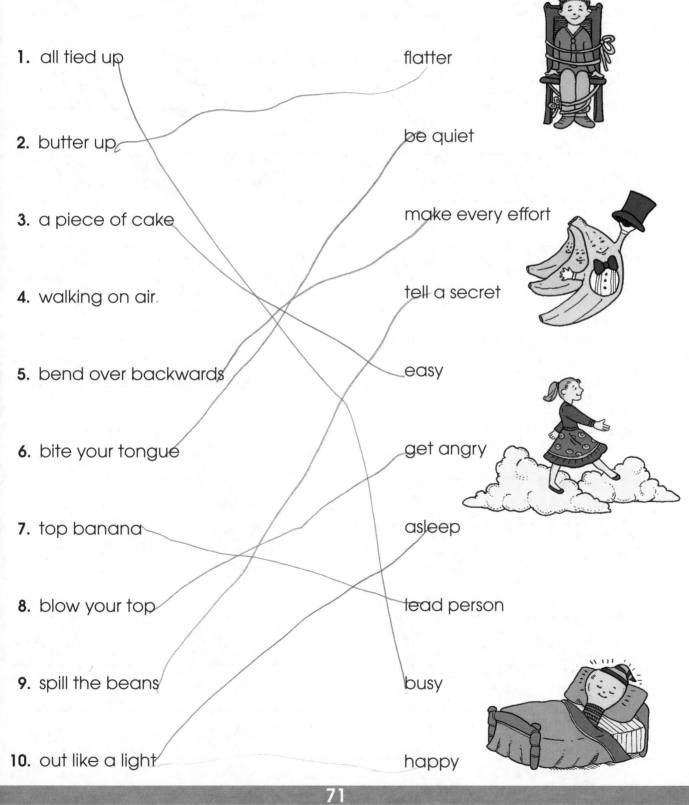

1. all tied up   flatter

2. butter up   be quiet

3. a piece of cake   make every effort

4. walking on air.   tell a secret

5. bend over backwards   easy

6. bite your tongue   get angry

7. top banana   asleep

8. blow your top   lead person

9. spill the beans   busy

10. out like a light   happy

Idioms

Study the alphabet chart. Then trace the letters.

Cursive Writing

Study the alphabet chart. Then trace the letters.

©School Zone Publishing Company 06320

Cursive Writing

Cursive Writing

Look at the arrows. Practice writing each letter.

Direct oval letters

Upper-loop letters, direct oval

Upper-loop letters, indirect oval

Cone-stem letters

Cursive Writing

Cursive Writing

Look at the arrows. Practice writing each letter.

Compound-curve letters

Lower-loop letters

Boat-ending letters

Indirect oval letters

©School Zone Publishing Company 06320

Cursive Writing

Cursive Writing

Look at the arrows. Practice writing each letter.

Undercurve beginnings: minimum letters

i u w e n s

Intermediate letters

t d p

Lower-loop letters

j g p y z q f

Tick-check letters

n b o w n s

©School Zone Publishing Company 06320

Look at the arrows. Practice writing each letter.

Undercurve beginnings: upper-loop letters

Overcurve beginnings: hump-letters

Downcurve beginnings: small oval group

Cursive Writing

Practice writing the letter. Practice writing the sentence.

$\mathcal{A}$ $\mathcal{A}$ $\mathcal{A}$

a a a

Ant ate an apple.

Cursive Writing   ©School Zone Publishing Company 06320

Cursive Writing

Practice writing the letter. Practice writing the sentence.

$\mathcal{B}$ $\mathcal{B}$ $\mathcal{B}$

b b b

HELLO
MY NAME IS
Bob

Big Bob is a bear.

©School Zone Publishing Company 06320

Cursive Writing

Practice writing the letter. Practice writing the sentence.

$\mathcal{C}$ $\mathcal{C}$ $\mathcal{C}$ $\mathcal{C}$

$\mathcal{C}$ $\mathcal{C}$ $\mathcal{C}$ $\mathcal{C}$

Cat collects cookies.

COOKIES

Cursive Writing

Practice writing the letter. Practice writing the sentence.

$\mathscr{D}$ $\mathscr{D}$ $\mathscr{D}$

d d d

Dan is a diver.

Cursive Writing

Cursive Writing

Practice writing the letter. Practice writing the sentence.

$\mathcal{E}$ $\mathcal{E}$ $\mathcal{E}$

e e e

Ed eats everything.

Cursive Writing

Practice writing the letter. Practice writing the sentence.

F F F

f f f

Fish feels funny.

©School Zone Publishing Company 06320

Cursive Writing

Cursive Writing

Practice writing the letter. Practice writing the sentence.

$\mathcal{G}$ $\mathcal{G}$ $\mathcal{G}$

g g g

Goat likes grass.

Cursive Writing

Practice writing the letter. Practice writing the sentence.

$\mathcal{H}$ $\mathcal{H}$ $\mathcal{H}$

h h h

$\mathcal{H}olly\ has\ a\ hat.$

Cursive Writing

Cursive Writing

Practice writing the letter. Practice writing the sentence.

$\mathcal{I}$ $\mathcal{I}$ $\mathcal{I}$

i i i

Iris eats ice cream.

Cursive Writing

Practice writing the letter. Practice writing the sentence.

$\mathcal{J}$ $\mathcal{J}$ $\mathcal{J}$ $\mathcal{J}$

j j j j

Joe juggles jars.

©School Zone Publishing Company 06320

Cursive Writing

Cursive Writing

Practice writing the letter. Practice writing the sentence.

K K K

k k k

Kim kept the kite.

Cursive Writing

Practice writing the letter. Practice writing the sentence.

$\mathscr{L}$ $\mathscr{L}$ $\mathscr{L}$ $\mathscr{L}$

ℓ ℓ ℓ ℓ

Lion loves leaves.

Cursive Writing

Practice writing the letter. Practice writing the sentence.

M M M

m m m

Monkey is mighty.

Cursive Writing

Practice writing the letter. Practice writing the sentence.

$\mathcal{N}$ $\mathcal{N}$ $\mathcal{N}$

$\mathcal{M}$ $\mathcal{M}$ $\mathcal{M}$

Nurse had a note.

Cursive Writing

Cursive Writing

Practice writing the letter. Practice writing the sentence.

O O O

o o o

Ollie is an octopus.

©School Zone Publishing Company 06320

Cursive Writing

Practice writing the letter. Practice writing the sentence.

P P P

p p p

Pig plays the piano.

©School Zone Publishing Company 06320

Cursive Writing

Practice writing the letter. Practice writing the sentence.

2   2   2

q   q   q

Queen quit quilting.

Cursive Writing

Practice writing the letter. Practice writing the sentence.

R R R R

n n n n

Raccoon likes to rock.

Cursive Writing

Cursive Writing

Practice writing the letter. Practice writing the sentence.

$\mathcal{S}$ $\mathcal{S}$ $\mathcal{S}$

s s s

Seal swims to school.

Cursive Writing

Practice writing the letter. Practice writing the sentence.

Tom talks to turtles.

Practice writing the letter. Practice writing the sentence.

$\mathcal{U}$ $\mathcal{U}$ $\mathcal{U}$

w w w

Umpire is unhappy.

Cursive Writing

Practice writing the letter. Practice writing the sentence.

$\mathcal{V}$ $\mathcal{V}$ $\mathcal{V}$

$\mathcal{N}$ $\mathcal{N}$ $\mathcal{N}$

Violet wants a vase.

    Cursive Writing

Cursive Writing

Practice writing the letter. Practice writing the sentence.

$\mathcal{W}$ $\mathcal{W}$ $\mathcal{W}$

w w w

Walrus has a wagon.

Cursive Writing

Practice writing the letter. Practice writing the sentence.

X X X

x x x

Xavier had an x-ray.

Cursive Writing

Cursive Writing

Practice writing the letter. Practice writing the sentence.

Y Y Y

y y y

Yak wants a yo-yo.

Cursive Writing

Practice writing the letter. Practice writing the sentence.

Zebra loves the zoo.

Cursive Writing

A Authors

Write the name of the author for each book title.

| A.A. Milne | Mark Twain | Beatrix Potter | Dr. Seuss | E.B. White |

1. The Adventures of Tom Sawyer

2. The Tale of Peter Rabbit

3. Winnie-the-Pooh

4. The Cat in the Hat

5. Charlotte's Web

Cursive Writing Practice

B Buildings

Write the name of the building that matches each clue.

library	school	hospital	museum	hotel

1. where you go when you are sick

2. where you would go to see a mummy

3. where you go to learn

4. where you go to borrow a book

5. where you can stay when you are on vacation

Cursive Writing Practice

Write the name of the coin that matches each clue.

| penny | nickel | dime | quarter | half dollar |

1. the coin with President Abraham Lincoln on it

_____

_____

_____

2. the coin with President Thomas Jefferson on it

_____

_____

_____

3. the coin with President Franklin Roosevelt on it

_____

_____

_____

4. the coin with President George Washington on it

_____

_____

_____

5. the coin with President John F. Kennedy on it

_____

_____

_____

Cursive Writing Practice

D Dogs

Write the name of the dog that matches each clue.

| husky | boxer | greyhound | pointer | beagle |

1. This dog is not a bus!

2. This dog points the way.

3. This dog might chase rabbits.

4. This dog does not wear gloves.

5. This dog looks like a wolf.

Cursive Writing Practice

E Ecosystems

Write the answer that completes each sentence.

Ecology	habitat	oxygen	Meteorology	botany

1. The environment in which a species lives is its _____ .

2. _____ is the study of how plants and animals act together.

3. The study of plants is called _____ .

4. _____ is the science of weather.

5. Plants and animals need water and_____ to live.

F Farm Animals

Write the name of the animal that matches each clue.

sheep	horse	cow	chicken	pig

1. This animal is raised on a dairy farm.

2. This animal is raised on a hog farm.

3. This animal is raised mainly for riding.

4. This animal is raised for wool.

5. This animal is raised for eggs.

Cursive Writing Practice

G Board Games

Write the name of the board game that matches each clue.

Candy Land®   **Chess**   **Monopoly®**   **Clue®**   **Scrabble®**

1. In this game, you use play money to buy and sell.

2. In this game, you might go to Lollipop Woods.

3. In this game, you try to capture your opponent's king.

4. In this game, it helps to be good at spelling!

5. In this game, you work to solve a mystery.

Cursive Writing Practice
*Candy Land, Monopoly, Clue, and Scrabble are registered trademarks of Hasbro.
©School Zone Publishing Company 06320

H Habitats

Write the habitat that matches each clue.

deserts	oceans	swamps	rainforests	grasslands

1. These are very dry places.

2. These are wide areas covered with grasses and trees.

3. These are hot and humid parts of the world.

4. These are homes to fish and mammals.

5. These are wetlands that are flooded all the time.

©School Zone Publishing Company 06320   Cursive Writing Practice

I Insects

Write the name of the insect that matches each clue.

ladybug	firefly	mosquito	termite	ant

1. This insect wants to eat your house!

2. This insect might show up at your picnic.

3. This insect is like a tiny vampire.

4. This insect makes its own light.

5. This insect is covered with small black spots.

J Jokes

Write the answer that makes each joke funny.

palm　　She wanted rich soil.　　It gets unhoppy.　　bedbug　　three days old

1. What is an insect after it is two days old?

2. What happens when a frog gets stuck in the mud?

3. Why did the gardener bury her money?

4. Which trees clap?

5. What kind of insect sleeps most?

Cursive Writing Practice

Label the bones with the correct words.

| skull | kneecap | ankle | shin | collarbone | elbow | jaw | pelvis |

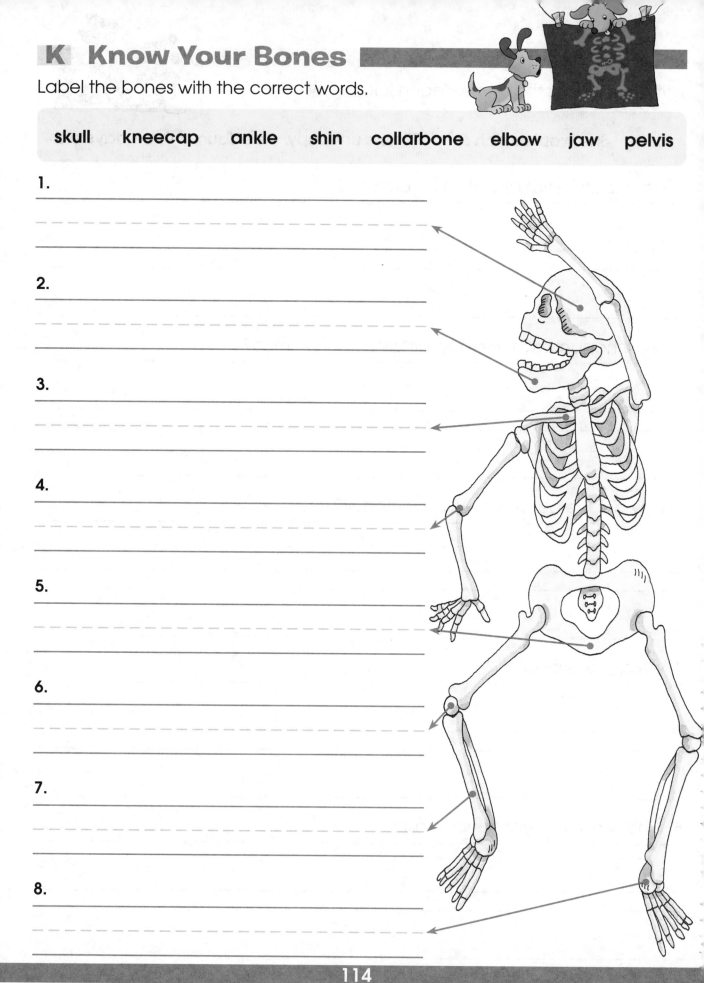

1. _____

2. _____

3. _____

4. _____

5. _____

6. _____

7. _____

8. _____

Cursive Writing Practice

©School Zone Publishing Company 06320

L Logic Puzzles

Patti, Mary, and Paul have different favorite foods.
Read the information in the charts below to complete the puzzle.
Write each child's favorite food on the line.

Patti _____

Mary _____

Paul _____

Patti does not like chicken.

	Patti	Mary	Paul
Pizza			
Spaghetti			
Chicken	no		

Mary will not eat foods that have tomatoes in them.
(Hint: Tomatoes are in spaghetti and pizza.)

	Patti	Mary	Paul
Pizza		no	
Spaghetti		no	
Chicken	no	yes	

Paul likes a food that starts with the same letter as his name.
(Hint: If Paul likes pizza, then spaghetti or chicken must not be his favorite.)

	Patti	Mary	Paul
Pizza		no	yes
Spaghetti		no	no
Chicken	no	yes	no

©School Zone Publishing Company 06320

Cursive Writing Practice

Write the name of the animal that matches each clue.

whale	elephant	bat	fox	giraffe

1. This mammal has a long neck.

2. This mammal carries a trunk.

3. The blue one is the largest mammal.

4. This is a flying mammal.

5. This mammal is a member of the dog family.

Solve the problems. Write the answers in the puzzle.

Across

A. 10 more than 25 = _____

B. 120 – 15 = _____

C. 51 + 35 = _____

D. 25¢ + 30¢ = _____¢

E. 137 – 64 = _____

F. one dozen = _____

G. 85, 90, 95, _____

H. 9 tens, 2 ones = _____

I. 6 x 8 = _____

J. 28 ÷ 2 = _____

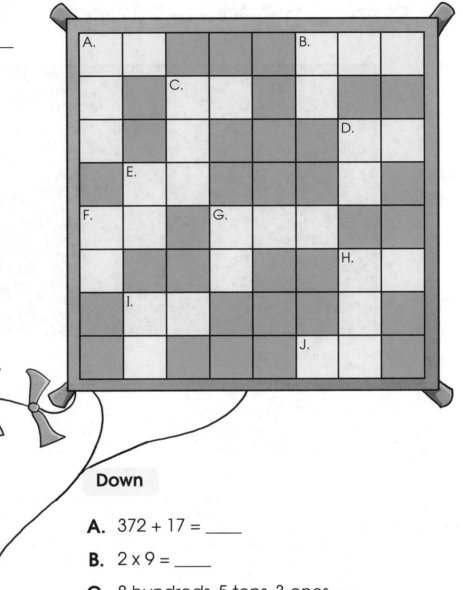

Down

A. 372 + 17 = _____

B. 2 x 9 = _____

C. 8 hundreds, 5 tens, 3 ones = _____

D. 105 – 54 = _____

E. 8 x 9 = _____

F. 4, 8, 12, _____

G. 45 ÷ 3 = _____

H. 9 hundreds, 7 tens, 4 ones = _____

I. 85¢ – 40¢ = _____¢

Cursive Writing Practice

O Oceans

Write on the lines to show where each ocean is located.

Atlantic Ocean	Indian Ocean	Pacific Ocean	Arctic Ocean	Antarctic Ocean

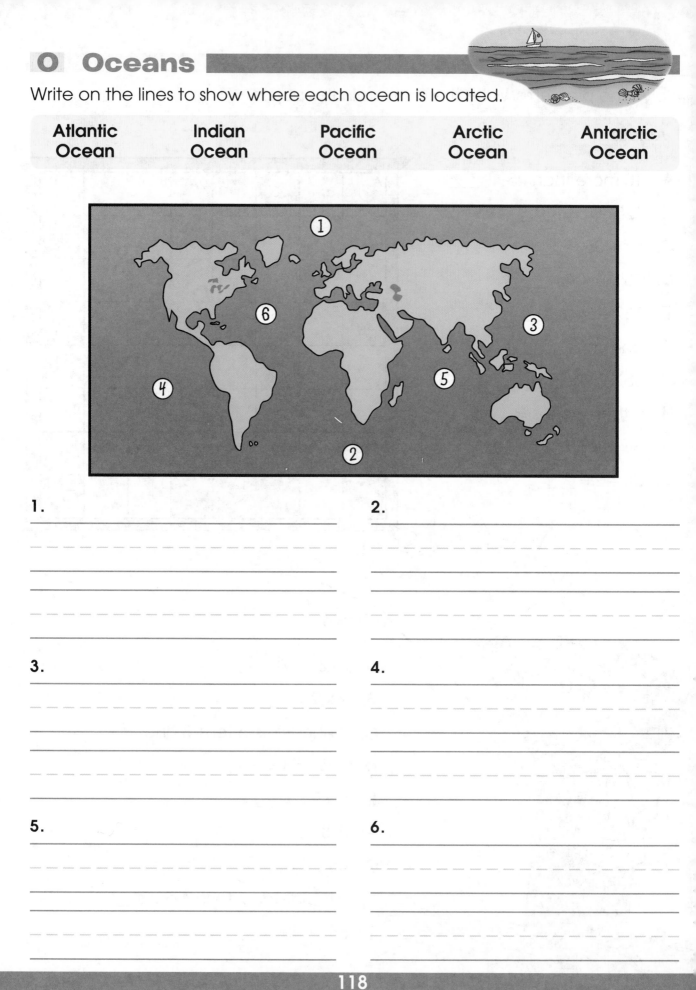

1. _____

2. _____

3. _____

4. _____

5. _____

6. _____

Cursive Writing Practice   ©School Zone Publishing Company 06320

P Presidents

Write the name of the president who matches each clue.

Lincoln	Washington	Jefferson	Reagan	Kennedy

1. He was the youngest elected president.

2. He was known as the "father" of his country.

3. He was an actor who became president.

4. He was the president during the Civil War.

5. He was the president who was also an inventor.

Cursive Writing Practice

The nouns are in the wrong similes. Write the correct noun on each line.

| silk | bear | feather | bug | night |

1. as light as a ~~rock~~

_____

_____

_____

2. as dark as ~~silk~~

_____

_____

_____

3. as hungry as a ~~wink~~

_____

_____

_____

4. as cute as a ~~bone~~

_____

_____

_____

5. as smooth as ~~night~~

_____

_____

_____

R Rivers

Write where each river is located.

North America	Africa	South America	Asia

1. Nile

2. Amazon

3. Yangtze

4. Mississippi

Cursive Writing Practice

Write the answer that completes each sentence.

energy	Galaxy	light	heat	gas	Milky Way

1. _____ is another word for star system.

2. The sun gives out _____ and _____ .

3. A star is made of _____ and has no solid surface.

4. Our galaxy is named the _____ _____ .

5. Light and heat are forms of _____ .

T Analogy Test

Write the word that completes each analogy.

computer	author	pound	rug	brake

1. Grass is to ground as _____ is to floor.

2. Bat is to baseball player as _____ is to writer.

3. Knife is to cut as hammer is to _____.

4. Artist is to painting as _____ is to novel.

5. Start is to go as _____ is to stop.

©School Zone Publishing Company 06320

Cursive Writing Practice

U United States

Write the answer that matches each clue.

Alaska	Michigan	New York	Hawaii	Missouri

1. Lake _____ is the largest lake within U.S. borders.

2. _____ is the newest state.

3. _____ is the largest state (in size).

4. The _____ River is the longest U.S. river.

5. _____ is the city with the most people.

V Vegetables

Write the name of each vegetable under the correct plant part.

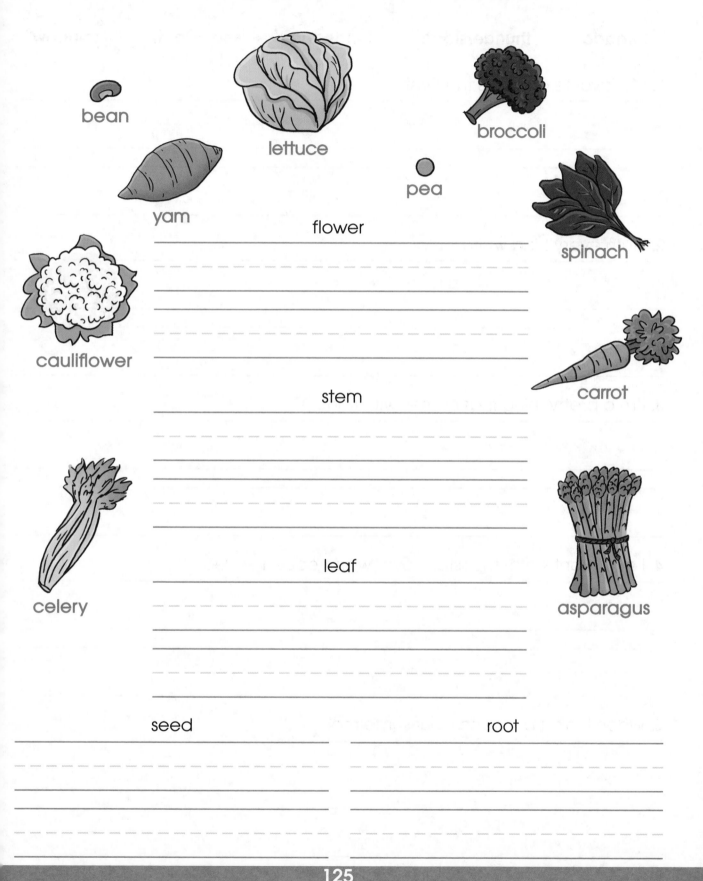

bean

lettuce

broccoli

yam

pea

spinach

flower

cauliflower

carrot

stem

celery

leaf

asparagus

seed

root

Cursive Writing Practice

W Weather

Write the answer that matches each clue.

tornado	thunderstorm	hurricane	snowstorm	rainbow

1. My favorite dance is the Twist.

2. I turn everything white.

3. I'm a pretty thing that comes with rain.

4. I'm a giant storm that starts over warm ocean water.

5. When I rain, I pour and pour some more.

Cursive Writing Practice   ©School Zone Publishing Company 06320

X X Marks the Spot

Write the name of the city found at each point.

J
I
H   St. Joseph   Hannibal
G   Kansas City
F   Sedalia   St. Louis
E   Jefferson City
D
C
B   Joplin   Springfield
A   Branson   New Madrid

0 1 2 3 4 5 6 7 8 9 10

Missouri

Ice cream cones were first served at the 1904 Louisiana Purchase Exposition World's Fair in St. Louis.

1. (4, A)

2. (2, B)

3. (8, F)

4. (2, G)

5. (6, H)

6. (4, F)

© School Zone Publishing Company 06320

Y Yellowstone National Park

Write the answer that completes each sentence.

Wyoming	glaciers	Louisiana	geysers	Grant

1. Yellowstone National Park was shaped by volcanoes and _____.

2. The Yellowstone region was acquired as part of the _____ Purchase.

3. Yellowstone National Park is located mainly in _____.

4. Old Faithful is one of the _____ in the park.

5. In 1872, President _____ made Yellowstone the first National Park.

Cursive Writing Practice   ©School Zone Publishing Company 06320

Z Zoo Quiz

Write the name of the animal that matches each clue.

| platypus | flea | ostrich | cheetah | chameleon |

1. I run up to 70 miles per hour.

2. I grow up to 9 feet tall and weigh 300 pounds.

3. I can jump up to 200 times the length of my own body.

4. I can change my color.

5. I am a mammal that lays eggs.

Cursive Writing Practice

Water Words

Write the word that matches each description.

tide	currents	salt	waves	sand

1. These are like giant rivers in the ocean.

2. This is something you can taste in the ocean water.

3. This is the daily rise and fall of ocean water.

4. These form when winds move ocean water toward the shore.

5. This is made up of tiny pieces of rock and coral.

Cursive Writing Practice   ©School Zone Publishing Company 06320

Idioms

Idioms are expressions or phrases that do not mean what they say.
Match each idiom with its meaning.

getting angry	telling a secret	taking a chance	being happy	being quiet

1. going out on a limb

2. walking on air

3. biting your tongue

4. blowing your top

5. spilling the beans

Cursive Writing Practice

Leaping Lizards!

Write the word that completes each sentence.

| tails | insects | iguana | tongue | dinosaurs |

1. Lizards have existed since the time of the _____ .

2. A chameleon catches bugs with its long, sticky _____ .

3. One lizard that eats plants is the _____ .

4. Some lizards eat _____ .

5. Some lizards drop their _____ when they're in trouble.

Cursive Writing Practice   ©School Zone Publishing Company 06320

Weather Words

Write the word that completes each sentence.

| wind | water | air pressure | precipitation | condensation |

1. Rain, snow, and hail are kinds of _____.

2. Drops of water on a cold can are _____.

3. The push of air on Earth is _____ _____.

4. Cold air can't hold as much _____ as warm air.

5. Moving air is _____.

Cursive Writing Practice

Sports

Write the word that matches each clue.

| baseball | football | squash | golf | soccer |

1. Batter up!

2. small ball

3. not a veggie

4. pointy ball

5. It's a kick!

Cursive Writing Practice

©School Zone Publishing Company 06320

Addition Clue Words

Some clue words tell you to **add**. These clue words are: **in all, altogether, sum,** and **total**. There are **6** steps to follow when solving all word problems.

1. Read the problem carefully.
2. Look for clue words and underline them.
3. Decide what you must do.
4. Write the number sentence.
5. Solve the problem.
6. Write a complete sentence that includes the answer.

Sara saw **23** butterflies when she was walking in the field. When she stopped to rest, she saw **10** grasshoppers. How many insects did she see **altogether**?

The number sentence:

$$\begin{array}{r} 23 \\ +\ 10 \\ \hline 33 \end{array}$$

The answer:

Sara saw **33** insects altogether.

Underline the word or words that give you the clue to **add**. Then use the **6** steps to solve the word problem.

1. While hiking in the woods, Calvin picked up **34** rocks. He then spotted **12** new rocks and picked them up also. What is the total number of rocks that Calvin found?

2. Yesterday Jamie saw **14** birds in her yard. Today she saw **39** birds in her yard. How many birds did she see in all?

©School Zone Publishing Company 06320   Addition Clue Words

Addition Word Problems

Underline the word or words that give you the clue to **add**. Solve the problem. Remember to follow the **6** steps.

1. Stephanie had **25** dolls in her collection. She received **11** more for her birthday. What is the total number of dolls Stephanie has in her collection?

2. Dalton had **31** baseball cards. His dad gave him **22** more. How many baseball cards does he have in all?

3. Andy counted **64** dandelions. Beth counted **26** violets. What is the sum of the flowers they counted?

4. Adam found **91** small twigs and **29** larger twigs for the campfire. How many twigs did he find altogether?

5. In her week of camping, Krista saw **15** chipmunks run for the safety of their homes. She also saw **15** squirrels climb into the trees. How many animals did Krista see in all?

6. Alesha caught **52** fish. Yumiko caught **39** fish. What is the total number of fish they caught?

Subtraction Clue Words

Some clue words tell you to **subtract**. These clue words are: **how many more, how many are left**, and **difference**. The same **6** steps you used for addition can also be used for subtraction problems.

1. Read the problem carefully.
2. Look for clue words and underline them.
3. Decide what you must do.
4. Write the number sentence.
5. Solve the problem.
6. Write a complete sentence that includes the answer.

Steve played **12** games with his baseball team. His team will be playing **57** games this season. **How many more** games will Steve need to play to complete the season?

The number sentence:

$$\begin{array}{r} 57 \\ -\ 12 \\ \hline 45 \end{array}$$

The answer:

Steve needs to play **45** more games to complete the season.

Underline the word or words that give you the clue to **subtract**. Then use the **6** steps to solve the word problems.

1. Chelsea threw the ball **29** feet. Meagan threw the ball **27** feet. What was the difference between their throws in feet?

2. Yesterday John kicked the soccer ball **68** times during the game. Today he kicked the ball **49** times. How many more times did he kick the ball yesterday?

©School Zone Publishing Company 06320

Subtraction Clue Words

Subtraction Word Problems

Underline the word or words that give you the clue to **subtract**. Then use the **6** steps to help you solve the word problems.

1. Sue delivered **46** newspapers. Tom delivered **35** newspapers. How many more newspapers did Sue deliver?

2. Jennifer sold **72** candy bars. Patti sold **56** candy bars. How many more candy bars did Jennifer sell?

3. Kim wants to do **75** cartwheels. She has already done **16** cartwheels. How many cartwheels are left for Kim to do?

4. Eric ran the race in **43** seconds. Scott ran the race in **46** seconds. What was the difference between their times in seconds?

5. Elliot wants to hit the tennis ball against the wall **100** times. He has hit the ball against the wall **66** times. How many hits are left for him to do?

Add or Subtract

On this page you will need to decide whether to **add** or **subtract**. Remember the **6** steps.

1. Read the problem carefully.
2. Look for clue words and underline them.
3. Decide what you must do.
4. Write the number sentence.
5. Solve the problem.
6. Write a complete sentence that includes the answer.

There are **178** sixth grade students and **106** fifth grade students. How many more sixth grade students are there?

What to do: ___subtract___

The answer:

There are **72** more sixth grade students.

Underline the word or words that give you the clue to **add** or **subtract**. Then use the **6** steps to solve the word problem.

1. In our school there are **328** girls and **297** boys. How many children are there in our school altogether?

   What to do: _____

2. The class painted **10** pictures on Monday and **13** pictures on Tuesday. How many more pictures did they paint on Tuesday?

   What to do: _____

3. Jessica brought **45** pennies to school and Sam brought **25** pennies to school. How many pennies did they bring in all?

   What to do: _____

4. Miss Bracken had **160** pieces of chalk. She broke **73** of them. How many pieces were left unbroken?

   What to do: _____

Add or Subtract

Addition & Subtraction Problems

Write the number sentence. Solve the problem.

1. There were **16** spotted butterflies in the field. They were joined by **18** plain butterflies. What is the sum of the butterflies in the field?

2. There are **15** spiders on the porch. If **10** of those spiders leave the porch, how many spiders will be left?

3. There are **98** grasshoppers in the grass. There are also **65** beetles in the grass. How many more grasshoppers are there?

4. There were **120** brown ants and **92** black ants marching down the ant hill. How many more brown ants were there?

5. There are **127** big flies buzzing around the pond. Also buzzing around are **112** little flies. How many flies are there altogether?

6. There are **25** bees and **13** hornets flying near the bush. How many insects are there in all?

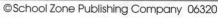

Addition & Subtraction Problems

When adding money, keep the decimal point in line.

Jacob bought a pencil for **$0.92** He also bought an eraser for **$0.37**. How much money did he spend altogether?

The number sentence:
$$\begin{array}{r} \$0.92 \\ + \ \$0.37 \\ \hline \$1.29 \end{array}$$

The answer:

He spent **$1.29** altogether.

Write the number sentence. Solve the problem.

1. Molly bought a box of cat food for **$1.64**. She then went to the candy store and bought some gum for **$0.35**. How much money did she spend in all?

2. Mandi bought a book that cost **$5.00**. Her friend Justin bought a used book that cost **$0.25**. How much more did Mandi spend?

3. Jaric saw a bottle of shampoo that cost **$1.72**. He also saw conditioner that cost **$1.18**. If he purchased both items, what would the sum be?

4. At a garage sale, Nancy bought a baseball card that cost **$3.01**. She also purchased a ring for **$0.45**. How much money did she spend in all?

5. Lauren bought some beads for **$2.60**. She later bought some string for **$0.55**. How much more money did she spend on the beads?

©School Zone Publishing Company 06320

Addition and Subtraction Problems

Addition & Subtraction Problems

Write the number sentence. Solve the problem.

1. The band marched **65** minutes in the morning and **45** minutes in the afternoon. How many minutes did the band march altogether?

2. The band has **25** tubas and **19** trombones. How many more tubas does the band have?

3. The band went on a field trip. It traveled **275** miles going and **280** miles returning. How many miles did the band travel in all?

4. There are **29** flutes in the band and **20** drums. What is the difference in number between these instruments?

5. There are **125** people in the band. There are only **65** uniforms. How many more uniforms are needed?

6. Jill knows how to play **26** marching songs. Jack knows how to play **32**. What is the total number of songs they know?

Addition and Subtraction Problems　　　　　　　　©School Zone Publishing Company 06320

Drawing Multiplication Word Problems

It is sometimes helpful to draw a picture of the information given to you in word problems. Using a graph will help you to organize and keep your information accurate. Here is an example:

Miss Halt stopped **5** rows of cars.　　　　There were **9** cars in each row.

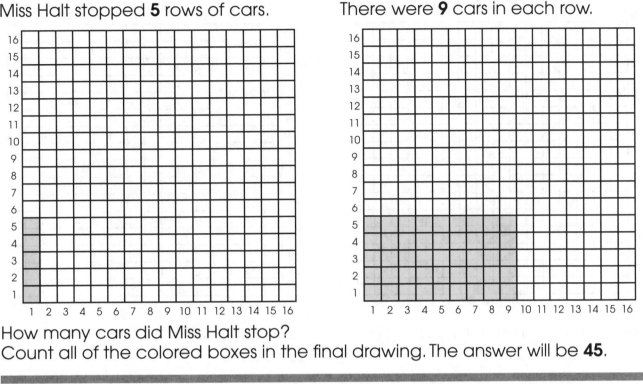

How many cars did Miss Halt stop?
Count all of the colored boxes in the final drawing. The answer will be **45**.

Read and solve each problem using the drawing method shown above.

1. Miss Halt helps about **15** people across the street each week.

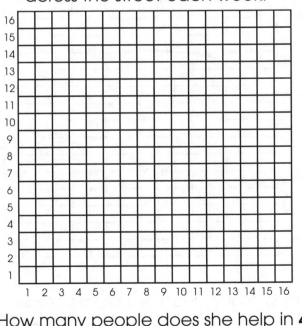

How many people does she help in **4** weeks? _____

2. Suppose Miss Halt gave **12** tickets in a day.

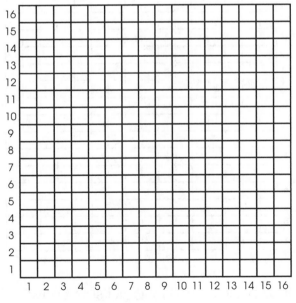

If she did this for **6** days, how many tickets would she give? _____

　　　　　　Drawing Multiplication Word Problems

Drawing Multiplication Word Problems

Read and solve each problem using the drawing method shown on page 143.

1. Miss Halt practiced directing traffic. She practiced for **7** hours a day. She practiced for **11** days.

How many hours did she practice?

_____

2. Miss Halt has **10** boxes. In each box she has **10** whistles.

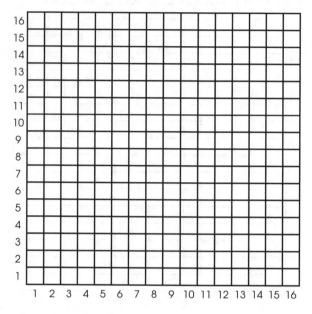

How many whistles does she have?

_____

3. Miss Halt blew her whistle **12** times in one day. Let's say she blew it that many times for **3** days.

How many times would she blow her whistle? _____

4. Miss Halt gave directions to **14** people. Each person asked **5** questions.

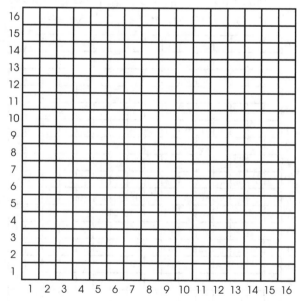

How many questions were asked?

_____

Drawing Division Word Problems

It is sometimes helpful to draw a picture of the information given to you in word problems. Here is another example:

Carl has **3** toolboxes. He needs to divide **15** hammers equally into all his toolboxes.

First draw **3** toolboxes. Then, beginning with the first box, draw one dot in each box. Each dot will represent one hammer. Repeat until all **15** hammers are drawn.

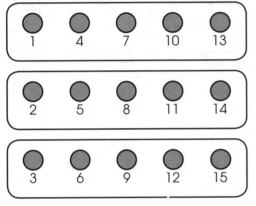

How many hammers will he place in each box?
Count the number of dots that were drawn in one box. The answer will be **5**.

Read and solve each problem using the drawing method shown above.

1. There are **4** construction workers. There are a total of **32** nails. How many nails does each worker get in order to have an equal amount of nails? _____

2. There are **8** construction workers. They have **56** screwdrivers. How many screwdrivers will each worker get in order to have an equal amount of screwdrivers? _____

Drawing Division Word Problems

Read and solve each problem using the drawing method shown on page 145.

1. There are **4** trucks. There are **32** pieces of wood. How many pieces of wood would be placed into each truck so that each truck has an equal amount of wood?

2. There are **7** toolboxes. There are **49** saws. How many saws will be in each box in order to have an equal amount in each box?

3. There were **8** people with drills. There were **48** holes drilled into the wall. Each person drilled an equal number of holes. How many holes did each person drill?

4. There were **6** toolboxes. There were **42** wrenches. Each toolbox contained an equal number of wrenches. How many wrenches were in each box?

Multiplication Clue Words

Some clue words tell you to **multiply**. These clue words are: **how many** and **how much**. Remember that multiplying is a quicker form of addition. Use the **6** steps to help you solve the word problems.

There were **15** people ready to begin the race. Each person had **2** water bottles at the finish line. **How many** water bottles were there at the finish line?

The number sentence:

$$\begin{array}{r} 15 \\ \times\ 2 \\ \hline 30 \end{array}$$

The answer:

There were **30** water bottles at the finish line.

Underline the clue words that tell you to **multiply**. Then solve the word problem.

1. There are **7** swimmers waiting for their finishing ribbons. Each swimmer will receive **3** ribbons. How many finishing ribbons are there altogether?

2. Amy trained for **5** hours every day to get ready for her big game. She trained for **30** days. How much time, in hours, did she spend training?

3. There were **72** bikers at the start of the race. Each biker had **1** helmet. How many helmets were there?

Multiplication Word Problems

Underline the clue words that tell you to **multiply**.
Then solve the word problem.

1. There were **16** golfers from each school at the tournament. **5** schools participated. How many golfers were there altogether?

2. Dana drove his snowmobile **37** miles a day for **8** days. How many miles did he drive in all?

3. Curtis trained for **39** days to get ready for the race. He drank **8** glasses of water every day that he trained. How many glasses of water did Curtis drink throughout his training?

4. There were **8** rows of bikers. There were **6** bikers in each row. How many bikers were there altogether?

5. There were **96** swimmers waiting to race. Each swimmer brought **4** friends to watch the race. How many friends were there at the race?

Multiplication Word Problems   ©School Zone Publishing Company 06320

More Multiplication Word Problems

Write the number sentence. Then solve the word problem.

1. There were **57** skaters at the start of the race. Each skater had **2** knee pads. How many knee pads were there?

2. Keli practiced for **19** days to prepare for her dance recital. Every day she practiced for **3** hours. How many hours did she practice in all?

3. Daniel has **3** cases to hold his toy planes. Each case holds **18** planes. How many planes can Daniel store in his cases?

4. Nadia's classroom has **12** rows of chairs. Each row has **5** chairs. How many chairs are in Nadia's classroom?

149

Division Clue Words

Some clue words mean to **divide**. These clue words are: **how many** and **each**. To solve each word problem use the **6** steps.

Kim planted **32** flowers. In **each** row there were **4** flowers. **How many** rows of flowers were there?

The number sentence:

$$4\overline{)32}^{\,8}$$

The answer:

There were **8** rows of flowers.

Underline the clue words that tell you to **divide**. Solve the problems.

1. Alesha planted **7** rows of carrots in her garden. Later, she pulled up the same number of carrots from each row. She counted **56** carrots. How many carrots did she pull from each row?

2. Scott and Brad had **48** flowers. They put **6** flowers in each vase. How many vases did they have?

3. Amy and John planted **30** rose bushes in **10** rows. Each row had the same number of bushes. How many rose bushes were in each row?

150

Division Word Problems

Underline the word or words that give you the clue to **divide**.
Solve the problems.

1. Jory had some bags and **56** pieces of candy. If he put **8** pieces into each bag, how many bags would he have?

2. Jamal planted **20** rows of onions in his garden. He pulled the same number of onions from each row. He counted **100** onions. How many onions did he pull from each row?

3. James was planting pine trees for his parents' tree farm. He planted **81** trees. There were **9** trees in each row. How many rows were there?

4. Margie has **45** plants in the tray she bought. The tray is divided into **9** rows. How many plants are in each row?

5. George picked **63** apples from **7** trees. He picked the same number of apples from each tree. How many apples did he pick from each tree?

More Division Word Problems

Write the number sentence. Then solve the word problem.

1. Katlin had **30** dolls. She divided them equally between herself and four friends while playing. How many dolls did each of the **5** girls have?

2. Jason swam **81** laps over a **9**-day period. If he swam the same distance every day, how many laps did he swim each day?

3. Dorry likes to send postcards to her friends. She mailed **24** postcards to **12** of her friends. Each friend received the same number of cards. How many postcards did each friend receive?

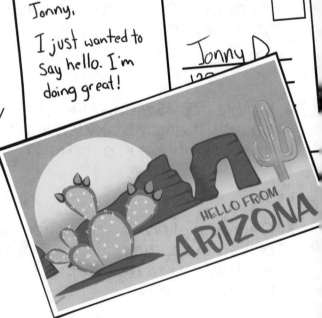

4. If a stamp costs **$0.29**, how many stamps could you buy with **$14.50**?

©School Zone Publishing Company 06320

Multiplication & Division Word Problems

Write the number sentence. Solve the problem.

1. Jamie bought **17** stamps. Andrew bought **3** times as many stamps. How many stamps did Andrew buy?

2. There are **40** letters in the mail bag. They are for **5** people. If each person gets the same number of letters, how many letters will each person get?

3. Miss James delivered **48** packets of letters. Each packet had **9** letters in it. How many letters did Miss James deliver?

4. Donna has pen pals in **15** countries. Suppose she has **3** pen pals in each country. How many pen pals would she have?

5. Mr. Koontz had **72** postcards. He put them in **9** equal piles. How many postcards were in each pile?

6. Miss James delivered **63** packages. She took **9** packages to each house. How many houses had packages delivered to them by Miss James?

©School Zone Publishing Company 06320

Multiplication and Division Word Problems

Multiplication & Division Word Problems

Write the number sentence. Solve the problem.

1. The Smiths drove **55** miles an hour for **5** hours. How many miles did they drive?

2. Tina Smith collects postcards. She has **81** postcards. She keeps equal amounts of them in **9** envelopes. How many postcards are in each envelope?

3. Mrs. Smith took pictures of the trip. If she took **125** pictures a day for **7** days, how many pictures would she take?

4. Ann Smith saw bears on **9** mountains. Suppose each mountain had **32** bears on it. How many bears would there be?

5. Mr. Smith packed **12** shirts. He packed them into **4** suitcases. If there were an equal number of shirts in each suitcase, how many shirts would be in each?

6. The Smiths rode on a cable car. There were **25** people waiting in line. Each cable cars holds **5** people. How many cable cars were needed?

Fractions

A **fraction** is a number that names part of a whole.

$\dfrac{2}{3}$ — **numerator**
    — **denominator**

$\dfrac{2}{3}$ = **2** pieces out of **3** equal parts.

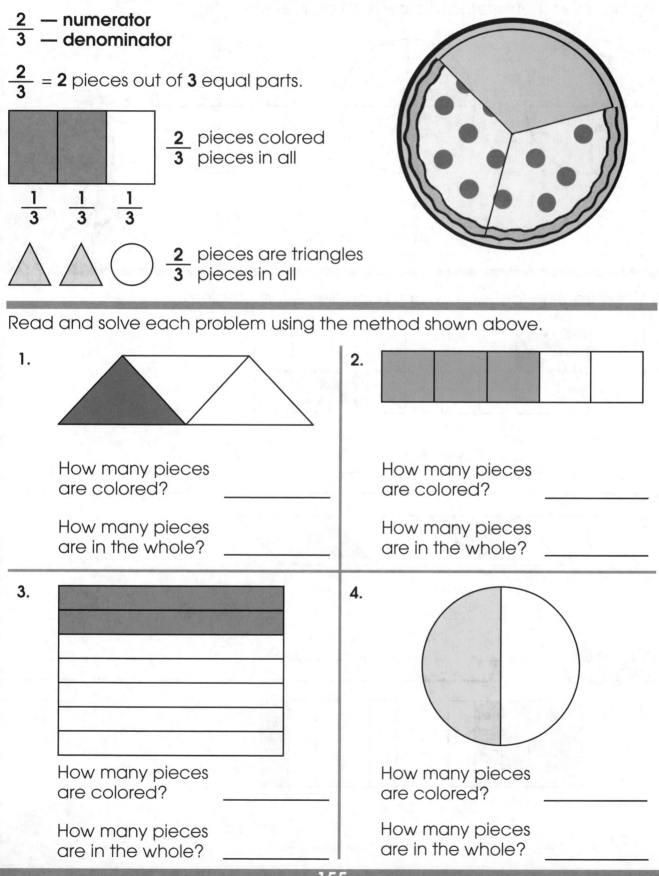

$\dfrac{2}{3}$ pieces colored
pieces in all

$\dfrac{1}{3}$ $\dfrac{1}{3}$ $\dfrac{1}{3}$

$\dfrac{2}{3}$ pieces are triangles
pieces in all

Read and solve each problem using the method shown above.

1.

How many pieces
are colored? _____

How many pieces
are in the whole? _____

2.

How many pieces
are colored? _____

How many pieces
are in the whole? _____

3.

How many pieces
are colored? _____

How many pieces
are in the whole? _____

4.

How many pieces
are colored? _____

How many pieces
are in the whole? _____

Adding & Subtracting Fractions

When you add or subtract fractions, you use only the top numbers (numerators). Below is an example:

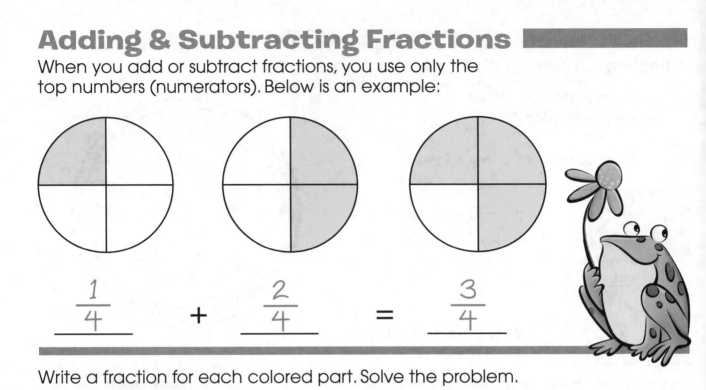

$$\frac{1}{4} \; + \; \frac{2}{4} \; = \; \frac{3}{4}$$

Write a fraction for each colored part. Solve the problem.

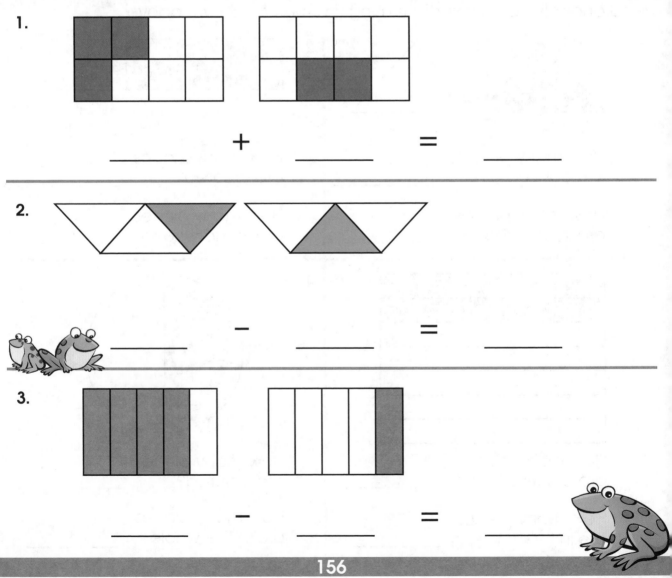

1.

___ + ___ = ___

2.

___ - ___ = ___

3.

___ - ___ = ___

Adding and Subtracting Fractions   ©School Zone Publishing Company 06320

Fractions in Word Problems

Sometimes you have fractions in word problems. Look for the clue words that tell you to add or subtract. Remember to add or subtract only the top number (numerator) of the fractions.

1. Read the problem carefully.
2. Look for clue words and underline them.
3. Decide what you must do.
4. Write the number sentence.
5. Solve the problem.
6. Write a complete sentence that includes the answer.

Mary planted $\frac{2}{7}$ of the garden with corn and $\frac{3}{7}$ with beans. How much of the garden did she use?

The number sentence:

$$\frac{2}{7} + \frac{3}{7} = \frac{5}{7}$$

The answer:

Mary used $\frac{5}{7}$ of the garden.

Using the **6** steps solve the word problems.

1. Wanda picked corn. She picked $\frac{8}{9}$ of a bushel on Wednesday. She picked $\frac{5}{9}$ of a bushel on Thursday. How much more did she pick on Wednesday than Thursday?

2. Kim dug $\frac{2}{4}$ of the garden in the morning and $\frac{1}{4}$ in the evening. How much of the garden did she dig altogether?

3. Suzanne must plant $\frac{8}{16}$ of the garden. She has planted $\frac{2}{16}$ so far. How much more must she plant?

Fractions in Word Problems

More Fractions in Word Problems

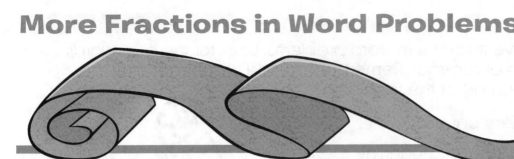

Read and solve each problem.

1. Todd bought $\frac{3}{8}$ of a yard of red fabric and $\frac{2}{8}$ of a yard of purple fabric. How much fabric did Todd buy?

2. Mom has only $\frac{9}{12}$ of an hour to paint. She painted for $\frac{3}{12}$ of an hour. How much more time does Mom have to paint?

3. Karen bought $\frac{5}{7}$ of a roll of flowered wallpaper. She used $\frac{3}{7}$. How much wallpaper does she have left?

4. Lucky used $\frac{2}{3}$ of a can of paint to paint a chair. He used $\frac{1}{3}$ of a can to paint a stool. How much more paint did it take for the chair?

5. Luis used $\frac{1}{4}$ cup of paste in one tray and $\frac{2}{4}$ cup in the other. How much paste did he use altogether?

6. Margie has one piece of wallpaper that is $\frac{12}{18}$ of a yard long. She has another that is $\frac{6}{18}$ of a yard long. What is the difference?

More Fractions in Word Problems

Logic Puzzles

Story problems give you information that helps you to solve a problem. These puzzles below give you a limited amount of information, but enough to solve the puzzle if you take some time to think. All of these puzzles will have a chart provided for you to record important information.

There are three children named Jenny, Tom, and Aaron. Each has a different favorite snack of applesauce, granola bars, or oranges. You need to decide what snack is the favorite for each child using the information below.

Jenny does not like oranges.

	Jenny	Tom	Aaron
Applesauce			
Granola Bar			
Oranges	no		

Tom will not eat foods that have apples in them. (*Hint: If Tom does not like foods with apples, then he must like oranges.*)

	Jenny	Tom	Aaron
Applesauce		no	
Granola Bar		no	
Oranges	no	yes	

Aaron likes a food that starts with the same letter as his name. (*Hint: If Aaron likes applesauce, then granola bars or oranges must not be his favorite.*)

	Jenny	Tom	Aaron
Applesauce		no	yes
Granola Bar		no	no
Oranges	no	yes	no

1. What is each child's favorite food according to the information given?

Jenny _____

Tom _____

Aaron _____

Logic Puzzles

Logic Puzzles

Here are a few logic puzzles for you to try. The charts are provided for you to record important information. Have fun!

1. Rachel's height is in between Nick's and Sam's.
Nick is taller than Sam.
What is the height of each child?

	Rachel	Nick	Sam
4'2"			
4'5"			
4'7"			

Rachel _____

Nick   _____

Sam   _____

2. Maggie is **9** years old. Susan is older than Maggie.
James is younger than Susan. Joe is the oldest. Can you
discover the ages of Maggie, Susan, Joe, and James?

	Maggie	Susan	Joe	James
8 years				
9 years				
10 years				
11 years				

Maggie is _____

Susan is _____

Joe is _____

James is _____

Logic Puzzles

Two-Step Problems

Sometimes you must use two steps to solve a problem. These problems are called two-step word problems.

There are **9** girls on the basketball team. Each girl needs a shirt and shorts for the games. A shirt costs **$3.50**. A pair of shorts cost **$5.00**. What is the total cost of all the outfits?

Step 1: Add to get the cost of one outfit.
Step 2: Multiply to get the cost of all the outfits.

Step 1:
$5.00 for a pair of shorts
+ $3.50 for a shirt
$8.50 total per outfit

Step 2:
$8.50 per outfit
x 9 number of girls
$76.50 for 9 outfits

The answer:
The total cost of all the outfits is **$76.50**.

Tell what the two steps are. Then solve the problem.

1. Angie has gym class **40** minutes a day. She has it **3** times a week. Nancy has gym class **90** minutes a week. How much longer does Angie have gym class compared to Nancy?

2. Craig put **208** tennis balls into **4** wire baskets. He put the same number of balls in each basket. Then he took **3** baskets of balls outdoors. How many tennis balls did Craig take outdoors?

3. P.J. sold **4** rabbits for **$3.75** each and **1** rabbit for **$4.50**. How much money did he get altogether?

4. Tim bought **6** tickets to the County Fair. Each ticket cost **$1.50**. How much change did he get from **$10.00**?

Two-Step Problems

Venn Diagrams

A Venn diagram uses circles to represent sets and their relationships.

Enjoy biking   Enjoy in-line skating

Ten children were surveyed to discover whether they enjoyed bicycling, in-line skating, or both. The **Venn diagram** above gives you all the information you need to answer the following questions. Hint: Where the **Venn diagram** intersects, the children are in both circles.

1. Which activity does Tamara enjoy? _____

2. Naomi and Sam enjoy the same activity. Which one is it? _____

3. How many children enjoy biking? _____

4. How many children enjoy in-line skating? _____

5. Who enjoys both biking and in-line skating? _____

6. How many children enjoy both biking and in-line skating? _____

Picture Graphs

A picture graph gives you information. Read it carefully. Make certain you understand what facts are being presented.

Enrollment in Joy School									
Boys	😊	😊	😊	😊	😊	😊			
Girls	😊	😊	😊	😊	😊	😊	😊		

Each symbol 😊 stands for **20** students.

1. How many boys are in Joy School? <u>120 boys</u> **(20 x 6 = 120)**

2. How many girls are in Joy School? <u>140 girls</u> **(20 x 7 = 140)**

Read the graph carefully. Make certain you understand what facts are being presented. Then answer the questions below.

Days Riding Bikes to School									
Nancy	🚲	🚲	🚲	🚲					
Kim	🚲	🚲							
Luis	🚲	🚲	🚲	🚲	🚲	🚲			
Ramona	🚲	🚲	🚲	🚲	🚲	🚲	🚲	🚲	
Fred	🚲								

Each bike 🚲 stands for **3** days.

1. Who rode to school the most days? _____

2. How many days did he or she ride to school? _____

3. How many days did Luis ride to school? _____

4. Nancy rode to school more days than Kim.
   How many more days did Nancy ride to school? _____

163

Bar Graphs

A bar graph gives you information. Read it carefully. Make sure you understand what facts are being presented.

Attendance at the School Play	50	100	150	200	250	300	350	400	450	500	550	600	650	700	750
WED.	■	■	■	■	■	■	■	■	■	■	■				
THURS.	■	■	■	■	■	■	■	■	■	■	■	■	■		
FRIDAY	■	■	■	■	■	■	■	■	■	■	■	■			

1. On what day did the most people attend the play? _____Thursday_____

2. How many people came that day? _____650_____

3. How many people came altogether? _____1,800_____

Study the graph. Then answer the questions below.

Tickets sold to the School Play	10	20	30	40	50
Albert					
Jennifer					
Lucy					
Todd					
Shirley					

1. Who sold the most tickets? _____

2. How many did Albert and Jennifer sell altogether? _____

3. How many did Lucy and Todd sell in total? _____

4. Todd sold more tickets than Shirley.
   How many more tickets did Todd sell? _____

5. Shirley sold more tickets than Albert.
   How many more tickets did Shirley sell? _____

164

Play Ball!

Multiplication is a short way to add equal groups.
The **x** sign means to multiply.

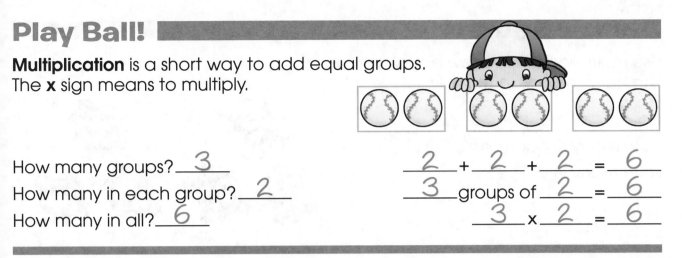

How many groups? __3__

How many in each group? __2__

How many in all? __6__

$\underline{2}$ + $\underline{2}$ + $\underline{2}$ = $\underline{6}$

$\underline{3}$ groups of $\underline{2}$ = $\underline{6}$

$\underline{3}$ x $\underline{2}$ = $\underline{6}$

How many are there? Fill in the blanks.

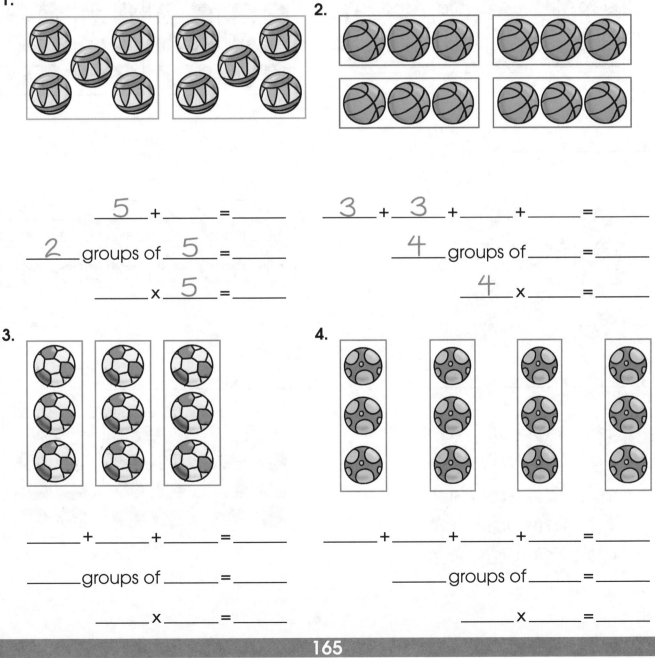

1.

$\underline{5}$ + _____ = _____

$\underline{2}$ groups of $\underline{5}$ = _____

_____ x $\underline{5}$ = _____

2.

$\underline{3}$ + $\underline{3}$ + _____ + _____ = _____

$\underline{4}$ groups of _____ = _____

$\underline{4}$ x _____ = _____

3.

_____ + _____ + _____ = _____

_____ groups of _____ = _____

_____ x _____ = _____

4.

_____ + _____ + _____ + _____ = _____

_____ groups of _____ = _____

_____ x _____ = _____

Understand Multiplication: Add Equal Groups

Animal Roundup

Use multiplication to show equal groups.
The **x** sign means to multiply.

How many groups? _2_

How many in each group? _3_

How many in all? _6_

___2___ x ___3___ = ___6___

Write a multiplication sentence to find how many.

   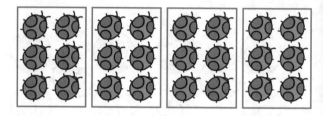

1. _____ x _____ = _____   **2.** _____ x _____ = _____

   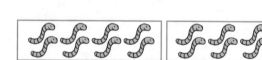

3. _____ x _____ = _____   **4.** _____ x _____ = _____

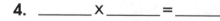
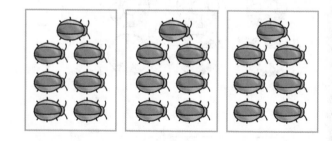

5. _____ x _____ = _____   **6.** _____ x _____ = _____

Make Snakes!

Find how many groups.
Find how many in each group.

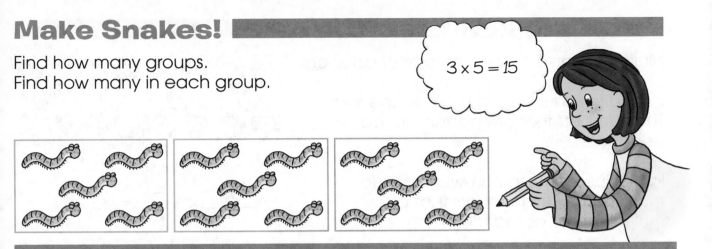

$3 \times 5 = 15$

Draw groups of snakes for each multiplication problem.
Then tell how many in all.

1. $2 \times 4 =$ _____

2. $5 \times 3 =$ _____

Draw more snakes. How many are there?

3. $2 \times 3 =$ _____

4. $3 \times 4 =$ _____

Understand Multiplication: Equal Groups

Addition, Addition

Multiplication is a different form of addition.

In addition, the answer is called the **sum**. The numbers that are added are called **addends**.

In multiplication, the answer is called the **product**. The numbers that are multiplied are called **factors**.

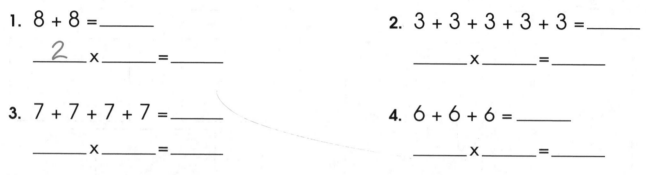

addends →$5 + 5 + 5 + 5 = \underline{20}$ ←sum

$\underline{\quad 4 \quad} \times \underline{\quad 5 \quad} = \underline{20}$

↑ factors ↑   ↑ product

Write each addition problem as a multiplication problem.
Find each sum and product.

1. $8 + 8 = \underline{\quad\quad}$

   $\underline{\quad 2 \quad} \times \underline{\quad\quad} = \underline{\quad\quad}$

2. $3 + 3 + 3 + 3 + 3 = \underline{\quad\quad}$

   $\underline{\quad\quad} \times \underline{\quad\quad} = \underline{\quad\quad}$

3. $7 + 7 + 7 + 7 = \underline{\quad\quad}$

   $\underline{\quad\quad} \times \underline{\quad\quad} = \underline{\quad\quad}$

4. $6 + 6 + 6 = \underline{\quad\quad}$

   $\underline{\quad\quad} \times \underline{\quad\quad} = \underline{\quad\quad}$

Write each multiplication problem as an addition problem.
Find each product and sum.

5. $5 \times 4 = \underline{\quad\quad}$

   $\underline{\quad\quad} + \underline{\quad\quad} + \underline{\quad\quad} + \underline{\quad\quad} + \underline{\quad\quad} = \underline{\quad\quad}$

6. $3 \times 7 = \underline{\quad\quad}$

   $\underline{\quad\quad} + \underline{\quad\quad} + \underline{\quad\quad} = \underline{\quad\quad}$

7. The sum and the product are the same in each problem.

   Multiplying is a different way of $\underline{\quad\quad\quad\quad\quad\quad\quad\quad\quad}$.

Understand Multiplication: Repeated Addition   ©School Zone Publishing Company 06320

You're a Problem Solver!

A book of stamps has 2 rows with 4 stamps in each row.
How many stamps are there?

$4 + 4 = 8$

$2 \times 4 = 8$

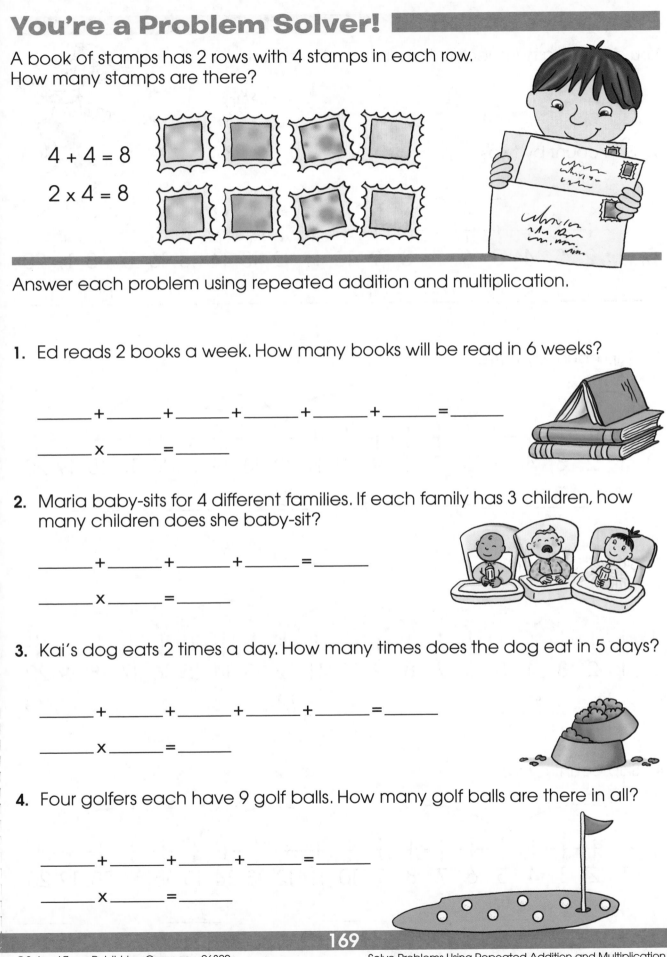

Answer each problem using repeated addition and multiplication.

1. Ed reads 2 books a week. How many books will be read in 6 weeks?

   _____ + _____ + _____ + _____ + _____ + _____ = _____

   _____ x _____ = _____

2. Maria baby-sits for 4 different families. If each family has 3 children, how many children does she baby-sit?

   _____ + _____ + _____ + _____ = _____

   _____ x _____ = _____

3. Kai's dog eats 2 times a day. How many times does the dog eat in 5 days?

   _____ + _____ + _____ + _____ + _____ = _____

   _____ x _____ = _____

4. Four golfers each have 9 golf balls. How many golf balls are there in all?

   _____ + _____ + _____ + _____ = _____

   _____ x _____ = _____

169

Solve Problems Using Repeated Addition and Multiplication

Skip on the Line!

You can use a number line to help you skip count.

skip, skip,
skip on the line...

1. Skip count by twos.

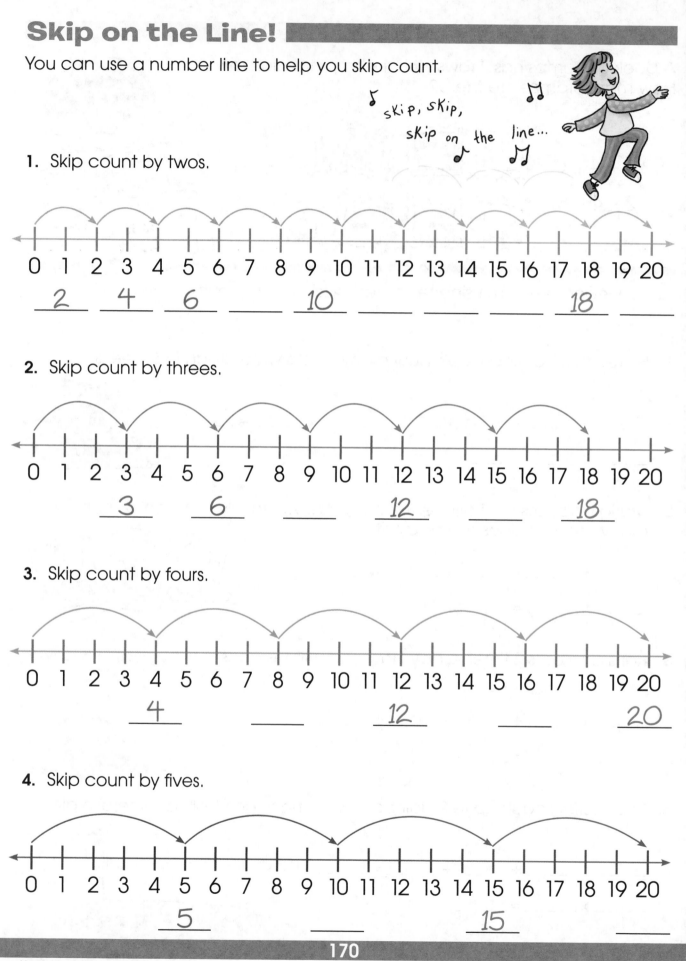

0 1 2 3 4 5 6 7 8 9 10 11 12 13 14 15 16 17 18 19 20

_2_ _4_ _6_ ___ _10_ ___ ___ ___ _18_ ___

2. Skip count by threes.

0 1 2 3 4 5 6 7 8 9 10 11 12 13 14 15 16 17 18 19 20

_3_ _6_ ___ _12_ ___ _18_

3. Skip count by fours.

0 1 2 3 4 5 6 7 8 9 10 11 12 13 14 15 16 17 18 19 20

_4_ ___ _12_ ___ _20_

4. Skip count by fives.

0 1 2 3 4 5 6 7 8 9 10 11 12 13 14 15 16 17 18 19 20

_5_ ___ _15_ ___

Use a Number Line to Skip Count

Little Critters

Practice skip counting. Connect the dots in each picture.

Start at the star. Skip count by threes.

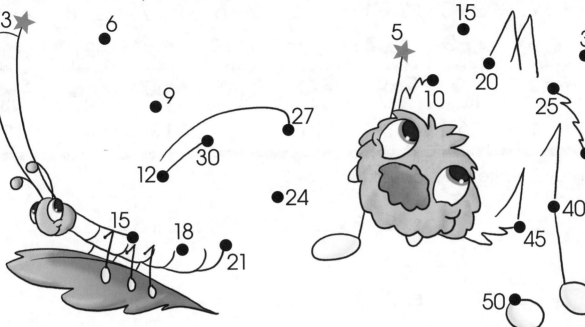

Start at the star. Skip count by fives.

Start at the star. Skip count by twos.

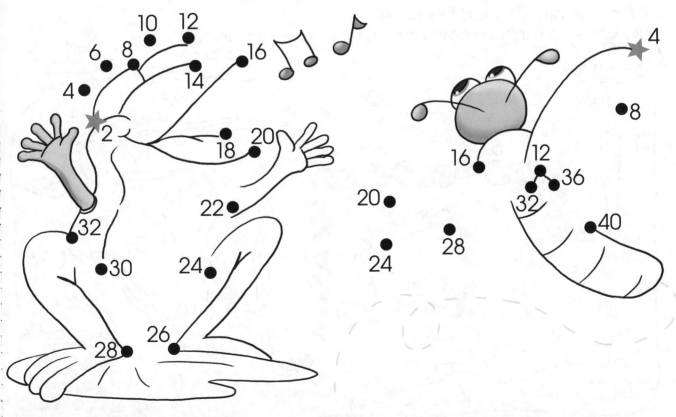

Start at the star. Skip count by fours.

Practice Skip Counting

Twice the Fun

When objects are in equal groups, you can skip count to find how many there are in all. To multiply by 2, skip count by twos. Find the products.

2×1	2×2	2×3	2×4	2×5	2×6	2×7	2×8	2×9
2	4	6	8	10	12	14	16	18

Multiply by 2. Write the product.

1. $2 \times 2 =$ _____

2. $2 \times 8 =$ _____

3. $2 \times 5 =$ _____

4. $2 \times 7 =$ _____

5. $2 \times 1 =$ _____

6. $2 \times 6 =$ _____

7. $2 \times 9 =$ _____

8. $2 \times 3 =$ _____

9. $2 \times 4 =$ _____

Start at the arrow to find the cake.
Follow the path in the same order as your answers above.

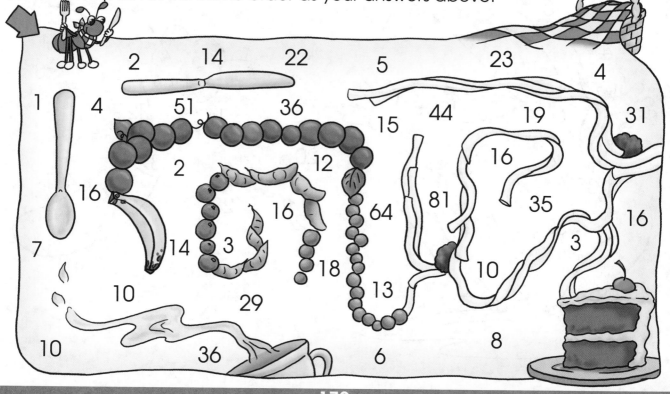

Multiply by 2

Do the Twos

2... 4... 6... 8...

1. Practice the facts.

$2 \times 1 = \underline{\hspace{1.5cm}}$

$2 \times 2 = \underline{\hspace{1.5cm}}$

$2 \times 3 = \underline{\hspace{1.5cm}}$

$2 \times 4 = \underline{\hspace{1.5cm}}$

$2 \times 5 = \underline{\hspace{1.5cm}}$

$2 \times 6 = \underline{\hspace{1.5cm}}$

$2 \times 7 = \underline{\hspace{1.5cm}}$

$2 \times 8 = \underline{\hspace{1.5cm}}$

$2 \times 9 = \underline{\hspace{1.5cm}}$

Count by twos to
check your answers.

2. Practice the facts.

$$\begin{array}{r} 4 \\ \times\,2 \\ \hline \end{array} \qquad \begin{array}{r} 8 \\ \times\,2 \\ \hline \end{array} \qquad \begin{array}{r} 5 \\ \times\,2 \\ \hline \end{array}$$

$$\begin{array}{r} 1 \\ \times\,2 \\ \hline \end{array} \qquad \begin{array}{r} 3 \\ \times\,2 \\ \hline \end{array} \qquad \begin{array}{r} 2 \\ \times\,2 \\ \hline \end{array}$$

$$\begin{array}{r} 9 \\ \times\,2 \\ \hline \end{array} \qquad \begin{array}{r} 3 \\ \times\,2 \\ \hline \end{array} \qquad \begin{array}{r} 8 \\ \times\,2 \\ \hline \end{array}$$

$$\begin{array}{r} 7 \\ \times\,2 \\ \hline \end{array} \qquad \begin{array}{r} 9 \\ \times\,2 \\ \hline \end{array} \qquad \begin{array}{r} 6 \\ \times\,2 \\ \hline \end{array}$$

3. When you multiply by 2, the product ends with a $\underline{\;2\;}$, $\underline{\hspace{1cm}}$, $\underline{\;6\;}$, $\underline{\hspace{1cm}}$,
or $\underline{\;0\;}$.

4. Complete the table.

x	0	1	2	3	4	5	6	7	8	9
2										

Multiply by 2

Three's a Breeze

To multiply by 3, skip count by threes to find the product.

3×1	3×2	3×3	3×4	3×5	3×6	3×7	3×8	3×9
3	6	9	12	15	18	21	24	27

Multiply by 3. Write the product.

1. $3 \times 4 = $ _____

2. $3 \times 1 = $ _____

3. $3 \times 5 = $ _____

4. $3 \times 6 = $ _____

5. $3 \times 8 = $ _____

6. $3 \times 2 = $ _____

7. $3 \times 7 = $ _____

8. $3 \times 9 = $ _____

9. $3 \times 3 = $ _____

Write a multiplication fact for each problem.

10. _____ x _____ = _____

11. _____ x _____ = _____

12. _____ x _____ = _____

13. _____ x _____ = _____

Multiply by 3

Three's Company

1. Practice the facts.

$3 \times 1 = \underline{\quad}$

$3 \times 2 = \underline{\quad}$

$3 \times 3 = \underline{\quad}$

$3 \times 4 = \underline{\quad}$

$3 \times 5 = \underline{\quad}$

$3 \times 6 = \underline{\quad}$

$3 \times 7 = \underline{\quad}$

$3 \times 8 = \underline{\quad}$

$3 \times 9 = \underline{\quad}$

Count by threes to check your answers.

2. Practice the facts.

$$\begin{array}{r} 5 \\ \times\ 3 \\ \hline \end{array} \qquad \begin{array}{r} 8 \\ \times\ 3 \\ \hline \end{array} \qquad \begin{array}{r} 4 \\ \times\ 3 \\ \hline \end{array}$$

$$\begin{array}{r} 2 \\ \times\ 3 \\ \hline \end{array} \qquad \begin{array}{r} 1 \\ \times\ 3 \\ \hline \end{array} \qquad \begin{array}{r} 2 \\ \times\ 3 \\ \hline \end{array}$$

$$\begin{array}{r} 6 \\ \times\ 3 \\ \hline \end{array} \qquad \begin{array}{r} 9 \\ \times\ 3 \\ \hline \end{array} \qquad \begin{array}{r} 8 \\ \times\ 3 \\ \hline \end{array}$$

$$\begin{array}{r} 9 \\ \times\ 3 \\ \hline \end{array} \qquad \begin{array}{r} 7 \\ \times\ 3 \\ \hline \end{array} \qquad \begin{array}{r} 6 \\ \times\ 3 \\ \hline \end{array}$$

Complete the table.

3.

x	0	1	2	3	4	5	6	7	8	9
3										

4.

x	6	3	1	0	2	7	4	9	5	8
3										

Multiply by 3

What's an Array?

An **array** shows objects in rows and columns. You can use an array to multiply. One factor is the number of rows. The other factor is the number of columns.

4 columns

3 rows

3 x 4 = 12

You can count all the objects in the array to make sure you have the correct answer.

Write a multiplication sentence to describe each array.

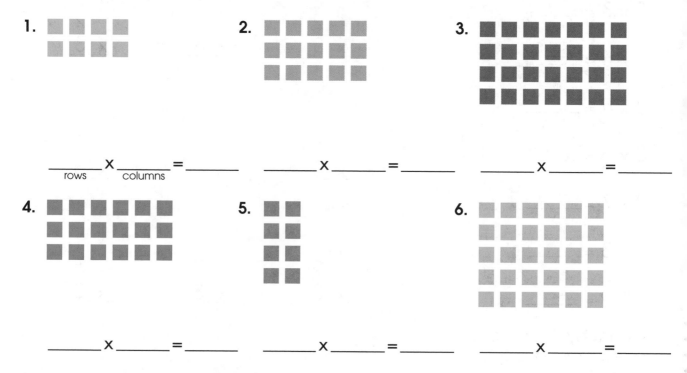

1. _____ x _____ = _____
     rows   columns

2. _____ x _____ = _____

3. _____ x _____ = _____

4. _____ x _____ = _____

5. _____ x _____ = _____

6. _____ x _____ = _____

Circle the pictures that show arrays.
Write a multiplication sentence for each array.

7.

8.

9.

_____

_____

_____

Understand Multiplication: Use Arrays   ©School Zone Publishing Company 06320

Display Arrays

To show an array, draw objects in neat rows and columns.

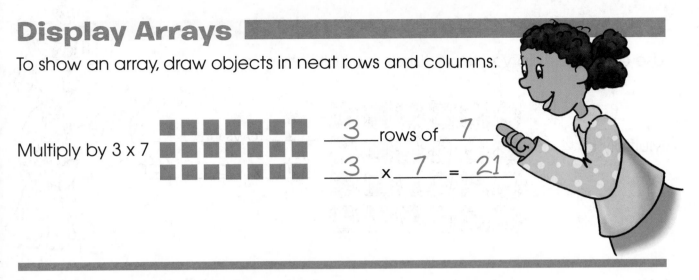

Multiply by 3 x 7

__3__ rows of __7__

__3__ x __7__ = __21__

Draw an array to find each product.

1. 2 x 6 = _____

2. 4 x 5 = _____

3. 5 x 3 = _____

4. 3 x 9 = _____

5. 2 x 8 = _____

6. 4 x 6 = _____

Understand Multiplication: Use Arrays

Explore the Fours

Use arrays to help you learn these multiplication facts.

Multiply by 4 x 6

___4___ rows of ___6___

___4___ x ___6___ = ___24___

Write a multiplication sentence for each array.

1.

_____ rows of _____

_____ x _____ = _____

2.

_____ rows of _____

_____ x _____ = _____

3. Practice the facts.

4 x 1 = _____

4 x 2 = _____

4 x 3 = _____

4 x 4 = _____

4 x 5 = _____

4 x 6 = _____

4 x 7 = _____

4 x 8 = _____

4 x 9 = _____

Count by fours to check your answers.

4. Practice the facts.

5	3	1	7	6	9	4	8
x 4	x 4	x 4	x 4	x 4	x 4	x 4	x 4

Multiply by 4

Serving Up a Riddle

Multiply.

I	N	L
1. $\begin{array}{r} 1 \\ \times\ 4 \\ \hline \end{array}$	2. $\begin{array}{r} 3 \\ \times\ 4 \\ \hline \end{array}$	3. $\begin{array}{r} 7 \\ \times\ 4 \\ \hline \end{array}$

A	E	B
4. $\begin{array}{r} 5 \\ \times\ 4 \\ \hline \end{array}$	5. $\begin{array}{r} 9 \\ \times\ 4 \\ \hline \end{array}$	6. $\begin{array}{r} 4 \\ \times\ 4 \\ \hline \end{array}$

T	L	S
7. $\begin{array}{r} 6 \\ \times\ 4 \\ \hline \end{array}$	8. $\begin{array}{r} 7 \\ \times\ 4 \\ \hline \end{array}$	9. $\begin{array}{r} 2 \\ \times\ 4 \\ \hline \end{array}$

Use your answers to decode the riddle below.
Write the letter for each answer on the correct blank.

What can you serve but never eat?

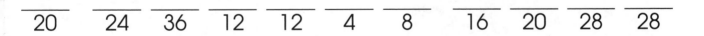

__ __ __ __ __ __ __ __ __ __ __
20   24   36   12   12   4   8   16   20   28   28

10. Complete the table.

x	0	1	2	3	4	5	6	7	8	9
4										

Multiply by 4

Save Your Nickels

A nickel is worth 5¢.
You can skip count to find the total amount of money.

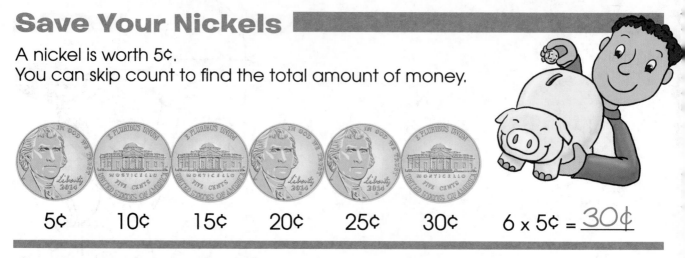

5¢   10¢   15¢   20¢   25¢   30¢   6 x 5¢ = _30¢_

Count the nickels. Fill in the missing numbers.

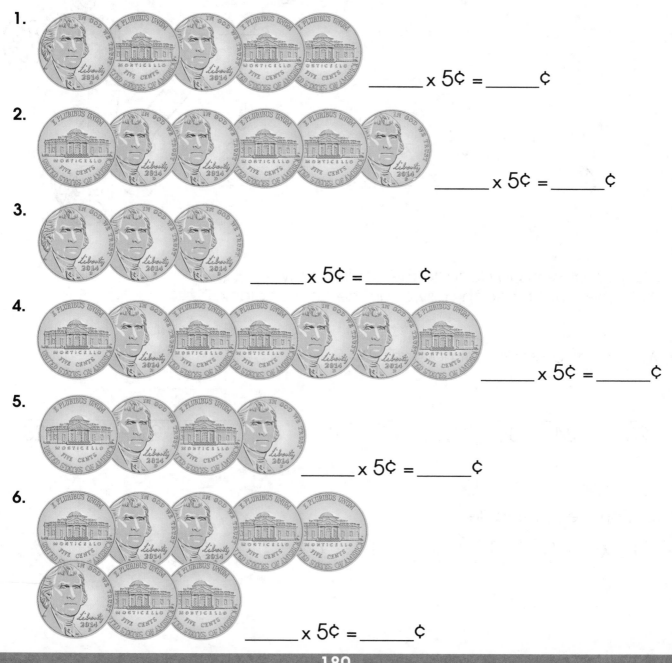

1. _____ x 5¢ = _____¢

2. _____ x 5¢ = _____¢

3. _____ x 5¢ = _____¢

4. _____ x 5¢ = _____¢

5. _____ x 5¢ = _____¢

6. _____ x 5¢ = _____¢

Multiply by 5   ©School Zone Publishing Company 06320

Five Alive!

1. Practice the facts.

$5 \times 1 = $ _____

$5 \times 2 = $ _____

$5 \times 3 = $ _____

$5 \times 4 = $ _____

$5 \times 5 = $ _____

$5 \times 6 = $ _____

$5 \times 7 = $ _____

$5 \times 8 = $ _____

$5 \times 9 = $ _____

Count by fives to
check your answers.

2. Practice the facts.

$$\begin{array}{r} 3 \\ \times\ 5 \\ \hline \end{array} \qquad \begin{array}{r} 1 \\ \times\ 5 \\ \hline \end{array} \qquad \begin{array}{r} 5 \\ \times\ 5 \\ \hline \end{array}$$

$$\begin{array}{r} 8 \\ \times\ 5 \\ \hline \end{array} \qquad \begin{array}{r} 6 \\ \times\ 5 \\ \hline \end{array} \qquad \begin{array}{r} 2 \\ \times\ 5 \\ \hline \end{array}$$

$$\begin{array}{r} 7 \\ \times\ 5 \\ \hline \end{array} \qquad \begin{array}{r} 6 \\ \times\ 5 \\ \hline \end{array} \qquad \begin{array}{r} 4 \\ \times\ 5 \\ \hline \end{array}$$

$$\begin{array}{r} 9 \\ \times\ 5 \\ \hline \end{array} \qquad \begin{array}{r} 5 \\ \times\ 4 \\ \hline \end{array} \qquad \begin{array}{r} 5 \\ \times\ 7 \\ \hline \end{array}$$

3. When you multiply by 5, the product ends with a _____ or a _____.

4. Complete the table.

x	0	1	2	3	4	5	6	7	8	9
5										

Multiply by 5

Skip Ahead!

Skip count to finish each pattern.

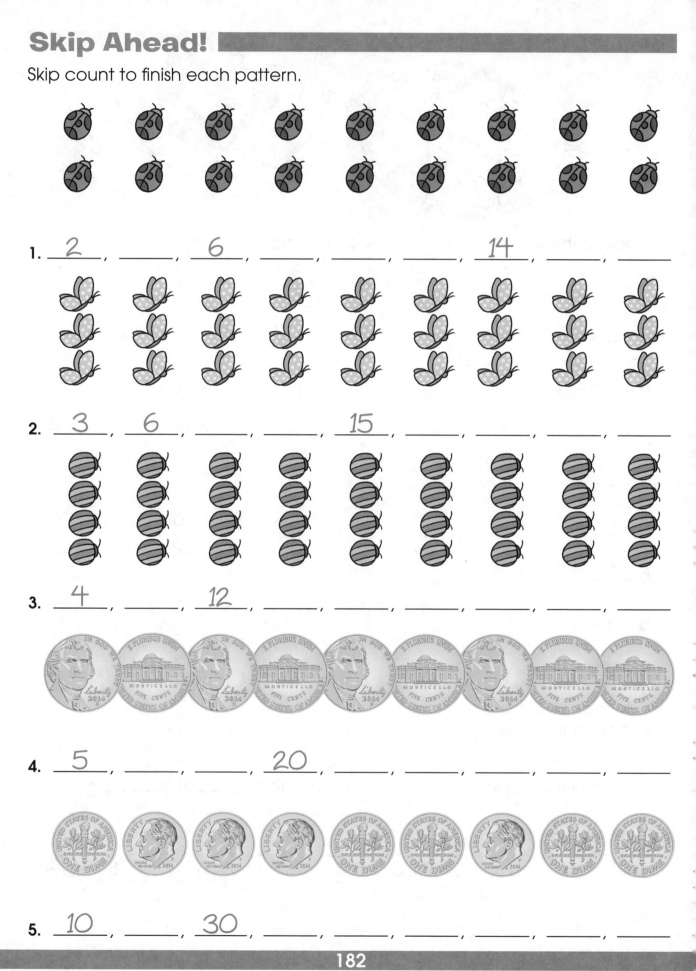

1. __2__, _____, __6__, _____, _____, _____, __14__, _____, _____

2. __3__, __6__, _____, _____, __15__, _____, _____, _____, _____

3. __4__, _____, __12__, _____, _____, _____, _____, _____, _____

4. __5__, _____, _____, __20__, _____, _____, _____, _____, _____

5. __10__, _____, __30__, _____, _____, _____, _____, _____, _____

Quick Count

Circle groups of 5. Then skip count.

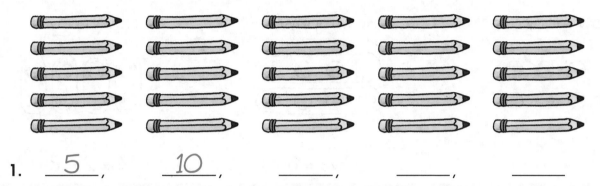

1. ___5___, ___10___, _____, _____, _____

Circle groups of 4. Then skip count.

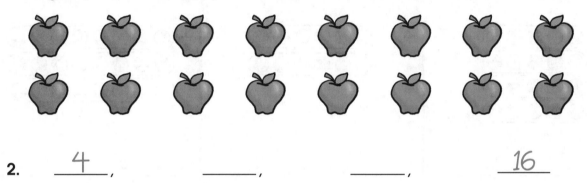

2. ___4___, _____, _____, ___16___

Circle groups of 2. Then skip count.

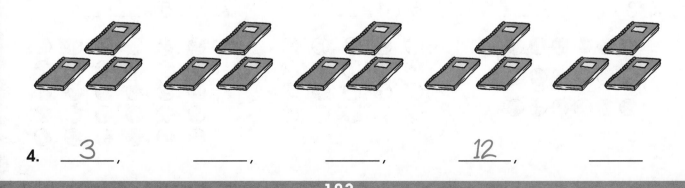

3. ___2___, _____, _____, _____, ___10___, _____, _____

Circle groups of 3. Then skip count.

4. ___3___, _____, _____, ___12___, _____

183

Skip Counting

In Any Order

You can multiply factors in any order and get the same product.

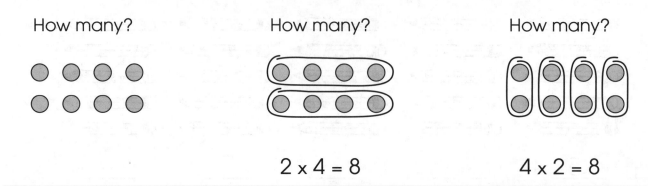

How many?	How many?	How many?
	2 x 4 = 8	4 x 2 = 8

Write a multiplication sentence for each array.

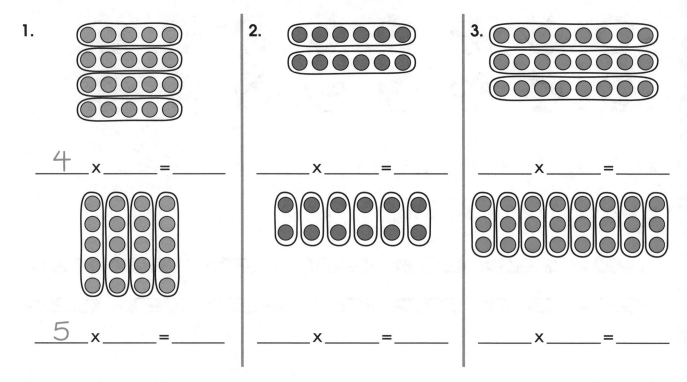

1. ____4____ x _____ = _____

____5____ x _____ = _____

2. _____ x _____ = _____

_____ x _____ = _____

3. _____ x _____ = _____

_____ x _____ = _____

Draw circles around the rows or columns in the array to show the multiplication problem. Then write the product.

4. 3 x 6 = _____

5. 5 x 4 = _____

6. 6 x 5 = _____

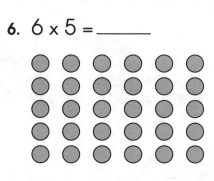

Commutative (order) Property of Multiplication

Draw a Winner

When two numbers are multiplied, they can be in any order. The products are the same.

3 groups of 2

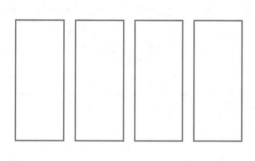

$3 \times 2 = 6$

2 groups of 3

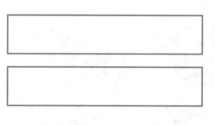

$2 \times 3 = 6$

Draw groups of ◯s to show each problem. Then write the product.

1. $4 \times 2 = $ _____

2. $5 \times 3 = $ _____

3. $3 \times 4 = $ _____

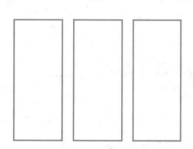

$2 \times 4 = $ _____

$3 \times 5 = $ _____

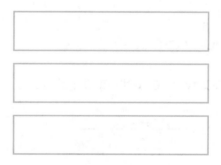

$4 \times 3 = $ _____

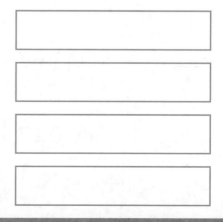

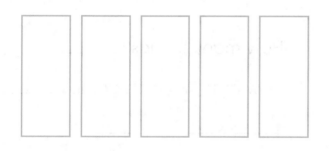

Commutative (order) Property of Multiplication

Multiply by 1 and 0

Any number times 1 equals that number. Any number times 0 equals 0.

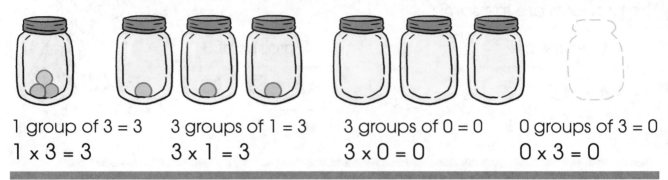

1 group of 3 = 3
$1 \times 3 = 3$

3 groups of 1 = 3
$3 \times 1 = 3$

3 groups of 0 = 0
$3 \times 0 = 0$

0 groups of 3 = 0
$0 \times 3 = 0$

Count the number in each group. Multiply to find the answer.

1.

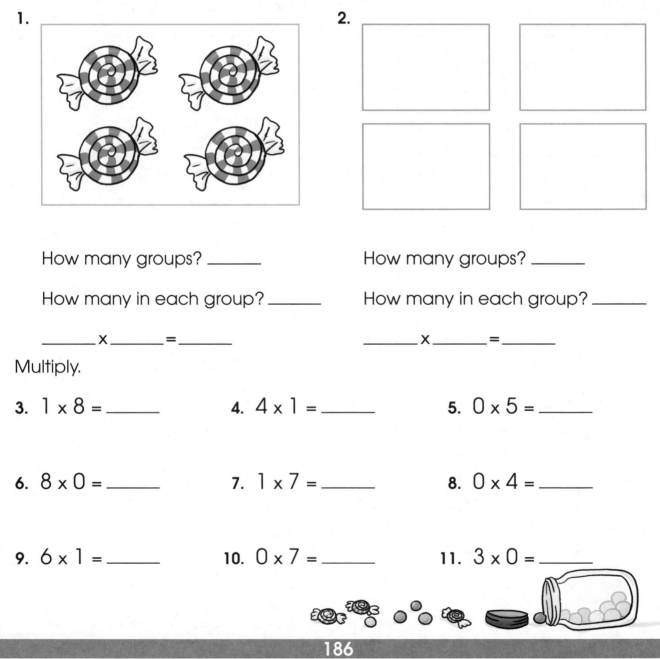

2.

How many groups? _____

How many in each group? _____

_____ x _____ = _____

How many groups? _____

How many in each group? _____

_____ x _____ = _____

Multiply.

3. $1 \times 8 =$ _____

4. $4 \times 1 =$ _____

5. $0 \times 5 =$ _____

6. $8 \times 0 =$ _____

7. $1 \times 7 =$ _____

8. $0 \times 4 =$ _____

9. $6 \times 1 =$ _____

10. $0 \times 7 =$ _____

11. $3 \times 0 =$ _____

Multiply by 1 and 0

©School Zone Publishing Company 06320

Easy Ones!

1. Complete the table.

x	0	1	2	3	4	5	6	7	8	9
0										
1										

2. Any number times 0 equals _____.

3. Any number times 1 equals _____.

4. Practice the facts.

$1 \times 3 =$ _____

$5 \times 1 =$ _____

$1 \times 8 =$ _____

$6 \times 1 =$ _____

$1 \times 4 =$ _____

$9 \times 1 =$ _____

5. Practice the facts.

$0 \times 3 =$ _____

$4 \times 0 =$ _____

$0 \times 8 =$ _____

$7 \times 0 =$ _____

$0 \times 9 =$ _____

$0 \times 0 =$ _____

6. Practice the facts.

$$\begin{array}{cccccccc} 5 & 3 & 1 & 0 & 6 & 9 & 4 & 8 \\ \underline{\times\,1} & \underline{\times\,0} & \underline{\times\,4} & \underline{\times\,4} & \underline{\times\,0} & \underline{\times\,1} & \underline{\times\,0} & \underline{\times\,1} \end{array}$$

7. Try these!

$$\begin{array}{cccccccc} 25 & 37 & 43 & 97 & 60 & 99 & 74 & 82 \\ \underline{\times\,0} & \underline{\times\,1} & \underline{\times\,1} & \underline{\times\,0} & \underline{\times\,1} & \underline{\times\,0} & \underline{\times\,1} & \underline{\times\,0} \end{array}$$

©School Zone Publishing Company 06320

Multiply by 1 and 0

Try a Table

You can use a multiplication table to learn new facts and to find products.

In $4 \times 2 =$ _____ , the factors are 4 and 2.

The factors are shown in the top row and in the first column.

Step 1: Find the 4 row.

Step 2: Find the 2 column.

Step 3: Find where the 4 row and the 2 column meet.
That is the product of 4 x 2.

$4 \times 2 = 8$

x	0	1	2	3	4	5
0	0	0	0	0	0	0
1	0	1	2	3	4	5
2	0	2	4	6	8	10
3	0	3	6	9	12	15
4	0	4	8	12	16	20
5	0	5	10	15	20	25

Name the factors. Then use the multiplication table to find the product.

	Factors	Product

1. $3 \times 2 =$ _____ _____   _____

2. $5 \times 5 =$ _____ _____   _____

3. $0 \times 1 =$ _____ _____   _____

4. $2 \times 4 =$ _____ _____   _____

5. $5 \times 0 =$ _____ _____   _____

6. $4 \times 3 =$ _____ _____   _____

7. $3 \times 3 =$ _____ _____   _____

8. $1 \times 5 =$ _____ _____   _____

Use Multiplication Facts Table

It's in the Table!

1. Complete the table.

x	0	1	2	3	4	5	6	7	8	9
0	0	0					0			
1				4				7		
2							12			
3						15				
4	0								32	
5		5								

Look for patterns in the table.

2. Look at the **2** row.
   When you multiply by 2, the product ends in_____, _____, _____, _____,

   or _____.

3. Look at the **5** row.
   When you multiply by 5, the product ends in_____ or _____.

4. Look at the **0** row. What is each product?_____

5. Look at the **1** row. What do you notice about each product?_____

   _____

6. Multiply: $3 \times 5 =$ _____ and $5 \times 3 =$ _____

   $3 \times 2 =$ _____ and $2 \times 3 =$ _____

©School Zone Publishing Company 06320   Review Multiplication Facts and Properties

Know the Facts

Multiply. Start with the number in the center of each circle.
The first one is done for you.

Multiplication Art

1. How many buttons are on the coat? _____

   How many buttons would be on 7 coats? _____

   How many buttons would be on 4 coats? _____

2. How many red stripes are on the hat? _____

   How many red stripes would be on 5 hats? _____

   How many red stripes would be on 9 hats? _____

3. How many patches are on the pants? _____

   How many patches would be on 8 pairs of pants? _____

   How many patches would be on 6 pairs of pants? _____

Practice Multiplication Facts

Gopher It!

Multiply by 6.

6 x 1	6 x 2	6 x 3	6 x 4	6 x 5	6 x 6	6 x 7	6 x 8	6 x 9
6	12	18	24	30	36	42	48	54

Help the gopher find his way home. Multiply and then color the even number products. (Even numbers end in 2, 4, 6, 8, or 0.)

6 x 4	3 x 3	6 x 9	3 x 6	6 x 7
6 x 6	5 x 9	0 x 6	3 x 9	1 x 6
4 x 6	1 x 7	5 x 6	5 x 7	6 x 9
2 x 6	6 x 3	6 x 8	1 x 9	6 x 2

Complete the table.

x	0	1	2	3	4	5	6	7	8	9
6										

Multiply by 6 ©School Zone Publishing Company 06320

Write a multiplication sentence for each array.

1.

_____6_____ rows of _____7_____

_____ x _____ = _____

2.

_____ rows of _____

_____ x _____ = _____

3. Practice the facts.

6 x 1 = _____

6 x 2 = _____

6 x 3 = _____

6 x 4 = _____

6 x 5 = _____

6 x 6 = _____

6 x 7 = _____

6 x 8 = _____

6 x 9 = _____

Count by sixes to check your answers.

4. Practice the facts.

5	6	1	7	6	9	6	8
x 6	x 4	x 6	x 6	x 8	x 6	x 3	x 6

Multiply by 6

Lucky Seven

You can use multiplication facts that you already know to learn new facts.

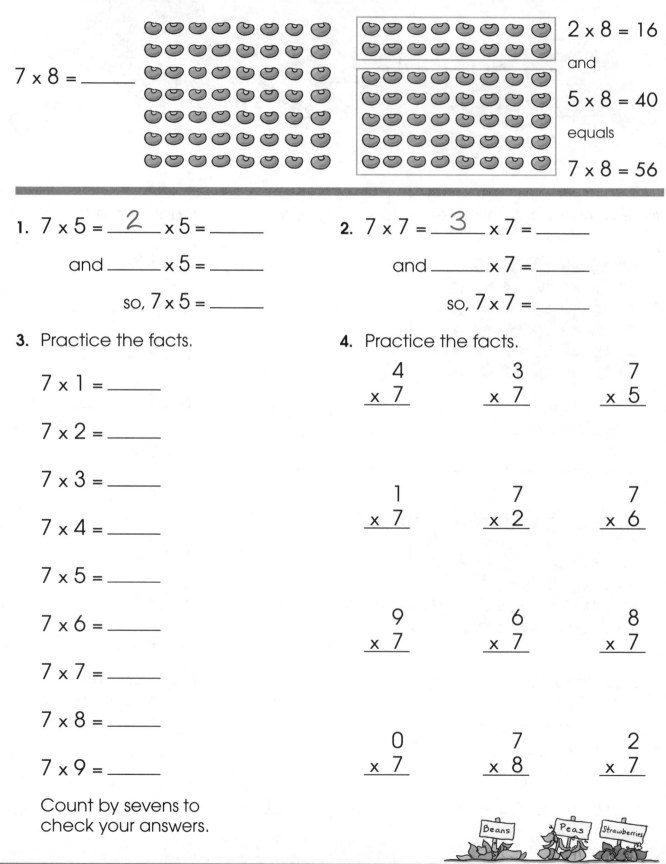

$7 \times 8 =$ _____

$2 \times 8 = 16$

and

$5 \times 8 = 40$

equals

$7 \times 8 = 56$

1. $7 \times 5 = \underline{2} \times 5 =$ _____

   and _____ $\times 5 =$ _____

   so, $7 \times 5 =$ _____

2. $7 \times 7 = \underline{3} \times 7 =$ _____

   and _____ $\times 7 =$ _____

   so, $7 \times 7 =$ _____

3. Practice the facts.

   $7 \times 1 =$ _____

   $7 \times 2 =$ _____

   $7 \times 3 =$ _____

   $7 \times 4 =$ _____

   $7 \times 5 =$ _____

   $7 \times 6 =$ _____

   $7 \times 7 =$ _____

   $7 \times 8 =$ _____

   $7 \times 9 =$ _____

   Count by sevens to
   check your answers.

4. Practice the facts.

$$\begin{array}{r} 4 \\ \times\ 7 \\ \hline \end{array} \qquad \begin{array}{r} 3 \\ \times\ 7 \\ \hline \end{array} \qquad \begin{array}{r} 7 \\ \times\ 5 \\ \hline \end{array}$$

$$\begin{array}{r} 1 \\ \times\ 7 \\ \hline \end{array} \qquad \begin{array}{r} 7 \\ \times\ 2 \\ \hline \end{array} \qquad \begin{array}{r} 7 \\ \times\ 6 \\ \hline \end{array}$$

$$\begin{array}{r} 9 \\ \times\ 7 \\ \hline \end{array} \qquad \begin{array}{r} 6 \\ \times\ 7 \\ \hline \end{array} \qquad \begin{array}{r} 8 \\ \times\ 7 \\ \hline \end{array}$$

$$\begin{array}{r} 0 \\ \times\ 7 \\ \hline \end{array} \qquad \begin{array}{r} 7 \\ \times\ 8 \\ \hline \end{array} \qquad \begin{array}{r} 2 \\ \times\ 7 \\ \hline \end{array}$$

Multiply by 7

The Richest Fish

Multiply.

1. $7 \times 4 = $ _____ F

2. $7 \times 9 = $ _____ L

3. $7 \times 2 = $ _____ H

4. $7 \times 6 = $ _____ O

5. $7 \times 3 = $ _____ S

6. $7 \times 5 = $ _____ I

7. $7 \times 0 = $ _____ A

8. $7 \times 8 = $ _____ G

9. $7 \times 7 = $ _____ D

Use your answers to decode the riddle below.
Write the letter for each answer on the correct blank.

What is the richest fish?

__ __ __ __ __ __ __ __ __
0   56   42   63   49   28   35   21   14

10. Complete the table.

x	0	1	2	3	4	5	6	7	8	9
7										

Multiply by 7

Find the Facts

Multiply to find the product for each problem. Look across and down to find the problems and products in the number search.

1. $4 \times 3 =$ _12_   2. $8 \times 0 =$ _____

3. $2 \times 8 =$ _____   4. $7 \times 2 =$ _____

5. $5 \times 4 =$ _____   6. $3 \times 9 =$ _____

7. $6 \times 4 =$ _____   8. $7 \times 9 =$ _____

9. $5 \times 5 =$ _____   10. $6 \times 6 =$ _____

11. $4 \times 7 =$ _____   12. $3 \times 5 =$ _____

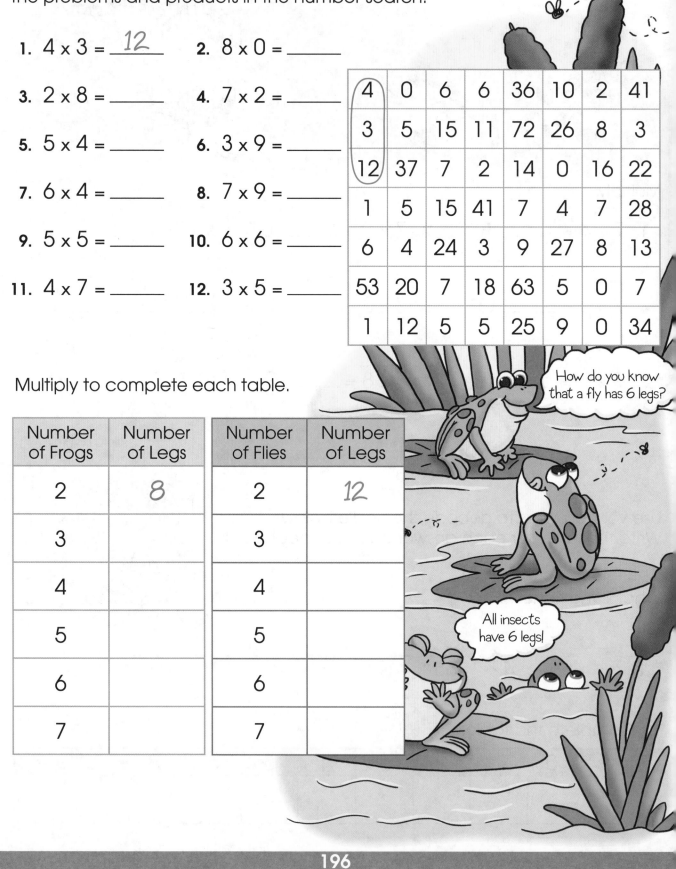

4	0	6	6	36	10	2	41
3	5	15	11	72	26	8	3
12	37	7	2	14	0	16	22
1	5	15	41	7	4	7	28
6	4	24	3	9	27	8	13
53	20	7	18	63	5	0	7
1	12	5	5	25	9	0	34

Multiply to complete each table.

Number of Frogs	Number of Legs
2	8
3	
4	
5	
6	
7	

Number of Flies	Number of Legs
2	12
3	
4	
5	
6	
7	

How do you know that a fly has 6 legs?

All insects have 6 legs!

Review Multiplication Facts 0-7

©School Zone Publishing Company 06320

Products in a Pyramid

Multiply. Write the products in the puzzle.

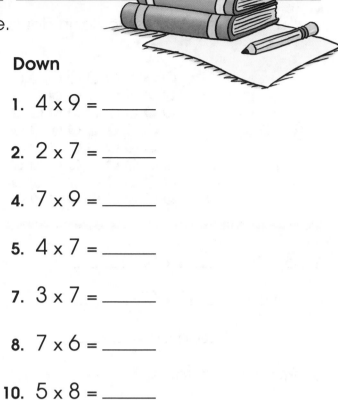

Across

1. 7 x 5 = _35_

2. 4 x 4 = _____

3. 7 x 8 = _____

5. 3 x 8 = _____

6. 4 x 8 = _____

8. 6 x 8 = _____

9. 2 x 7 = _____

11. 8 x 4 = _____

12. 7 x 0 = _____

Down

1. 4 x 9 = _____

2. 2 x 7 = _____

4. 7 x 9 = _____

5. 4 x 7 = _____

7. 3 x 7 = _____

8. 7 x 6 = _____

10. 5 x 8 = _____

©School Zone Publishing Company 06320

Review Multiplication Facts 0–7

Double the Fours

If you know the 4 facts, you can double those products to learn the 8 facts.

Use the facts you know.

$8 \times 9 = \underline{\hspace{1cm}}$

$4 \times 9 = 36$

and

$4 \times 9 = 36$

equals

$8 \times 9 = 72$

---

1. $8 \times 6 = \underline{\quad 4 \quad} \times 6 = \underline{\hspace{1cm}}$

   and $\underline{\hspace{1cm}} \times 6 = \underline{\hspace{1cm}}$

   so, $8 \times 6 = \underline{\hspace{1cm}}$

2. $8 \times 7 = \underline{\quad 4 \quad} \times 7 = \underline{\hspace{1cm}}$

   and $\underline{\hspace{1cm}} \times 7 = \underline{\hspace{1cm}}$

   so, $8 \times 7 = \underline{\hspace{1cm}}$

3. Practice the facts.

   $8 \times 1 = \underline{\hspace{1cm}}$

   $8 \times 2 = \underline{\hspace{1cm}}$

   $8 \times 3 = \underline{\hspace{1cm}}$

   $8 \times 4 = \underline{\hspace{1cm}}$

   $8 \times 5 = \underline{\hspace{1cm}}$

   $8 \times 6 = \underline{\hspace{1cm}}$

   $8 \times 7 = \underline{\hspace{1cm}}$

   $8 \times 8 = \underline{\hspace{1cm}}$

   $8 \times 9 = \underline{\hspace{1cm}}$

   Count by eights to
   check your answers.

4. Practice the facts.

$$\begin{array}{r} 3 \\ \times\ 8 \\ \hline \end{array} \qquad \begin{array}{r} 5 \\ \times\ 8 \\ \hline \end{array} \qquad \begin{array}{r} 8 \\ \times\ 2 \\ \hline \end{array}$$

$$\begin{array}{r} 8 \\ \times\ 7 \\ \hline \end{array} \qquad \begin{array}{r} 1 \\ \times\ 8 \\ \hline \end{array} \qquad \begin{array}{r} 7 \\ \times\ 8 \\ \hline \end{array}$$

$$\begin{array}{r} 9 \\ \times\ 8 \\ \hline \end{array} \qquad \begin{array}{r} 6 \\ \times\ 8 \\ \hline \end{array} \qquad \begin{array}{r} 8 \\ \times\ 9 \\ \hline \end{array}$$

$$\begin{array}{r} 8 \\ \times\ 6 \\ \hline \end{array} \qquad \begin{array}{r} 0 \\ \times\ 8 \\ \hline \end{array} \qquad \begin{array}{r} 4 \\ \times\ 8 \\ \hline \end{array}$$

Eight Is Great

Multiply.

1. $8 \times 3 =$ _____ E

2. $8 \times 6 =$ _____ L

3. $8 \times 4 =$ _____ P

4. $8 \times 8 =$ _____ B

5. $8 \times 1 =$ _____ A

6. $8 \times 9 =$ _____ Y

7. $8 \times 5 =$ _____ H

8. $8 \times 7 =$ _____ N

9. $8 \times 2 =$ _____ T

Use your answers to decode the riddle below.
Write the letter for each answer on the correct blank.

What does an elephant have that no other animals have?

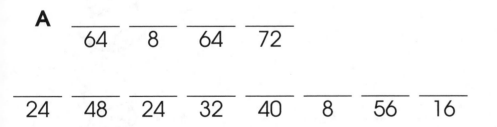

A _____ _____ _____ _____
   64   8   64   72

_____ _____ _____ _____ _____ _____ _____ _____
24   48   24   32   40   8   56   16

10. Complete the table.

x	0	1	2	3	4	5	6	7	8	9
8										

Multiply by 8

Nine Is Fine

When you multiply 9 by a single digit, the sum of the digits of the product is 9.

$2 \times 9 = ?$

$2 \times 9 = 18 \longrightarrow 1 + 8 = 9$

$5 \times 9 = ?$

$5 \times 9 = 45 \longrightarrow 4 + 5 = 9$

Multiply. Add the digits of the product to check your answer.

1. $9 \times 4 =$ _36_ $\longrightarrow$ _3_ + _6_ = _9_

2. $9 \times 7 =$ _____ $\longrightarrow$ _____ + _____ = _____

3. $9 \times 3 =$ _____ $\longrightarrow$ _____ + _____ = _____

4. $9 \times 8 =$ _____ $\longrightarrow$ _____ + _____ = _____

5. $9 \times 5 =$ _____ $\longrightarrow$ _____ + _____ = _____

6. $9 \times 6 =$ _____ $\longrightarrow$ _____ + _____ = _____

7. $9 \times 9 =$ _____ $\longrightarrow$ _____ + _____ = _____

8. Complete the table.

x	0	1	2	3	4	5	6	7	8	9
9										

Multiply by 9

Find Nines

Multiply.

1.
$$\begin{array}{r} 3 \\ \times\ 9 \\ \hline \end{array}\qquad \begin{array}{r} 5 \\ \times\ 9 \\ \hline \end{array}\qquad \begin{array}{r} 7 \\ \times\ 9 \\ \hline \end{array}\qquad \begin{array}{r} 1 \\ \times\ 9 \\ \hline \end{array}\qquad \begin{array}{r} 8 \\ \times\ 9 \\ \hline \end{array}\qquad \begin{array}{r} 0 \\ \times\ 9 \\ \hline \end{array}\qquad \begin{array}{r} 6 \\ \times\ 9 \\ \hline \end{array}\qquad \begin{array}{r} 2 \\ \times\ 9 \\ \hline \end{array}$$

2.
$$\begin{array}{r} 4 \\ \times\ 9 \\ \hline \end{array}\qquad \begin{array}{r} 9 \\ \times\ 6 \\ \hline \end{array}\qquad \begin{array}{r} 9 \\ \times\ 3 \\ \hline \end{array}\qquad \begin{array}{r} 9 \\ \times\ 0 \\ \hline \end{array}\qquad \begin{array}{r} 9 \\ \times\ 5 \\ \hline \end{array}\qquad \begin{array}{r} 9 \\ \times\ 7 \\ \hline \end{array}\qquad \begin{array}{r} 9 \\ \times\ 9 \\ \hline \end{array}\qquad \begin{array}{r} 9 \\ \times\ 8 \\ \hline \end{array}$$

Start at the arrow to find the carrot.
Follow the path in the same order as your answers above.

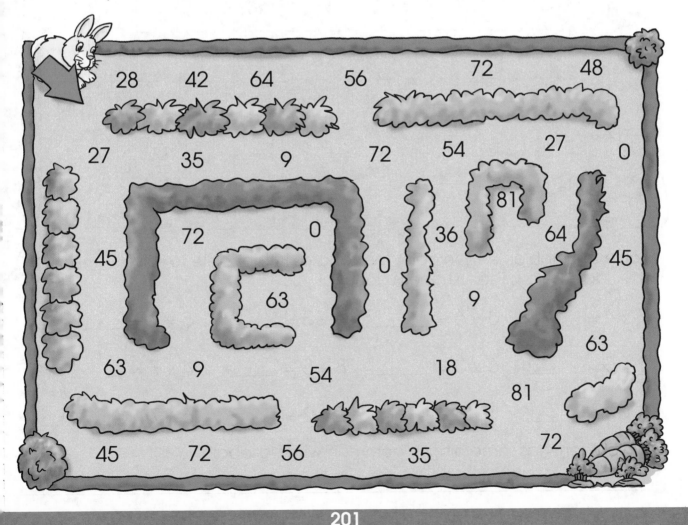

©School Zone Publishing Company 06320

Multiply by 9

Home Run Riddle

Complete the multiplication table.

> The first factor is the row, and the second factor is the column.

x	0	1	2	3	4	5	6	7	8	9
0		0						0		
1				3						
2	0							14		
3										27
4		4								
5					25					
6	0									
7			28							63
8										
9							54			

Solve the problems. Then color the squares in the table to solve the riddle below. The first one is done for you.

$7 \times 4 = \underline{28}$ $3 \times 6 = \underline{}$ $4 \times 3 = \underline{}$ $5 \times 8 = \underline{}$

$2 \times 5 = \underline{}$ $6 \times 3 = \underline{}$ $8 \times 5 = \underline{}$ $4 \times 7 = \underline{}$

$3 \times 4 = \underline{}$ $7 \times 6 = \underline{}$ $5 \times 2 = \underline{}$ $6 \times 7 = \underline{}$

Which gem has something in common with baseball?

_____

Practice Multiplication Facts 0–9

Cross Out!

When two numbers are multiplied, they can be in any order. The answers will be the same.

$4 \times 3 = 12$ $3 \times 4 = 12$

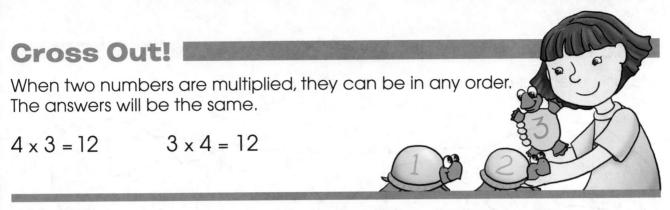

Multiply. Draw lines that connect the matching problems. To answer the riddle, write the letters from top to bottom that aren't crossed out.

$7 \times 9 =$ _____ •

W

R

T

$6 \times 8 =$ _____ •

I

N

$8 \times 7 =$ _____ •

S

$8 \times 0 =$ _____ •   **D**   **E**

A

$5 \times 7 =$ _____ •

O

$9 \times 6 =$ _____ •

W

P

$7 \times 6 =$ _____ •   **C**

M

$8 \times 9 =$ _____ •   **S**

• $0 \times 8 =$ _____

• $9 \times 7 =$ _____

• $6 \times 9 =$ _____

• $7 \times 5 =$ _____

• $8 \times 6 =$ _____

• $9 \times 8 =$ _____

• $6 \times 7 =$ _____

• $7 \times 8 =$ _____

What invention allows you to see through walls?

_____ _____ _____ _____   _____ _____ _____ _____

Commutative (order) Property of Multiplication

Out of This World

Multiply. Use your answers to color the picture.

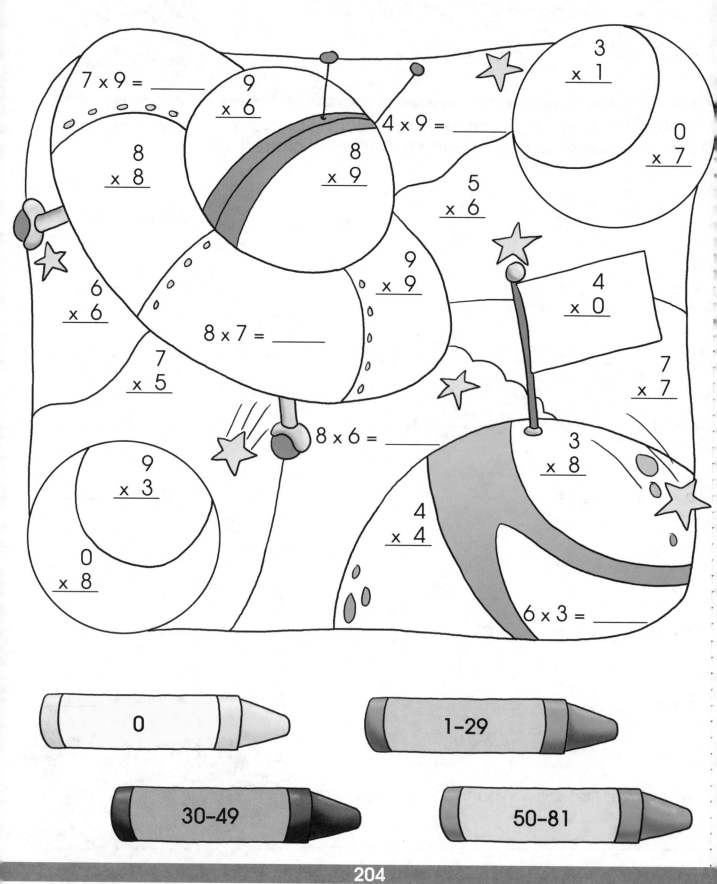

$7 \times 9 = \underline{\hspace{1cm}}$

$\begin{array}{r} 9 \\ \times\ 6 \\ \hline \end{array}$

$4 \times 9 = \underline{\hspace{1cm}}$

$\begin{array}{r} 3 \\ \times\ 1 \\ \hline \end{array}$

$\begin{array}{r} 8 \\ \times\ 8 \\ \hline \end{array}$

$\begin{array}{r} 8 \\ \times\ 9 \\ \hline \end{array}$

$\begin{array}{r} 0 \\ \times\ 7 \\ \hline \end{array}$

$\begin{array}{r} 5 \\ \times\ 6 \\ \hline \end{array}$

$\begin{array}{r} 6 \\ \times\ 6 \\ \hline \end{array}$

$\begin{array}{r} 9 \\ \times\ 9 \\ \hline \end{array}$

$\begin{array}{r} 4 \\ \times\ 0 \\ \hline \end{array}$

$8 \times 7 = \underline{\hspace{1cm}}$

$\begin{array}{r} 7 \\ \times\ 5 \\ \hline \end{array}$

$\begin{array}{r} 7 \\ \times\ 7 \\ \hline \end{array}$

$8 \times 6 = \underline{\hspace{1cm}}$

$\begin{array}{r} 3 \\ \times\ 8 \\ \hline \end{array}$

$\begin{array}{r} 9 \\ \times\ 3 \\ \hline \end{array}$

$\begin{array}{r} 4 \\ \times\ 4 \\ \hline \end{array}$

$\begin{array}{r} 0 \\ \times\ 8 \\ \hline \end{array}$

$6 \times 3 = \underline{\hspace{1cm}}$

0

1–29

30–49

50–81

Practice Multiplication Facts 0–9

Bunches of Facts

Write all the multiplication facts that have the following products.
A pair of facts like 3 x 4 = 12 and 4 x 3 = 12 will count as one fact since they have the same factors.

1. Products 10 -19:

   _____, _____, _____, _____,

   _____, _____, _____, _____, _____

2. Products 20-29:

   _____, _____, _____, _____,

   _____, _____, _____

3. Products 30-39:

   _____, _____, _____, _____, _____

4. Products 40-49:

   _____, _____, _____, _____, _____

5. Products 50-59:

   _____, _____

6. Products 60-69:

   _____, _____

7. Products 70-79:

   _____

8. Products 80-89:

   _____

Look! It's easy to remember these facts. There are only one or two facts in each bunch.

Review Multiplication Facts 0–9

Triangle Times

Multiply. Use the numbers in the triangle.
Write a product in each circle.

It's a puzzler...

Review Multiplication Facts 0-9

©School Zone Publishing Company 06320

Fast Facts!

Practice the facts. Time yourself. Can you solve
all of these problems in less than 10 minutes?

1. $2 \times 8 =$ _____ $4 \times 5 =$ _____ $6 \times 4 =$ _____ $3 \times 7 =$ _____

2. $5 \times 3 =$ _____ $3 \times 8 =$ _____ $5 \times 5 =$ _____ $4 \times 8 =$ _____

3. $7 \times 4 =$ _____ $4 \times 9 =$ _____ $7 \times 3 =$ _____ $8 \times 6 =$ _____

4. $5 \times 9 =$ _____ $6 \times 1 =$ _____ $2 \times 9 =$ _____ $4 \times 9 =$ _____

5. $8 \times 3 =$ _____ $7 \times 2 =$ _____ $5 \times 8 =$ _____ $8 \times 7 =$ _____

6. $7 \times 9 =$ _____ $8 \times 8 =$ _____ $3 \times 6 =$ _____ $0 \times 9 =$ _____

7. $4 \times 7 =$ _____ $9 \times 6 =$ _____ $6 \times 8 =$ _____ $9 \times 7 =$ _____

8. $9 \times 9 =$ _____ $3 \times 0 =$ _____ $8 \times 4 =$ _____ $6 \times 9 =$ _____

9. $5 \times 8 =$ _____ $7 \times 7 =$ _____ $4 \times 6 =$ _____ $7 \times 8 =$ _____

10. $9 \times 5 =$ _____ $5 \times 7 =$ _____ $8 \times 0 =$ _____ $9 \times 8 =$ _____

11. $4 \times 4 =$ _____ $7 \times 6 =$ _____ $5 \times 9 =$ _____ $7 \times 4 =$ _____

12. $9 \times 3 =$ _____ $0 \times 7 =$ _____ $8 \times 9 =$ _____ $0 \times 0 =$ _____

Practice Multiplication Facts 0–9

Bright Idea

Remember! In multiplication, the numbers that are multiplied are called **factors**.

factors

product

Write a factor on each light bulb so that the pair of factors equals the product shown. Use the numbers 2–9 as factors.

Multiply.

9. $7 \times 4 =$ _____ V

10. $8 \times 3 =$ _____ A

11. $9 \times 5 =$ _____ I

12. $6 \times 6 =$ _____ R

13. $8 \times 6 =$ _____ R

14. $2 \times 4 =$ _____ E

Use your answers to decode the riddle below.
Write the letter for each answer on the correct blank.

What has a big mouth but doesn't say a word?

___ ___ ___ ___ ___ ___
24   36   45   28   8   48

Factor Pairs

Find the missing factors.

$$\begin{array}{r} 3 \\ \times\ \boxed{?} \\ \hline 15 \end{array}$$ 3 times what number equals 15? $$\begin{array}{r} 3 \\ \times\ \boxed{5} \\ \hline 15 \end{array}$$

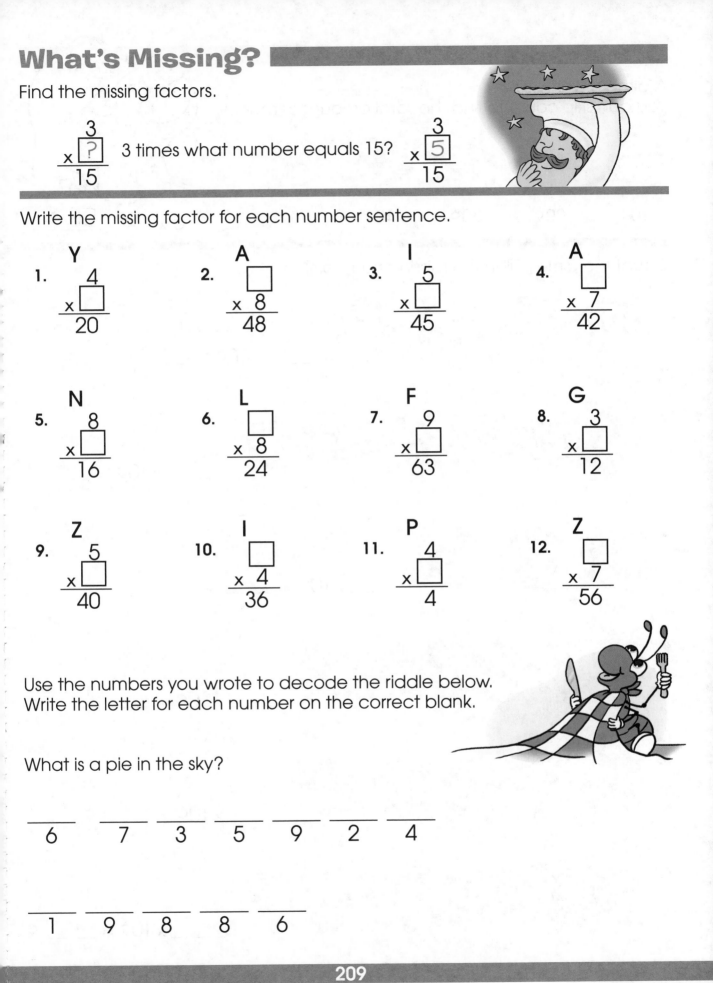

Write the missing factor for each number sentence.

Y
1. $$\begin{array}{r} 4 \\ \times\ \square \\ \hline 20 \end{array}$$

A
2. $$\begin{array}{r} \square \\ \times\ 8 \\ \hline 48 \end{array}$$

I
3. $$\begin{array}{r} 5 \\ \times\ \square \\ \hline 45 \end{array}$$

A
4. $$\begin{array}{r} \square \\ \times\ 7 \\ \hline 42 \end{array}$$

N
5. $$\begin{array}{r} 8 \\ \times\ \square \\ \hline 16 \end{array}$$

L
6. $$\begin{array}{r} \square \\ \times\ 8 \\ \hline 24 \end{array}$$

F
7. $$\begin{array}{r} 9 \\ \times\ \square \\ \hline 63 \end{array}$$

G
8. $$\begin{array}{r} 3 \\ \times\ \square \\ \hline 12 \end{array}$$

Z
9. $$\begin{array}{r} 5 \\ \times\ \square \\ \hline 40 \end{array}$$

I
10. $$\begin{array}{r} \square \\ \times\ 4 \\ \hline 36 \end{array}$$

P
11. $$\begin{array}{r} 4 \\ \times\ \square \\ \hline 4 \end{array}$$

Z
12. $$\begin{array}{r} \square \\ \times\ 7 \\ \hline 56 \end{array}$$

Use the numbers you wrote to decode the riddle below.
Write the letter for each number on the correct blank.

What is a pie in the sky?

$$\overline{\ 6\ }\ \overline{\ 7\ }\ \overline{\ 3\ }\ \overline{\ 5\ }\ \overline{\ 9\ }\ \overline{\ 2\ }\ \overline{\ 4\ }$$

$$\overline{\ 1\ }\ \overline{\ 9\ }\ \overline{\ 8\ }\ \overline{\ 8\ }\ \overline{\ 6\ }$$

Missing Factors

Dime Time

A dime is worth 10¢.
You can skip count to find the total amount of money.

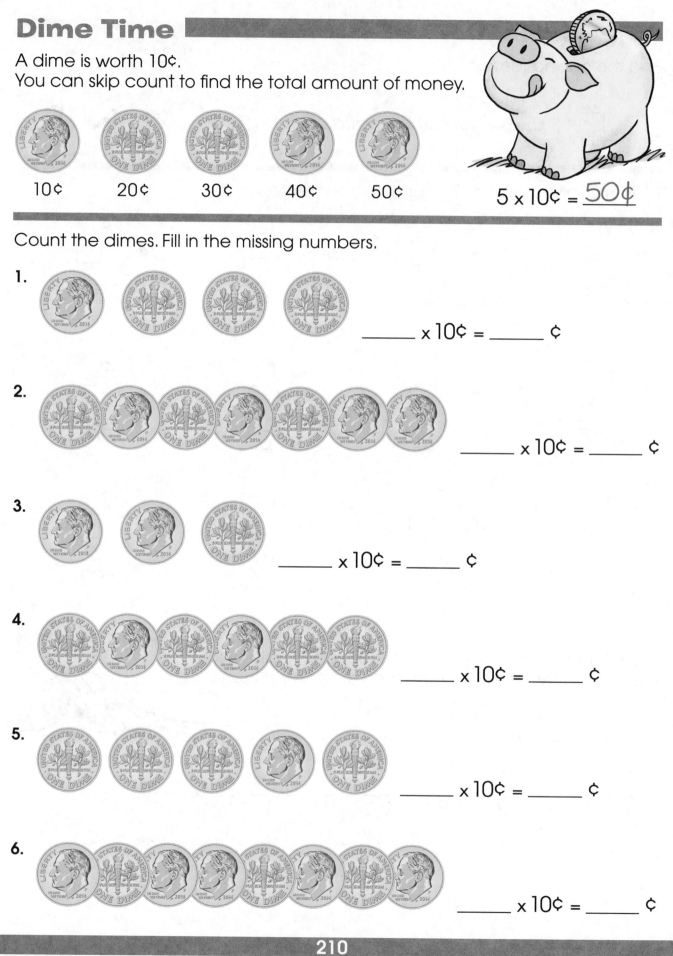

10¢   20¢   30¢   40¢   50¢

5 x 10¢ = <u>50¢</u>

Count the dimes. Fill in the missing numbers.

1.

_____ x 10¢ = _____ ¢

2.

_____ x 10¢ = _____ ¢

3.

_____ x 10¢ = _____ ¢

4.

_____ x 10¢ = _____ ¢

5.

_____ x 10¢ = _____ ¢

6.

_____ x 10¢ = _____ ¢

Multiply by 10

Ten Again

1. Practice the facts.　　**2.** Practice the facts.

$10 \times 1 =$ _____　　　$10 \times 6 =$ _____

$10 \times 2 =$ _____　　　$10 \times 4 =$ _____

$10 \times 3 =$ _____　　　$1 \times 10 =$ _____

$10 \times 4 =$ _____　　　$10 \times 3 =$ _____

$10 \times 5 =$ _____　　　$5 \times 10 =$ _____

$10 \times 6 =$ _____　　　$10 \times 8 =$ _____

$10 \times 7 =$ _____　　　$7 \times 10 =$ _____

$10 \times 8 =$ _____　　　$10 \times 0 =$ _____

$10 \times 9 =$ _____　　　$2 \times 10 =$ _____

Count by tens to
check your answers.　　$9 \times 10 =$ _____

3. When you multiply a number times 10, the
product ends with a _____ .

4. Complete the table.

x	0	1	2	3	4	5	6	7	8	9
10										

5. Try these!

$10 \times 10 =$ _____　　　$10 \times 11 =$ _____　　　$10 \times 12 =$ _____

　　　Multiply by 10

Double-Digit Time

To multiply by 11 times a number from 1 through 9, remember this clue:
The product is a two-digit number that repeats the factor.

11 x 1	11 x 2	11 x 3	11 x 4	11 x 5	11 x 6	11 x 7	11 x 8	11 x 9
11	22	33	44	55	66	77	88	99

Look across and down to find the problems
and products in the number search.

1. 11 x 3 = _33_

2. 11 x 7 = _____

3. 11 x 9 = _____

4. 11 x 4 = _____

5. 11 x 2 = _____

6. 11 x 8 = _____

7. 11 x 5 = _____

8. 11 x 1 = _____

9. 11 x 0 = _____

10. 11 x 6 = _____

11	17	1	28	11	7	77
5	11	4	44	16	48	11
55	32	63	11	0	0	3
0	11	8	88	11	38	33
24	9	56	71	1	15	41
65	99	36	23	11	2	22
18	11	6	66	43	0	17

11. Complete the table.

x	0	1	2	3	4	5	6	7	8	9
11										

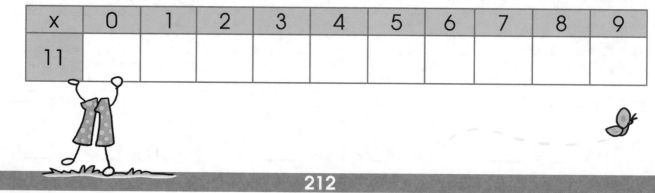

Multiply by 11

Ten and One

Since 11 = 10 + 1, here is another way to learn the 11 facts. Complete the pattern.

$11 \times 1 = (10 \times 1) + 1$

$= \underline{}10\underline{} + 1 = \underline{}$

$11 \times 7 = (10 \times \underline{}) + 7$

$= \underline{} + \underline{} = \underline{}$

$11 \times 2 = (10 \times 2) + 2$

$= \underline{} + 2 = \underline{}$

$11 \times 8 = (10 \times \underline{}) + \underline{}$

$= \underline{} + \underline{} = \underline{}$

$11 \times 3 = (10 \times 3) + 3$

$= \underline{}30\underline{} + \underline{} = \underline{}$

$11 \times 9 = (\underline{} \times 9) + 9$

$= \underline{} + 9 = \underline{}$

$11 \times 4 = (10 \times 4) + 4$

$= \underline{} + 4 = \underline{}$

$11 \times 10 = (10 \times 10) + 10$

$= \underline{} + 10 = \underline{}$

$11 \times 5 = (10 \times \underline{}) + 5$

$= \underline{} + 5 = \underline{}$

$11 \times 11 = (10 \times 11) + \underline{}$

$= \underline{}110\underline{} + \underline{} = \underline{}$

$11 \times 6 = (10 \times 6) + 6$

$= \underline{} + \underline{} = \underline{}$

$11 \times 12 = (10 \times 12) + 12$

$= \underline{} + \underline{} = \underline{}$

Try these!

$11 \times 15 = (10 \times 15) + 15$

$= \underline{} + \underline{} = \underline{}$

$11 \times 20 = (10 \times \underline{}) + \underline{}$

$= \underline{} + \underline{} = \underline{}$

Multiply by 11

Delve into Twelves

You can use multiplication facts to describe groups.

12 x 1	12 x 2	12 x 3	12 x 4	12 x 5	12 x 6	12 x 7	12 x 8	12 x 9
12	24	36	48	60	72	84	96	108

Multiply.

1. $12 \times 2 =$ _____ N

2. $12 \times 5 =$ _____ O

3. $12 \times 4 =$ _____ A

4. $12 \times 8 =$ _____ I

5. $12 \times 1 =$ _____ C

6. $12 \times 7 =$ _____ E

7. $12 \times 6 =$ _____ U

8. $12 \times 9 =$ _____ R

9. $12 \times 3 =$ _____ P

Use your answers to decode the riddle below.
Write the letter for each answer on the correct blank.

What pine has the sharpest needles?

___ ___ ___ ___ ___ ___ ___ ___ ___ ___
48   36   60 108   12   72   36   96   24   84

10. Complete the table.

x	0	1	2	3	4	5	6	7	8	9
12										

214

Double the Sixes

If you know the 6 facts, you can double those products to learn the 12 facts.
Use the facts you know.

$12 \times 7 =$ _____

$6 \times 7 = 42$

and

$6 \times 7 = 42$

equals

$12 \times 7 = 84$

Write a pair of 6 facts you know to help you find these products.

1. $12 \times 9 = \underline{6} \times 9 =$ _____

    and _____ $\times 9 =$ _____

    so, $12 \times 9 =$ _____

2. $12 \times 8 = \underline{6} \times 8 =$ _____

    and _____ $\times 8 =$ _____

    so, $12 \times 8 =$ _____

3. Practice the facts.

    $12 \times 1 =$ _____ $12 \times 7 =$ _____

    $12 \times 2 =$ _____ $12 \times 8 =$ _____

    $12 \times 3 =$ _____ $12 \times 9 =$ _____

    $12 \times 4 =$ _____ $12 \times 10 =$ _____

    $12 \times 5 =$ _____ $12 \times 11 =$ _____

    $12 \times 6 =$ _____ $12 \times 12 =$ _____

    Count by twelves to check your answers. Or, you can add 12 to the previous product.

4. Practice the facts.

    $12 \times 5 =$ _____ $7 \times 12 =$ _____ $12 \times 12 =$ _____ $9 \times 12 =$ _____

©School Zone Publishing Company 06320   Multiply by 12

Dozens More

12 eggs = 1 dozen

Solve each problem.

1. John bought 3 dozen apples to make some pies. How many apples did he buy?

_____

2. Kevin is a dozen years old. How old is he?

_____

3. The third grade class planted 10 dozen trees on Arbor Day. How many trees did they plant?

_____

4. Kayla bought 3 dozen buttons. Then she bought 2 dozen more to complete her project. How many buttons did she buy?

_____

A gross is 12 dozen.

Did You Know?
A "baker's dozen" is 13.

Try these!

5. Jan's teacher bought a gross of pencils. How many pencils did she buy?

_____

6. Tennis balls are sold in cans of 3. How many cans of balls must you buy to have a dozen tennis balls?

_____

7. Some pairs of socks are sold in packages of 6. How many packages would you have to buy to have 3 dozen pairs of socks?

_____

8. Hot dog buns are sold in packages of 8. How many packages would you have to buy to have 4 dozen buns?

_____

Multiply by 12

Inches and Feet

Solve each problem.

1. Maria is 4 feet tall. How many inches tall is she?

_____

2. Maria's brother is 6 feet tall. How many inches tall is he?

_____

3. A yard is equal to 3 feet. How many inches are in 1 yard?

_____

4. The flagpole in front of the school is 10 feet tall. How many inches high is the flagpole?

_____

Try These! Hint: Draw a picture to help you solve a problem.

5. How many inches are around a 1-foot square tile?

_____

6. How many inches are around a rectangle that is 3 feet long and 2 feet wide?

_____

7. Ashton is 5 feet 3 inches tall. How many inches tall is she?

_____

8. Jesse is 4 feet tall. His sister is 8 inches taller. His older brother is 4 inches taller than his sister. How tall is Jesse's older brother?

_____

Multiply by 12

Who Am I?

Read each riddle. Write the answer.

1.
I am 9 x 8 or 6 x 12.

Who am I? _____

2.
I am 3 x 8, 4 x 6, or 2 x 12.

Who am I? _____

3.
I am 10 x 4 or 5 x 8.

Who am I? _____

4.
If you add 4 of me, you get 20.

Who am I? _____

5.
If you add 3 of me, you get the same answer as 6 x 5.

Who am I? _____

6.
If you multiply me by 5, you get 6 x 10.

Who am I? _____

7.
If you multiply me by 7 and then add 7 to the product, you get 6 x 7.

Who am I? _____

8.
If you multiply me by 9 and then add 7 to the product, you get 5 x 5.

Who am I? _____

9.
If you multiply me by 2 and then add 1 to the product, you get 9.

Who am I? _____

10.
If you add 5 of me and then add 5 more of me you get 65.

Who am I? _____

Review Multiplication Facts 0–12   ©School Zone Publishing Company 06320

Home Run Hit

Multiply. Write the products in the puzzle.

Across

1. $\begin{array}{r} 11 \\ \times\ 5 \\ \hline \end{array}$
3. $\begin{array}{r} 7 \\ \times\ 9 \\ \hline \end{array}$
5. $\begin{array}{r} 3 \\ \times\ 9 \\ \hline \end{array}$
7. $\begin{array}{r} 8 \\ \times\ 3 \\ \hline \end{array}$
9. $\begin{array}{r} 9 \\ \times\ 9 \\ \hline \end{array}$
11. $\begin{array}{r} 6 \\ \times\ 9 \\ \hline \end{array}$

Down

2. $\begin{array}{r} 7 \\ \times\ 8 \\ \hline \end{array}$
4. $\begin{array}{r} 8 \\ \times\ 4 \\ \hline \end{array}$
6. $\begin{array}{r} 12 \\ \times\ 6 \\ \hline \end{array}$
8. $\begin{array}{r} 8 \\ \times\ 6 \\ \hline \end{array}$
10. $\begin{array}{r} 3 \\ \times\ 5 \\ \hline \end{array}$
12. $\begin{array}{r} 10 \\ \times\ 4 \\ \hline \end{array}$

219

Review Multiplication Facts 0–12

Multiplication Challenges

Solve each problem.

1. Seven bicycles are parked in front of the library. How many wheels are there altogether?

_____

2. There are 3 spiders in a web. How many legs are there altogether?

_____

3. If there are exactly 8 more weeks of the year left, how many days are left?

_____

4. A small singing group calls itself "The Triple Trio." How many people are in the singing group?

_____

5. Two baseball teams are playing ball. How many players are there?

_____

6. How many fingers are on 8 hands?

_____

7. Eight insects are sitting on a lily pad. How many legs are there altogether?

_____

8. Roger had 8 strikes in a row last week when he went bowling. How many pins did he knock down?

_____

9. Rico wants to save some money each month in order to go to college 9 years from now. For how many months will he have to save money?

_____

10. Six football teams are playing in a city park. How many players are in the park?

_____

Review Multiplication Facts

©School Zone Publishing Company 06320

Multiplication Table

Complete the table.

x	0	1	2	3	4	5	6	7	8	9
0										
1										
2										
3										
4										
5										
6										
7										
8										
9										

Multiplication Table

Multiplication Table

Complete the table.

x	0	1	2	3	4	5	6	7	8	9	10	11	12
0													
1													
2													
3													
4													
5													
6													
7													
8													
9													
10													
11													
12													

Finding Missing Factors

factor   factor   product

$5 \times \underline{\quad} = 35$

The missing factor is 7
because $5 \times 7 = 35$.

Find the missing factor.

1. $5 \times \underline{\quad} = 20$

2. $9 \times \underline{\quad} = 63$

3. $9 \times \underline{\quad} = 9$

4. $5 \times \underline{\quad} = 40$

5. $\underline{\quad} \times 8 = 32$

6. $\underline{\quad} \times 4 = 24$

7. $9 \times \underline{\quad} = 81$

8. $6 \times \underline{\quad} = 42$

9. $\underline{\quad} \times 7 = 14$

10. $\underline{\quad} \times 7 = 49$

11. $\underline{\quad} \times 1 = 9$

12. $\underline{\quad} \times 1 = 0$

13. $3 \times \underline{\quad} = 0$

14. $9 \times \underline{\quad} = 72$

15. $4 \times \underline{\quad} = 12$

16. $8 \times \underline{\quad} = 64$

©School Zone Publishing Company 06320

Finding Missing Factors

Multiplying Three Factors

Multiply the way that is easiest for you.

You can find the product of three factors by multiplying them in any order or grouping. This is the **associative property** of multiplication.

Multiply: $2 \times 10 \times 3$

$$
\begin{array}{lll}
(2 \times 10) \times 3 = & 2 \times (10 \times 3) = & (2 \times 3) \times 10 = \\
20 \times 3 = & 2 \times 30 = & 6 \times 10 = \\
60 & 60 & 60
\end{array}
$$

Remember these properties of multiplication:

Commutative Property of Multiplication
If you change the order of the factors, the product is the same.

$$3 \times 4 = 12 \text{ and } 4 \times 3 = 12$$

Identity Property of Multiplication
If you multiply a number and 1, the product is that number.

$$1 \times 8 = 8$$

Associative Property of Multiplication
If you change the grouping of the factors, the product is the same.

$$(2 \times 3) \times 4 = 24 \text{ and } 2 \times (3 \times 4) = 24$$

Zero Property of Multiplication
If you multiply a number and zero, the product is zero.

$$0 \times 7 = 0$$

Multiply the factors. Show your work. Be careful!

1. $2 \times 1 \times 8 =$ _____

2. $4 \times 10 \times 2 =$ _____

3. $5 \times 10 \times 0 =$ _____

4. $3 \times 10 \times 3 =$ _____

5. $10 \times 10 \times 1 =$ _____

6. $2 \times 3 \times 5 =$ _____

7. $8 \times 3 \times 2 =$ _____

8. $10 \times 2 \times 2 =$ _____

9. $3 \times 6 \times 1 =$ _____

10. $10 \times 1 \times 10 =$ _____

11. $2 \times 10 \times 3 =$ _____

12. $9 \times 1 \times 9 =$ _____

13. $10 \times 0 \times 10 =$ _____

14. $3 \times 3 \times 3 =$ _____

15. $9 \times 10 \times 10 =$ _____

Multiplying Three Factors; Multiplication Properties   ©School Zone Publishing Company 06320

What I Learned about Multiplication

Circle the answer.

1. Which of the following does **not** tell about this picture?

A. 4 + 6   **B.** 4 + 4 + 4 + 4 + 4 + 4

C. 6 x 4   **D.** 4 x 6

2. For the 2s multiplication facts, the ones digit is _____ in the products.

A. 1, 2, 3, 4, or 5

B. 2, 4, 6, 8, or 0

C. 1, 2, 4, or 8

D. 0 or 2

3. Which number makes this number sentence true?

$$6 \times 1 = \underline{\quad}$$

A. 0   **B.** 1   **C.** 6   **D.** 60

4. Which number makes this number sentence true?

$$2 \times 4 \times \underline{\quad} = 80$$

A. 6   **B.** 8   **C.** 10   **D.** 12

5. Which number makes this number sentence true?

$$5 \times \underline{\quad} = 0$$

A. 10   **B.** 5   **C.** 1   **D.** 0

6. In the fact 5 x 9 = 45, the 9 is a _____.

A. addend   **B.** divisor

C. factor   **D.** product

7. How many inches are in 6 feet?

A. 12   **B.** 60

C. 66   **D.** 72

8. How many eggs are in 9 dozen?

A. 12   **B.** 96

C. 108   **D.** 120

9. Which number makes this number sentence true?

$$6 \times \underline{\quad} = 60$$

A. 0   **B.** 1   **C.** 10   **D.** 12

10. 11 + 11 + 11 + 11 + 11 is **not** the same as _____.

A. 11 x 4   **B.** 5 x 11

C. 44 + 11   **D.** 33 + 11 + 11

225

Reviewing Multiplication Concepts and Facts

Learning about Division

6 divided into 3 groups = 2 in each group
$6 \div 3 = 2$

6 divided into 2 groups = 3 in each group
$6 \div 2 = 3$

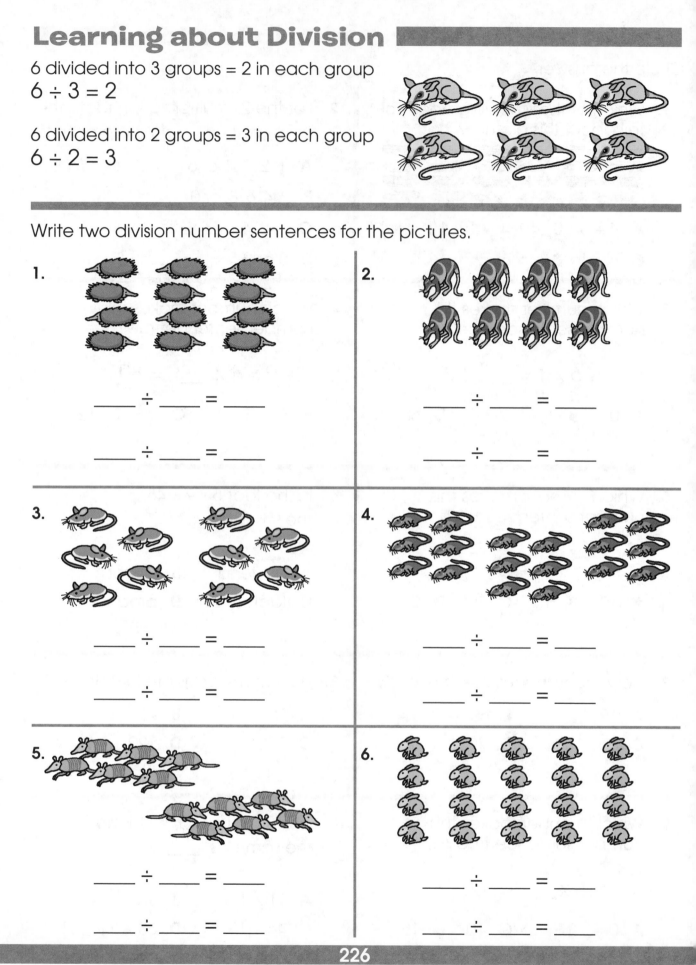

Write two division number sentences for the pictures.

1.

_____ ÷ _____ = _____

_____ ÷ _____ = _____

2.

_____ ÷ _____ = _____

_____ ÷ _____ = _____

3.

_____ ÷ _____ = _____

_____ ÷ _____ = _____

4.

_____ ÷ _____ = _____

_____ ÷ _____ = _____

5.

_____ ÷ _____ = _____

_____ ÷ _____ = _____

6.

_____ ÷ _____ = _____

_____ ÷ _____ = _____

Understanding Division

Learning about Division

If you know your multiplication facts, you are ready for division.

Here is a multiplication fact:
$$4 \times 3 = 12$$

Here are two related division facts:
$$12 \div 3 = 4 \text{ and } 12 \div 4 = 3$$

Write related division facts for each multiplication fact.

1. $8 \times 7 = 56$

    ___ $\div$ ___ = ___

    ___ $\div$ ___ = ___

2. $4 \times 9 = 36$

    ___ $\div$ ___ = ___

    ___ $\div$ ___ = ___

3. $5 \times 5 = 25$

    ___ $\div$ ___ = ___

4. $6 \times 7 = 42$

    ___ $\div$ ___ = ___

    ___ $\div$ ___ = ___

5. $3 \times 8 = 24$

    ___ $\div$ ___ = ___

    ___ $\div$ ___ = ___

6. $2 \times 7 = 14$

    ___ $\div$ ___ = ___

    ___ $\div$ ___ = ___

7. $7 \times 5 = 35$

    ___ $\div$ ___ = ___

    ___ $\div$ ___ = ___

8. $8 \times 9 = 72$

    ___ $\div$ ___ = ___

    ___ $\div$ ___ = ___

9. $4 \times 8 = 32$

    ___ $\div$ ___ = ___

    ___ $\div$ ___ = ___

Solve the problem.

10. Joshua has collected 63 stamps from different countries. He has to divide them into 7 different albums. How many stamps will go into each album?

    _____

Understanding Multiplication and Division

Dividing by 2 and 3

There are 15 fish.
There are 3 groups.
There are 5 fish in each group. $15 \div 3 = 5$

Draw circles around groups of fish to show the division fact. Then write the answer.

1. $14 \div 2 = $ _____

2. $12 \div 3 = $ _____

3. $8 \div 2 = $ _____

Practice these division facts.
Recall related multiplication facts.

4. $2 \div 2 = $ _____

$4 \div 2 = $ _____

$6 \div 2 = $ _____

$8 \div 2 = $ _____

$10 \div 2 = $ _____

$12 \div 2 = $ _____

$14 \div 2 = $ _____

$16 \div 2 = $ _____

$18 \div 2 = $ _____

5. $3 \div 3 = $ _____

$6 \div 3 = $ _____

$9 \div 3 = $ _____

$12 \div 3 = $ _____

$15 \div 3 = $ _____

$18 \div 3 = $ _____

$21 \div 3 = $ _____

$24 \div 3 = $ _____

$27 \div 3 = $ _____

Fill in the blanks.

6. If you know $2 \times 8 = 16$, then you know $16 \div 2 = $ _____.

7. If you know $3 \times 7 = 21$, then you know $21 \div $ _____ $= $ _____.

8. If you know $2 \times 9 = $ _____, then you know _____ $\div 2 = $ _____.

9. If you know _____ $\times 3 = 3$, then you know _____ $\div$ _____ $= $ _____.

10. Look at the facts above. What is a number divided by itself? _____

©School Zone Publishing Company 06320

Dividing by 4 and 5

Circle the fish to show the division fact. Write the answer.

1. 20 ÷ 4 = _____

2. 30 ÷ 5 = _____

Practice these division facts.
Recall related multiplication facts.

3. 4 ÷ 4 = _____

8 ÷ 4 = _____

12 ÷ 4 = _____

16 ÷ 4 = _____

20 ÷ 4 = _____

24 ÷ 4 = _____

28 ÷ 4 = _____

32 ÷ 4 = _____

36 ÷ 4 = _____

4. 5 ÷ 5 = _____

10 ÷ 5 = _____

15 ÷ 5 = _____

20 ÷ 5 = _____

25 ÷ 5 = _____

30 ÷ 5 = _____

35 ÷ 5 = _____

40 ÷ 5 = _____

45 ÷ 5 = _____

Divide.

5. 12 ÷ 4 = _____

10 ÷ 5 = _____

32 ÷ 4 = _____

40 ÷ 5 = _____

4 ÷ 4 = _____

20 ÷ 5 = _____

36 ÷ 4 = _____

28 ÷ 4 = _____

5 ÷ 5 = _____

24 ÷ 4 = _____

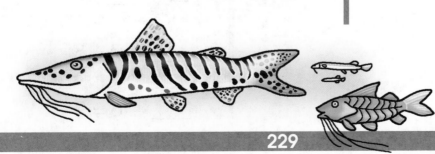

Dividing by 4 and 5

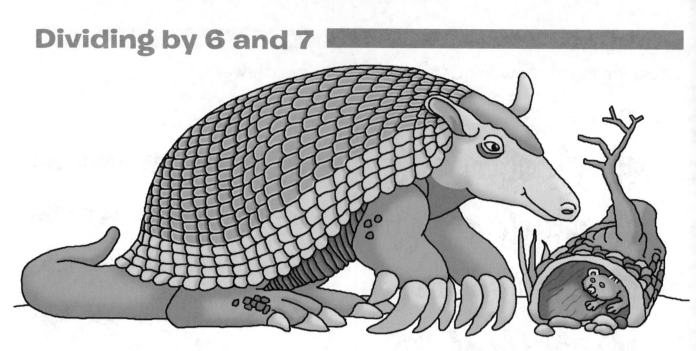

Practice these division facts.
Recall related multiplication facts.

1. 6 ÷ 6 = _____

12 ÷ 6 = _____

18 ÷ 6 = _____

24 ÷ 6 = _____

30 ÷ 6 = _____

36 ÷ 6 = _____

42 ÷ 6 = _____

48 ÷ 6 = _____

54 ÷ 6 = _____

2. 7 ÷ 7 = _____

14 ÷ 7 = _____

21 ÷ 7 = _____

28 ÷ 7 = _____

35 ÷ 7 = _____

42 ÷ 7 = _____

49 ÷ 7 = _____

56 ÷ 7 = _____

63 ÷ 7 = _____

3. Find the missing numbers.

36 ÷ _____ = 6

_____ ÷ 7 = 3

48 ÷ 6 = _____

_____ ÷ 7 = 7

18 ÷ _____ = 3

63 ÷ _____ = 9

21 ÷ _____ = 7

_____ ÷ 7 = 8

_____ ÷ 6 = 9

Dividing by 8 and 9

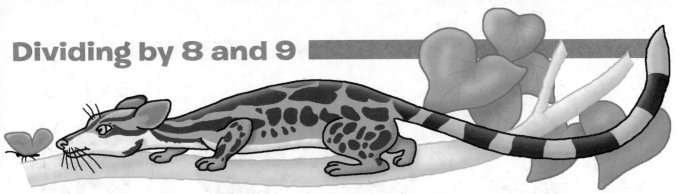

Practice these division facts.
Recall related multiplication facts.

1. 8 ÷ 8 = _____
16 ÷ 8 = _____
24 ÷ 8 = _____
32 ÷ 8 = _____
40 ÷ 8 = _____
48 ÷ 8 = _____
56 ÷ 8 = _____
64 ÷ 8 = _____
72 ÷ 8 = _____

2. 9 ÷ 9 = _____
18 ÷ 9 = _____
27 ÷ 9 = _____
36 ÷ 9 = _____
45 ÷ 9 = _____
54 ÷ 9 = _____
63 ÷ 9 = _____
72 ÷ 9 = _____
81 ÷ 9 = _____

Write a fact family for each group of numbers.

7.   7, 8, 56

_____ x _____ = _____

_____ x _____ = _____

_____ ÷ _____ = _____

_____ ÷ _____ = _____

8.   1, 9, 9

_____ x _____ = _____

_____ x _____ = _____

_____ ÷ _____ = _____

_____ ÷ _____ = _____

Fill in the missing numbers for each fact family.

3. 5 x 8 = _____
40 ÷ 5 = _____

8 x _____ = 40
40 ÷ 8 = _____

4. 9 x _____ = 54
54 ÷ 9 = _____

6 x 9 = _____
_____ ÷ 6 = 9

5. _____ x 8 = 72
72 ÷ 8 = _____

8 x _____ = 72
72 ÷ _____ = 8

6. 8 x 8 = _____

64 ÷ _____ = 8

9.   7, 9, 63

_____ x _____ = _____

_____ x _____ = _____

_____ ÷ _____ = _____

_____ ÷ _____ = _____

Dividing with 1 and 0

$$5 \div 5 = 1$$

$$5 \div 1 = 5$$

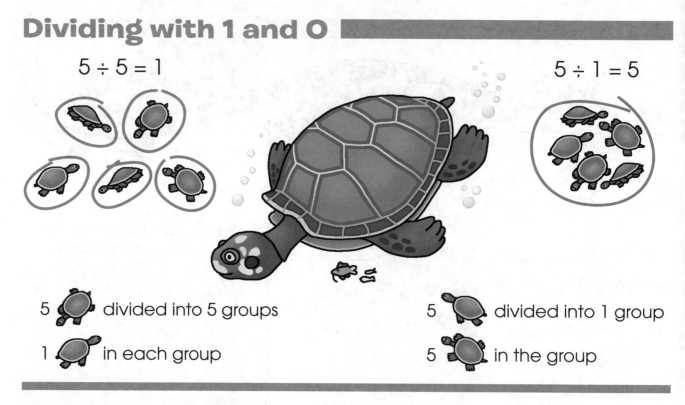

5 🐢 divided into 5 groups

1 🐢 in each group

5 🐢 divided into 1 group

5 🐢 in the group

Divide. Match the problems to the division rules.
The first one is done for you.

Here are some division rules:

$4 \div 4 = \underline{\;1\;}$

$0 \div 3 = \underline{\qquad}$

Any number divided by 1 equals that number.
$5 \div 1 = 5$

$10 \div 1 = \underline{\qquad}$

$12 \div 12 = \underline{\qquad}$

$7 \div 1 = \underline{\qquad}$

$2 \div 0 = \underline{\qquad}$

Any non-zero number divided by itself is 1.
$5 \div 5 = 1$

$0 \div 11 = \underline{\qquad}$

$25 \div 25 = \underline{\qquad}$

$8 \div 8 = \underline{\qquad}$

$0 \div 9 = \underline{\qquad}$

Zero divided by any non-zero number equals 0.
$0 \div 5 = 0$

$15 \div 0 = \underline{\qquad}$

$0 \div 25 = \underline{\qquad}$

$6 \div 1 = \underline{\qquad}$

$0 \div 0 = \underline{\qquad}$

You cannot divide by zero. You **cannot** do $5 \div 0$.

$12 \div 1 = \underline{\qquad}$

$11 \div 11 = \underline{\qquad}$

Writing Division Facts Two Ways

You can write a division problem two ways.
There are three parts to a division problem.

$12 \div 3 = 4$

Dividend
Divisor
Quotient

$$4 \leftarrow \text{Quotient}$$
$$3\overline{)12} \leftarrow \text{Dividend}$$
Divisor

Rewrite each division problem.

1. $36 \div 9 = 4$ $\overline{)}$

2. $10 \div 2 = 5$ $\overline{)}$

3. $56 \div 8 = 7$ $\overline{)}$

4. $63 \div 7 = 9$ $\overline{)}$

Complete each problem by finding the divisor and quotient.
Hint: there may be more than one answer for each problem.

5. $18 \div \underline{} = \underline{}$

6. $\underline{}\overline{)30}$

7. $\underline{}\overline{)45}$

8. $54 \div \underline{} = \underline{}$

9. $72 \div \underline{} = \underline{}$

10. $\underline{}\overline{)7}$

Divide.

11. $36 \div 4 = \underline{}$

12. $6\overline{)42}$

13. $27 \div 3 = \underline{}$

14. $7\overline{)63}$

15. $56 \div 8 = \underline{}$

16. $9\overline{)81}$

17. $8\overline{)8}$

18. $40 \div 5 = \underline{}$

19. $6\overline{)0}$

     Writing Division Facts Two Ways

Division Facts Review

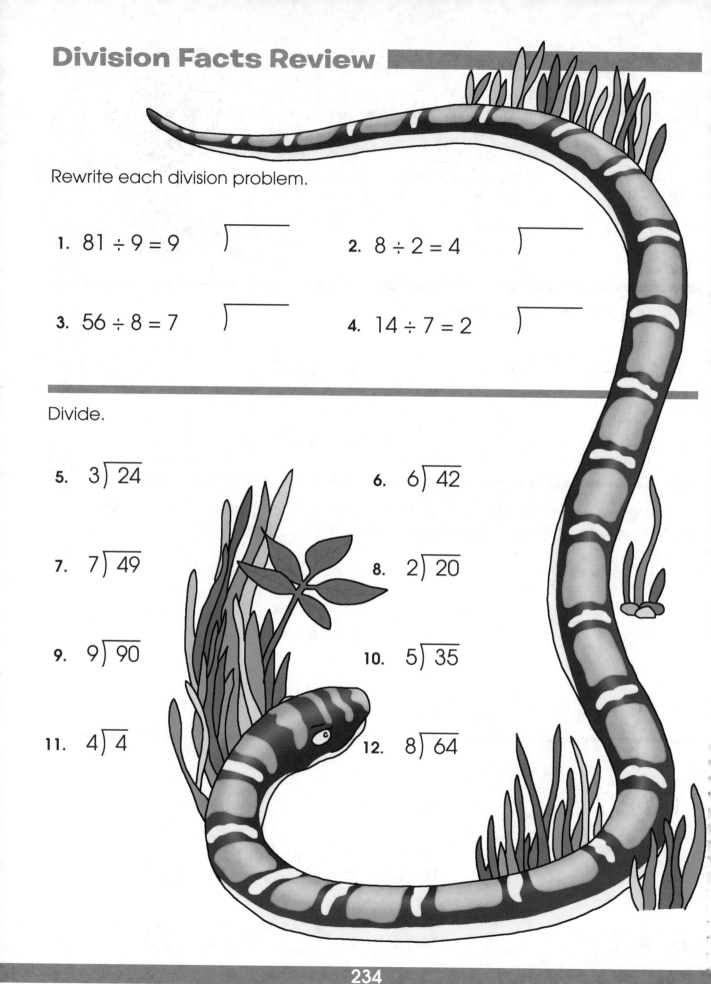

Rewrite each division problem.

1. $81 \div 9 = 9$ ⟌

2. $8 \div 2 = 4$ ⟌

3. $56 \div 8 = 7$ ⟌

4. $14 \div 7 = 2$ ⟌

Divide.

5. $3\overline{)24}$

6. $6\overline{)42}$

7. $7\overline{)49}$

8. $2\overline{)20}$

9. $9\overline{)90}$

10. $5\overline{)35}$

11. $4\overline{)4}$

12. $8\overline{)64}$

Multiplication and Division Word Problems ▪

To solve division problems, look for clue words like **how many groups** or **how many in each group**.

Write and solve a number sentence. Label the answer.

Joshua has 20 fish. He divided them equally into 4 fish bowls. How many fish are in each bowl?

$$\underline{20} \div \underline{4} = \underline{5}$$
$$\underline{5} \quad \underline{fish}$$

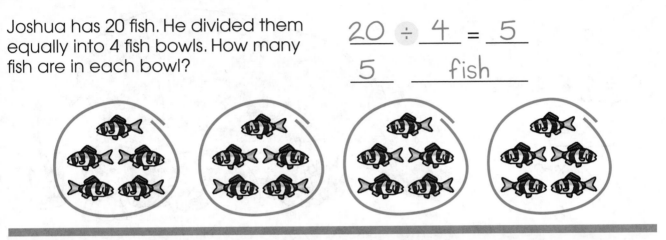

Write and solve a number sentence for each problem. Label your answer.

1. Joshua has 24 Brazil nuts that he has to divide among 6 friends. How many nuts will each friend get?

   ____ ⬤ ____ = ____

   ____ _____

2. Joshua and his two friends each bought 8 bananas. How many bananas did all 3 of them buy?

   ____ ⬤ ____ = ____

   ____ _____

3. Joshua put 6 stickers in each row on an album page. If there are 7 rows on each page, what is the total number of stickers on each page?

   ____ ⬤ ____ = ____

   ____ _____

4. Joshua has 9 toy boats. He put an equal number of them into 3 different boxes. How many boats are in each box?

   ____ ⬤ ____ = ____

   ____ _____

Solving Multiplication and Division Word Problems

Combining Multiplication and Division

Here's a fun activity for you using both multiplication and division. Multiply and/or divide the first four numbers in order to make the fifth number. You may want to use a calculator.

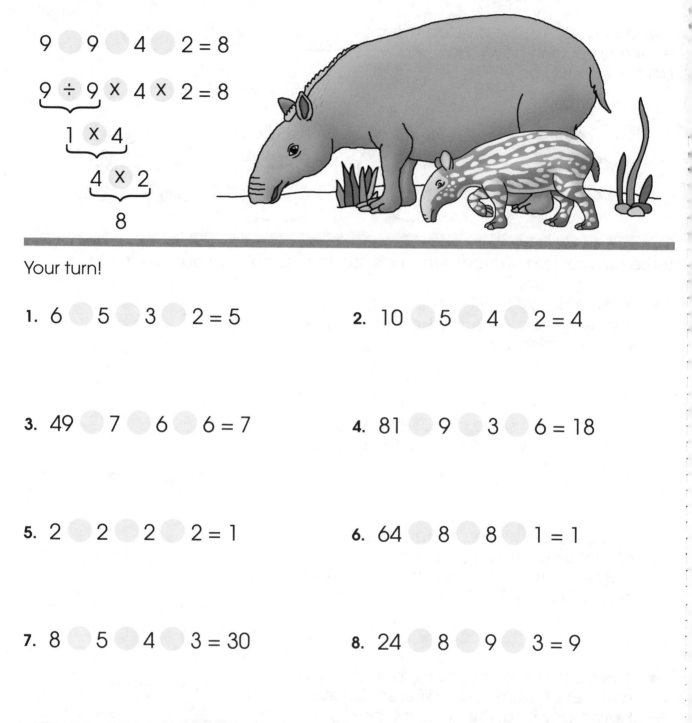

9 ◯ 9 ◯ 4 ◯ 2 = 8

9 ÷ 9 × 4 × 2 = 8

1 × 4

4 × 2

8

Your turn!

1. 6 ◯ 5 ◯ 3 ◯ 2 = 5

2. 10 ◯ 5 ◯ 4 ◯ 2 = 4

3. 49 ◯ 7 ◯ 6 ◯ 6 = 7

4. 81 ◯ 9 ◯ 3 ◯ 6 = 18

5. 2 ◯ 2 ◯ 2 ◯ 2 = 1

6. 64 ◯ 8 ◯ 8 ◯ 1 = 1

7. 8 ◯ 5 ◯ 4 ◯ 3 = 30

8. 24 ◯ 8 ◯ 9 ◯ 3 = 9

Reviewing Multiplication and Division Facts

©School Zone Publishing Company 06320

Multiplication and Division Puzzle

Complete the problems.
Then write the numbers in the puzzle.

Across

1. 5 groups of 8 is _____.

2. 7 x 8 = _____

3. 27 ÷ 9 = _____

4. 8 x _____ = 64

5. _____ ÷ 6 = 4

6. 9 groups of 4 is _____.

7. 2 x 7 = _____

8. 5 x 4 = _____

9. 9 x 8 = _____

10. 6 ÷ _____ = 6

11. _____ x 5 = 30

12. 4 x 7 = _____

13. _____ ÷ 4 = 6

14. 8 x 5 = _____

15. _____ ÷ 7 = 4

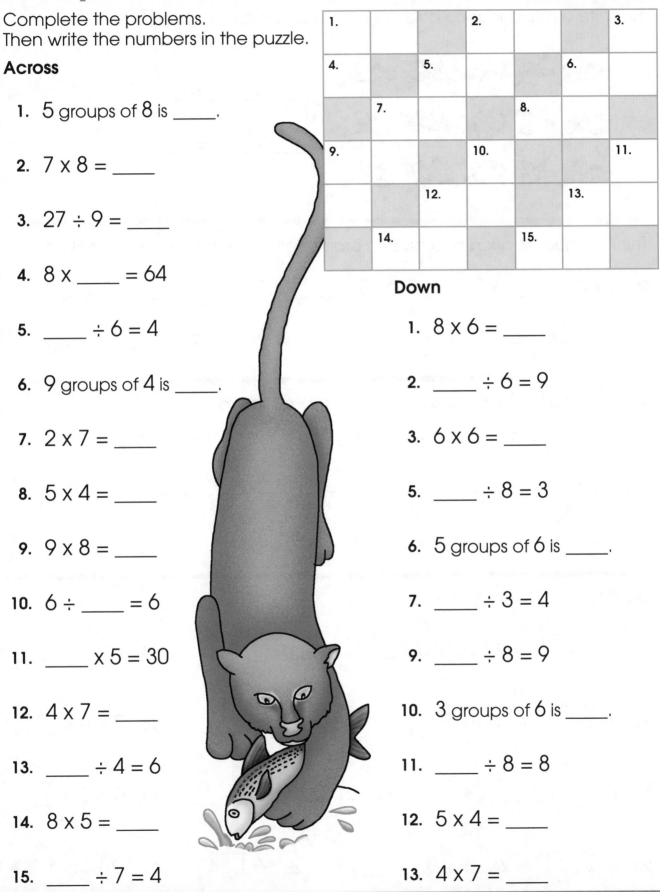

Down

1. 8 x 6 = _____

2. _____ ÷ 6 = 9

3. 6 x 6 = _____

5. _____ ÷ 8 = 3

6. 5 groups of 6 is _____.

7. _____ ÷ 3 = 4

9. _____ ÷ 8 = 9

10. 3 groups of 6 is _____.

11. _____ ÷ 8 = 8

12. 5 x 4 = _____

13. 4 x 7 = _____

©School Zone Publishing Company 06320   Reviewing Multiplication and Division Facts

What I Learned about Division

1. Write a multiplication and division sentence for the picture.

____ x ____ = ____

____ ÷ ____ = ____

Think of multiplication and division properties to complete each problem.

2. $3 \times 8 =$ ____ $\times 3$

3. $9 \div$ ____ $= 1$

4. ____ $\times 5 = 0$

5. ____ $\div 8 = 0$

6. $7 \div$ ____ $= 7$

7. $4 \div$ ____ $=$ cannot do

Write related division facts for each multiplication fact.

8. $6 \times 9 = 54$

9. $8 \times 1 = 8$

10. $7 \times 5 = 35$

____ ÷ ____ = ____

____ ÷ ____ = ____

____ ÷ ____ = ____

____ ÷ ____ = ____

____ ÷ ____ = ____

____ ÷ ____ = ____

Divide.

11. $6 \overline{)48}$

12. $30 \div 5 =$ ____

13. $7 \overline{)56}$

14. $9 \div 1 =$ ____

15. $8 \overline{)72}$

16. $36 \div 9 =$ ____

17. $0 \div 6 =$ ____

18. $7 \times 6 =$ ____

19. $6 \div 6 =$ ____

20. $8 \overline{)64}$

21. $81 \div 9 =$ ____

22. $0 \div 0 =$ ____

23. $7 \overline{)63}$

24. $3 \div 0 =$ ____

25. $6 \overline{)54}$

26. $9 \overline{)45}$

Reviewing Division Concepts and Facts

©School Zone Publishing Company 06320

Circle the answer.

27. Which number sentence does not tell about this picture?

A. $12 \div 6 = 2$ B. $12 - 6 = 2$

C. $12 \div 2 = 6$ D. $6 \times 2 = 12$

28. Joshua put 36 shells into 4 equal groups. Which number sentence would you use to find how many shells are in each group?

A. $4 \times 36 =$ ___

B. $4 + 36 =$ ___

C. $36 \div 4 =$ ___

D. $36 - 4 =$ ___

29. Which fact does **not** belong in the same fact family with the other choices?

A. $5 \times 6 = 30$ B. $30 \div 5 = 6$

C. $5 \times 1 = 5$ D. $30 \div 6 = 5$

30. Which option makes this number sentence true?

$$8 \div 0 =$$ ___

A. 0   B. 8   C. 80   D. cannot do

31. Which word names the part of this problem pointed to by the arrow?

$$6 \overline{)24} \leftarrow$$

with 4 above the 24

A. quotient   B. product

C. divisor   D. dividend

32. Which number makes this number sentence true?

$$9 \div 3 =$$ ___

A. 0   B. 1   C. 3   D. 27

33. Which number makes this number sentence true?

$$7 \div \_\_\_ = 7$$

A. 0   B. 1   C. 7   D. 49

34. Which of the following number sentences cannot be done?

A. $0 \div 4$ B. $4 \div 4$

C. $4 \div 1$ D. $4 \div 0$

Reviewing Division Concepts and Facts

Multiplication Patterns

If you know your multiplication facts, you can find these products mentally. Look for a pattern.

$3 \times 4 = 12$

$3 \times 40 = 120$

$3 \times 400 = 1,200$

3×4 ones = 12 ones

3×4 tens = 12 tens

3×4 hundreds = 12 hundreds

Practice the facts.

1. $8 \times 1 = $ _____

   $8 \times 10 = $ _____

   $8 \times 100 = $ _____

2. $7 \times 9 = $ _____

   $7 \times 90 = $ _____

   $7 \times 900 = $ _____

Fill in the blanks.

3. 6×1 ten = __6__ tens = __60__

4. 4×4 hundreds = _____ hundreds = _____

5. 3×9 hundreds = _____ hundreds = _____

6. 8×7 tens = _____ tens = _____

7. 5×8 tens = _____ tens = _____

8. 6×9 hundreds = _____ hundreds = _____

Multiply mentally.

9. $7 \times 100 = $ _____

10. $4 \times 90 = $ _____

11. $3 \times 500 = $ _____

12. $40 \times 7 = $ _____

13. $300 \times 8 = $ _____

14. $9 \times 50 = $ _____

15. $600 \times 7 = $ _____

16. $8 \times 50 = $ _____

17. $8 \times 900 = $ _____

18. Complete the chart.

x	10	30	80	100	400	900
5						
7				700		
8			640			

Using Basic Facts to Multiply Multiples

Estimating Products

Use rounding to estimate products.

Joshua has 3 tanks of fish.
There are 37 fish in each tank.
About how many fish is this?

3 x 37
↓   ↓

3 x 40 = 120   Round 37 to 40.   There are about 120 fish.

> If the number is 5 or more, round up.
> If the number is 4 or less, round down.

40
39
38
37
36
35
34
33
32
31
30

Estimate the product by rounding.

1. 4 x 62

____ X ____ = ____

2. 6 x 75

____ X ____ = ____

3. 3 x 191

____ X ____ = ____

4. 637 x 8

____ X ____ = ____

5. 7 x 213

____ X ____ = ____

6. 5 x 807

____ X ____ = ____

Estimate the product.

7. 3 x 71 _____

8. 4 x 795 _____

9. 7 x 678 _____

10. 459 x 4 _____

11. 2 x 925 _____

12. 88 x 6 _____

13. 5 x 304 _____

14. 7 x 77 _____

15. 605 x 9 _____

Solve the problem.

16. Joshua has 3 photo albums. There are 68
    photographs in each album. About how many
    photographs are in the albums?   _____

17. Joshua rides the bus to school. There are 42
    students on each bus. About how many students
    are on 6 buses?   _____

Estimating Products

Multiplying Two-Digit Numbers

If you know the multiplication facts, you can multiply any two numbers together.

Multiply the ones.

```
    tens ones
     2  3
  x     3
  --------
        9
```

Multiply the tens.

```
    tens ones
     2  3
  x     3
  --------
     6  9
```

Multiply.

1.
```
    14
  x  2
  -----
```

2.
```
    12
  x  4
  -----
```

3.
```
    23
  x  2
  -----
```

4.
```
    33
  x  3
  -----
```

5.
```
    24
  x  2
  -----
```

6.
```
    11
  x  7
  -----
```

7.
```
    32
  x  3
  -----
```

8.
```
    10
  x  4
  -----
```

9.
```
    13
  x  2
  -----
```

Solve the problem.

10. Joshua is filling 3 pages in his journal per day. How many pages will he fill in 12 days?

_____

Multiplying with Regrouping

Sometimes you need to regroup when you multiply.

Multiply the ones.
Regroup.

$$
\begin{array}{r}
^{3} \\
45 \\
\times\ \ 7 \\
\hline
5
\end{array}
$$

7 ones x 5 ones = 35 ones
Regroup as 3 tens and 5 ones.

Multiply the tens.
Add regrouped ones.

$$
\begin{array}{r}
^{3} \\
45 \\
\times\ \ 7 \\
\hline
315
\end{array}
$$

7 ones x 4 tens = 28 tens
28 tens + 3 tens = 31 tens
31 tens is 3 hundreds
and 1 ten.

Multiply.

1.	42 x 6	2.	98 x 2	3.	74 x 4	4.	34 x 3	5.	78 x 2	6.	64 x 5

7.	63 x 9	8.	18 x 3	9.	55 x 5	10.	19 x 9	11.	28 x 3	12.	45 x 5

Try these!

13. $4 \times 2 \times 3 =$ _____

14. $5 \times 2 \times 8 =$ _____

15. $6 \times 2 \times 3 =$ _____

Multiplying Three-Digit Numbers

Multiply the ones.
Regroup.

```
    1
  4 5 2
x     6
-------
      2
```

6 ones x 2 ones = 12 ones
Regroup as 1 ten and 2 ones.

Multiply the tens.
Add regrouped ones.
Regroup.

```
  3 1
  4 5 2
x     6
-------
    1 2
```

6 ones x 5 tens = 30 tens
30 tens + 1 ten = 31 tens
Regroup as 3 hundreds
and 1 ten.

Multiply the hundreds.
Add regrouped tens.

```
  3 1
  4 5 2
x     6
-------
2, 7 1 2
```

6 ones x 4 hundreds = 24 hundreds
24 hundreds + 3 hundreds = 27 hundreds

Estimate the product: 6 x 452 is about 6 x 500 = 3,000

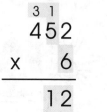

Multiply. Estimate to check your answer.

1.
```
  126        Estimate
x   4      x
```

2.
```
  472        Estimate
x   2      x
```

3.
```
  975        Estimate
x   4      x
```

4.
```
  134        Estimate
x   7      x
```

5.
```
  813        Estimate
x   3      x
```

6.
```
  144        Estimate
x   8      x
```

7.
```
  135        Estimate
x   2      x
```

8.
```
  292        Estimate
x   5      x
```

9.
```
  224        Estimate
x   9      x
```

Multiplying with Regrouping

©School Zone Publishing Company 06320

More Multiplication

Multiply. Estimate to check your answer.

1.
$$\begin{array}{r} 78 \\ \times\ 4 \\ \hline \end{array}$$
Estimate
x _____

2.
$$\begin{array}{r} 56 \\ \times\ 8 \\ \hline \end{array}$$
Estimate
x _____

3.
$$\begin{array}{r} 26 \\ \times\ 9 \\ \hline \end{array}$$
Estimate
x _____

4.
$$\begin{array}{r} 213 \\ \times\ 4 \\ \hline \end{array}$$
Estimate
x _____

5.
$$\begin{array}{r} 183 \\ \times\ 7 \\ \hline \end{array}$$
Estimate
x _____

6.
$$\begin{array}{r} 491 \\ \times\ 6 \\ \hline \end{array}$$
Estimate
x _____

7.
$$\begin{array}{r} 169 \\ \times\ 3 \\ \hline \end{array}$$
Estimate
x _____

8.
$$\begin{array}{r} 555 \\ \times\ 4 \\ \hline \end{array}$$
Estimate
x _____

9.
$$\begin{array}{r} 732 \\ \times\ 5 \\ \hline \end{array}$$
Estimate
x _____

Solve the problem.

10. The largest bird is the ostrich. An ostrich can weigh up to 345 pounds. How much would 4 ostriches weigh?

_____

11. How many ostriches might weigh about one ton? A ton is 2,000 pounds.

_____

©School Zone Publishing Company 06320

Multiplying with Regrouping

Multiplying with Zeros

Estimate to check.
8 x 300 = 2,400

$$\begin{array}{r} \overset{5}{3\,0\,7} \\ \times\quad 8 \\ \hline 2{,}4\,5\,6 \end{array}$$

Multiply the ones. Regroup.
Multiply the tens.
$8 \times 0 = 0$ and $0 + 5 = 5$
Multiply the hundreds.

Multiply. Estimate to check your answer.

1. $\begin{array}{r} 301 \\ \times\quad 3 \\ \hline \end{array}$

2. $\begin{array}{r} 190 \\ \times\quad 3 \\ \hline \end{array}$

3. $\begin{array}{r} 390 \\ \times\quad 5 \\ \hline \end{array}$

4. $\begin{array}{r} 705 \\ \times\quad 6 \\ \hline \end{array}$

5. $\begin{array}{r} 402 \\ \times\quad 6 \\ \hline \end{array}$

6. $\begin{array}{r} 450 \\ \times\quad 5 \\ \hline \end{array}$

7. $\begin{array}{r} 306 \\ \times\quad 5 \\ \hline \end{array}$

8. $\begin{array}{r} 409 \\ \times\quad 2 \\ \hline \end{array}$

9. $\begin{array}{r} 204 \\ \times\quad 7 \\ \hline \end{array}$

10. $\begin{array}{r} 350 \\ \times\quad 9 \\ \hline \end{array}$

11. $\begin{array}{r} 406 \\ \times\quad 9 \\ \hline \end{array}$

12. $\begin{array}{r} 670 \\ \times\quad 8 \\ \hline \end{array}$

Find the missing digits.

13. $\begin{array}{r} 3\ \bullet\ 2 \\ \times\quad 8 \\ \hline 2{,}\bullet16 \end{array}$

14. $\begin{array}{r} 605 \\ \times\quad\bullet \\ \hline 4{,}\bullet40 \end{array}$

15. $\begin{array}{r} 34\bullet \\ \times\quad 5 \\ \hline 1{,}\bullet00 \end{array}$

16. $\begin{array}{r} 2\bullet0 \\ \times\quad 7 \\ \hline 1{,}8\bullet0 \end{array}$

Multiplying with Zeros in the Factor

Multiplying Four-Digit Numbers

$$\begin{array}{r} {\scriptstyle 2 \quad 11} \\ 5,432 \\ \times \quad 6 \\ \hline 32,592 \end{array}$$

Multiply the ones. Regroup.
Multiply the tens. Regroup.
Multiply the hundreds. Regroup.
Multiply the thousands. 6 x 5 = 30 + 2 = 32

Multiply.

1.
$$\begin{array}{r} 2,222 \\ \times \quad 3 \\ \hline \end{array}$$

2.
$$\begin{array}{r} 3,141 \\ \times \quad 5 \\ \hline \end{array}$$

3.
$$\begin{array}{r} 1,338 \\ \times \quad 6 \\ \hline \end{array}$$

4.
$$\begin{array}{r} 9,214 \\ \times \quad 4 \\ \hline \end{array}$$

5.
$$\begin{array}{r} 7,768 \\ \times \quad 2 \\ \hline \end{array}$$

6.
$$\begin{array}{r} 5,261 \\ \times \quad 3 \\ \hline \end{array}$$

7.
$$\begin{array}{r} 3,105 \\ \times \quad 7 \\ \hline \end{array}$$

8.
$$\begin{array}{r} 2,025 \\ \times \quad 8 \\ \hline \end{array}$$

9.
$$\begin{array}{r} 6,350 \\ \times \quad 5 \\ \hline \end{array}$$

Solve the problem.

10. The largest reptile is the saltwater crocodile. A
saltwater crocodile weighs about 1,500 pounds.
How much would a half dozen of them weigh?

_____

©School Zone Publishing Company 06320   Multiplying Four-Digit Numbers by One-Digit Numbers

Multiplying Money

When you write amounts of money as dollars and cents, there are always two places for cents. Remember to put a decimal point in the answer after you multiply.

Multiply the numbers.

$$\begin{array}{r} {}^{6}\;{}^{4} \\ \$6.85 \\ \times \qquad 8 \\ \hline 5480 \end{array}$$

Write the dollar sign and decimal point in the answer.

$$\begin{array}{r} {}^{6}\;{}^{4} \\ \$6.85 \\ \times \qquad 8 \\ \hline \$54.80 \end{array}$$

↑ dollar sign   ↑ decimal

$6.85 is about $7.
8 x $7 is $56.
$54.80 is close to $56.

Estimate the product. Round each amount to the nearest dollar or 10 dollars. The first one is done for you.

1. $2.93
    x   6

    $3 x 6 = $18

2. $8.06
    x   7

3. $42.50
    x   3

4. $0.89
    x   9

Multiply.

5. $2.93
    x   6

6. $8.06
    x   7

7. $42.50
    x   3

8. $0.89
    x   9

9. $4.75
    x   6

10. $7.49
    x   4

11. $38.29
    x   3

12. $0.98
    x   6

Multiplying Money

Multiplication Word Problems

Look at the prices above to solve each problem.
Read the problems very carefully!

1. Joshua bought 3 t-shirts.
   How much did the t-shirts cost?

   _____

2. Joshua also bought 6 pairs of socks.
   How much did the socks cost?

   _____

3. Joshua and 3 friends each bought a
   new backpack. How much did all the
   backpacks cost?

   _____

4. The 4 campers bought 5 different bird
   books. How much did they spend on
   the books?

   _____

5. The 4 campers bought 2 boxes of raisins
   each for a snack on their hike. How much
   did they pay for all the boxes of raisins?

   _____

6. The 4 campers each bought a pair of
   sunglasses and a bottle of sunblock. What
   was the total cost of these items for all the
   campers?

   _____

©School Zone Publishing Company 06320   Multiplying Money

Multiplying with Multiples

Here's a shortcut for multiplying with multiples of 10.
Multiply the non-zero numbers. Then count all the
zeros and write that many zeros in the product.

$$\begin{array}{r} 80 \\ \times\ 40 \\ \hline 3,200 \end{array}$$

$8 \times 4 = 32$
There are two zeros.
The product is 32
followed by two zeros.

Multiply.

1. $\begin{array}{r} 20 \\ \times\ 30 \\ \hline \end{array}$

2. $\begin{array}{r} 80 \\ \times\ 70 \\ \hline \end{array}$

3. $\begin{array}{r} 60 \\ \times\ 50 \\ \hline \end{array}$

4. $\begin{array}{r} 20 \\ \times\ 80 \\ \hline \end{array}$

5. $\begin{array}{r} 60 \\ \times\ 60 \\ \hline \end{array}$

6. $\begin{array}{r} 70 \\ \times\ 60 \\ \hline \end{array}$

7. $\begin{array}{r} 50 \\ \times\ 80 \\ \hline \end{array}$

8. $\begin{array}{r} 90 \\ \times\ 40 \\ \hline \end{array}$

9. $\begin{array}{r} 30 \\ \times\ 40 \\ \hline \end{array}$

10. $\begin{array}{r} 90 \\ \times\ 30 \\ \hline \end{array}$

11. Complete the chart.

x	10	20	40	50	60	80
10						
30						
60						
70						
90						

Knowing how to multiply with multiples of 10 will help
you estimate products on the next few pages.

Multiplying with Multiples of 10   ©School Zone Publishing Company 06320

Multiplying by Two-Digit Numbers

Multiply by ones to find a partial product.

$$\begin{array}{r} \overset{3}{5}4 \\ \times\ 38 \\ \hline 432 \end{array}$$

$8 \times 54 = 432$

Multiply by tens to find another partial product.

$$\begin{array}{r} \overset{1}{5}4 \\ \times\ 38 \\ \hline 432 \\ 1620 \end{array}$$

3 tens x 54 = 162 tens
162 tens is 1,620.

Add the partial products.

$$\begin{array}{r} 54 \\ \times\ 38 \\ \hline 432 \\ +1620 \\ \hline 2,052 \end{array}$$

432 + 1620 = 2,052

Multiply. Estimate to check your answer.

1.
$$\begin{array}{r} 31 \\ \times\ 77 \\ \hline \end{array}$$
Estimate
x _____

2.
$$\begin{array}{r} 46 \\ \times\ 22 \\ \hline \end{array}$$
Estimate
x _____

3.
$$\begin{array}{r} 93 \\ \times\ 11 \\ \hline \end{array}$$
Estimate
x _____

4.
$$\begin{array}{r} 84 \\ \times\ 17 \\ \hline \end{array}$$
Estimate
x _____

5.
$$\begin{array}{r} 53 \\ \times\ 44 \\ \hline \end{array}$$
Estimate
x _____

6.
$$\begin{array}{r} 62 \\ \times\ 25 \\ \hline \end{array}$$
Estimate
x _____

Solve the problem.

7. Joshua has 23 classmates. He promised to send each of them a postcard from all of the 12 cities he plans to visit. How many postcards will he send? _____

©School Zone Publishing Company 06320

Multiplying Two–Digit Numbers

Multiplying by Multiples of Ten

Multiply by ones.
Multiply by tens.
Add partial products.

$$
\begin{array}{r}
{}^{1} \\
54 \\
\times \quad 30 \\
\hline
00 \leftarrow 0 \times 54 \\
+ 1620 \leftarrow 30 \times 54 \\
\hline
1{,}620
\end{array}
$$

Use a shortcut.
Write a zero in the ones place.
Multiply by tens.

$$
\begin{array}{r}
{}^{1} \\
54 \\
\times \quad 30 \\
\hline
1{,}620 \\
\uparrow
\end{array}
$$

Multiply.

1. $\begin{array}{r} 32 \\ \times\ 30 \\ \hline \end{array}$

2. $\begin{array}{r} 78 \\ \times\ 20 \\ \hline \end{array}$

3. $\begin{array}{r} 63 \\ \times\ 50 \\ \hline \end{array}$

4. $\begin{array}{r} 29 \\ \times\ 70 \\ \hline \end{array}$

5. $\begin{array}{r} 31 \\ \times\ 20 \\ \hline \end{array}$

6. $\begin{array}{r} 43 \\ \times\ 60 \\ \hline \end{array}$

7. $\begin{array}{r} 25 \\ \times\ 40 \\ \hline \end{array}$

8. $\begin{array}{r} 84 \\ \times\ 40 \\ \hline \end{array}$

9. $\begin{array}{r} 23 \\ \times\ 30 \\ \hline \end{array}$

10. $\begin{array}{r} 56 \\ \times\ 60 \\ \hline \end{array}$

11. $\begin{array}{r} 71 \\ \times\ 50 \\ \hline \end{array}$

12. $\begin{array}{r} 99 \\ \times\ 40 \\ \hline \end{array}$

Solve the problem.

13. About 45 species of orchids were found blooming in a single rainforest tree. If 20 trees had the same number of different species, how many kinds of orchids would you find?

_____

252

Greatest and Least Products

Use a digit only once in each problem to find the product. You may use a calculator.

3 2 9 6 5

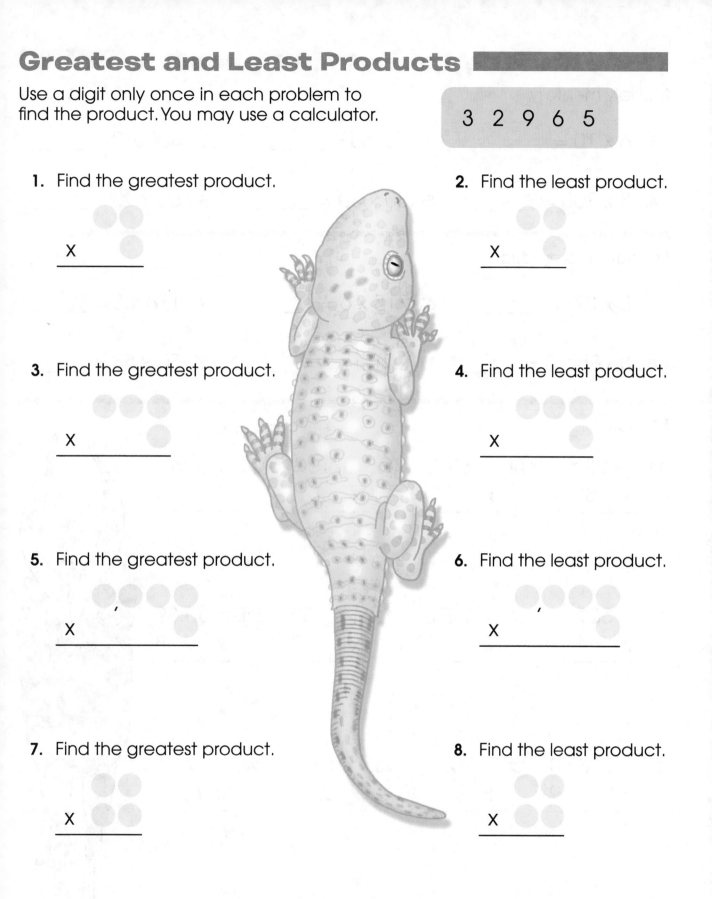

1. Find the greatest product.

◯◯
_____ X _____

2. Find the least product.

◯◯
_____ X _____

3. Find the greatest product.

◯◯◯
_____ X _____

4. Find the least product.

◯◯◯
_____ X _____

5. Find the greatest product.

◯◯,◯◯
_____ X _____

6. Find the least product.

◯◯,◯◯
_____ X _____

7. Find the greatest product.

◯◯
_____ X _____

8. Find the least product.

◯◯
_____ X _____

Understanding Factors and Products

What I Learned about Multiplication

Multiply mentally.

1. $6 \times 10 = $ _____

2. $7 \times 50 = $ _____

3. $400 \times 2 = $ _____

4. $8 \times 700 = $ _____

5. $30 \times 30 = $ _____

6. $60 \times 90 = $ _____

Estimate the product.

7. $5 \times 37 = $ _____

8. $715 \times 6 = $ _____

9. $178 \times 5 = $ _____

10. $\$6.85 \times 3 = $ _____

11. $2{,}190 \times 7 = $ _____

12. $50 \times 58 = $ _____

Multiply.

13. $\begin{array}{r} 23 \\ \times\ 3 \\ \hline \end{array}$

14. $\begin{array}{r} 69 \\ \times\ 7 \\ \hline \end{array}$

15. $\begin{array}{r} 713 \\ \times\ 3 \\ \hline \end{array}$

16. $\begin{array}{r} 825 \\ \times\ 6 \\ \hline \end{array}$

17. $\begin{array}{r} 509 \\ \times\ 4 \\ \hline \end{array}$

18. $\begin{array}{r} 4{,}273 \\ \times\ 3 \\ \hline \end{array}$

19. $\begin{array}{r} 6{,}035 \\ \times\ 7 \\ \hline \end{array}$

20. $\begin{array}{r} \$5.39 \\ \times\ 8 \\ \hline \end{array}$

21. $\begin{array}{r} \$23.50 \\ \times\ 9 \\ \hline \end{array}$

22. $\begin{array}{r} 47 \\ \times\ 23 \\ \hline \end{array}$

23. $\begin{array}{r} 74 \\ \times\ 30 \\ \hline \end{array}$

24. $\begin{array}{r} 60 \\ \times\ 82 \\ \hline \end{array}$

Reviewing Multiplication Skills ©School Zone Publishing Company 06320

Circle the answer.

25. Multiply: $7 \times 900 =$ _____

    A. 630

    B. 6,300

    C. 63,000

    D. 630,000

26. Multiply: $60 \times 80 =$ _____

    A. 480

    B. 4,800

    C. 48,000

    D. 480,000

27. Estimate: 476×3 is about _____.

    A. 400×3

    B. 500×3

    C. 400×4

    D. 500×4

28. Estimate: $\$6.81 \times 8$ is about _____.

    A. $7   **B.** $48

    C. $56   **D.** $63

29. Multiply:
$$\begin{array}{r} 863 \\ \times\ \ \ 7 \\ \hline \end{array}$$

    A. 5,601   **B.** 5,621

    C. 6,021   **D.** 6,041

30. Multiply:
$$\begin{array}{r} 508 \\ \times\ \ \ 6 \\ \hline \end{array}$$

    A. 348   **B.** 3,048

    C. 3,448   **D.** 34,048

31. Multiply: $5,431 \times 7 =$ _____

    A. 35,017   **B.** 37,017

    C. 37,817   **D.** 38,017

32. Multiply: $78 \times 32 =$ _____

    A. 156   **B.** 390

    C. 2,396   **D.** 2,496

Reviewing Multiplication Skills

Dividing Two-Digit Numbers

When you divide, there are five steps to remember.
Repeat them over and over until you finish dividing.

1. Divide	2. Multiply	3. Subtract	4. Compare	5. Bring Down
3 3)96	3 3)96 9	3 3)96 −9 0	3 3)96 −9 0	3 3)96 −9↓ 06
$9 \div 3 = 3$	$3 \times 3 = 9$	$9 - 9 = 0$	$3 > 0$ The divisor is greater than the difference.	Bring down the next number. Now you can do 3)6.

Repeat the five steps. Then check your answer.

1. Divide	2. Multiply	3. Subtract	4. Compare	5. Bring Down	Check:
32 3)96 −9 06	32 3)96 −9 06 6	32 3)96 −9 06 − 6 0	32 3)96 −9 06 − 6 0	There is no other number to bring down, so the dividing is finished.	Multiply the quotient by the divisor. 32 x 3 96
$6 \div 3 = 2$	$2 \times 3 = 6$	$6 - 6 = 0$	$3 > 0$		

Divide. Then check your answer.

1. 2)84   Check:
   _X____

2. 4)92   Check:
   _X____

3. 8)96   Check:
   _X____

4. 3)57   Check:
   _X____

5. 5)95   Check:
   _X____

6. 7)84   Check:
   _X____

Estimating Quotients

To estimate a quotient, think of a basic division fact.

Think.
$48 \div 8 = 6$

Estimate: $50 \div 8$

The estimate for $50 \div 8$ is about 6.

Estimate the quotient. Write the basic division fact under the problem.
The first one is done for you.

1. $37 \div 4$ is about __9__.

    __$36 \div 4 = 9$__

2. $62 \div 8$ is about ____.

    _____

3. $26 \div 8$ is about ____.

    _____

4. $29 \div 9$ is about ____.

    _____

5. $56 \div 6$ is about ____.

    _____

6. $29 \div 5$ is about ____.

    _____

Estimate the quotient.

7. $30 \div 7$ ____

8. $40 \div 9$ ____

9. $37 \div 5$ ____

10. $29 \div 5$ ____

11. $39 \div 4$ ____

12. $52 \div 5$ ____

13. $23 \div 3$ ____

14. $58 \div 7$ ____

15. $7\overline{)29}$

16. $6\overline{)55}$

17. $3\overline{)16}$

18. $8\overline{)67}$

19. $4\overline{)17}$

20. $4\overline{)21}$

21. $9\overline{)28}$

22. $5\overline{)37}$

23. $9\overline{)95}$

24. $4\overline{)85}$

Estimating Quotients Using Basic Facts

Quotients with Remainders

Sometimes a division problem has a **remainder**.

If 23 frogs were divided into groups of 3, there would be 7 groups of 3 and 2 frogs remaining.

The **R** stands for **remainder**.

$$3\overline{)23} \quad 7\text{ R}2$$
$$-21$$
$$2$$

Check: Multiply the quotient by the divisor. Then add the remainder.

$$
\begin{array}{r}
7 \\
\times\ 3 \\
\hline
21 \\
+\ \ 2 \\
\hline
23
\end{array}
$$

Divide. Then check your answer.

1. $4\overline{)47}$ Check:

2. $6\overline{)56}$ Check:

3. $5\overline{)29}$ Check:

4. $2\overline{)95}$ Check:

5. $7\overline{)89}$ Check:

6. $6\overline{)82}$ Check:

7. $4\overline{)39}$ Check:

8. $3\overline{)67}$ Check:

9. $5\overline{)52}$ Check:

©School Zone Publishing Company 06320

Dividing Three-Digit Numbers

Look closely at these two problems.
This one has a quotient
with 3 digits.

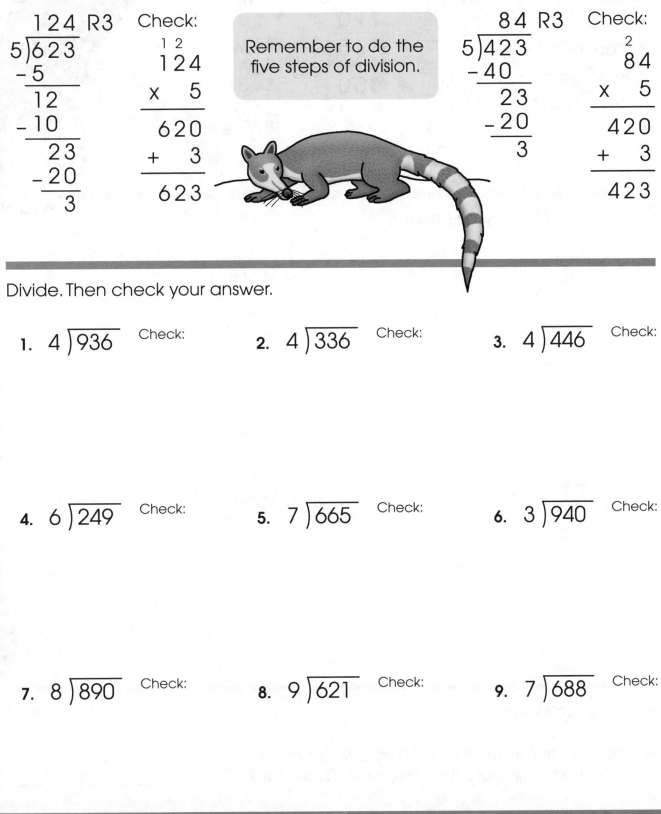

```
  124 R3      Check:
5)623          1 2
 -5            124
 ---         x   5
 12          -----
-10           620
 ---        +   3
 23         -----
-20           623
 ---
   3
```

Remember to do the
five steps of division.

```
   84 R3      Check:
5)423           2
 -40           84
 ---         x  5
 23          -----
-20           420
 ---        +   3
   3        -----
              423
```

Divide. Then check your answer.

1. 4)936   Check:

2. 4)336   Check:

3. 4)446   Check:

4. 6)249   Check:

5. 7)665   Check:

6. 3)940   Check:

7. 8)890   Check:

8. 9)621   Check:

9. 7)688   Check:

Dividing Three–Digit Numbers with Remainders

Zeros in the Quotient

Follow the five steps for division.

1. Divide
2. Multiply
3. Subtract
4. Compare
5. Bring Down

```
      120
  5)600
   -5
    10
   -10
     00
    - 0
       0
```

Check: Multiply the quotient by the divisor.

```
    1
   120
 x   5
  600
```

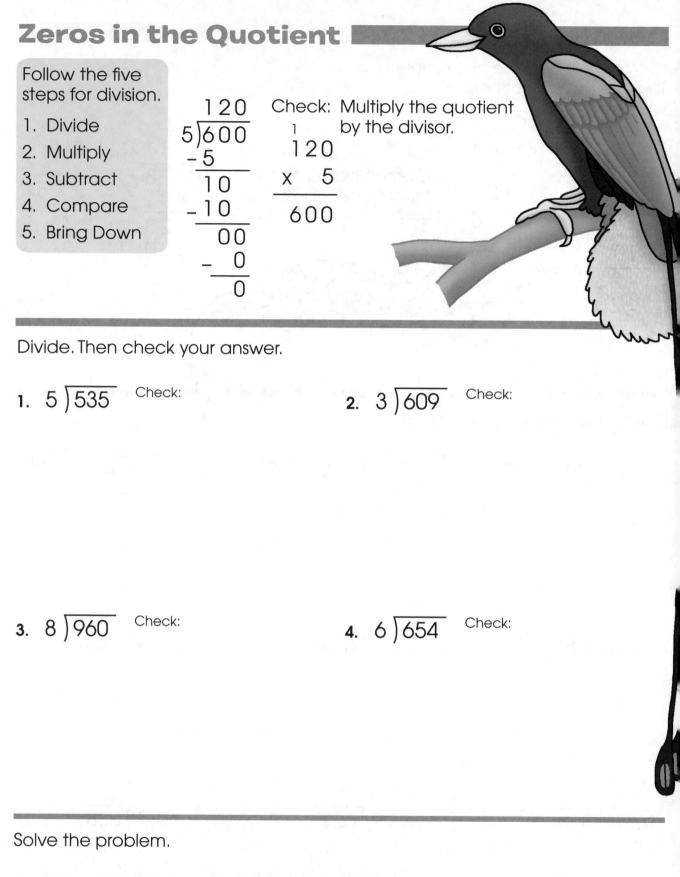

Divide. Then check your answer.

1. 5)535   Check:

2. 3)609   Check:

3. 8)960   Check:

4. 6)654   Check:

Solve the problem.

5. Joshua's family traveled 720 miles in 3 days.
How many miles did they average each day?   _____

Dividing with Zeros in the Quotient   ©School Zone Publishing Company 06320

Division Puzzle

Divide.

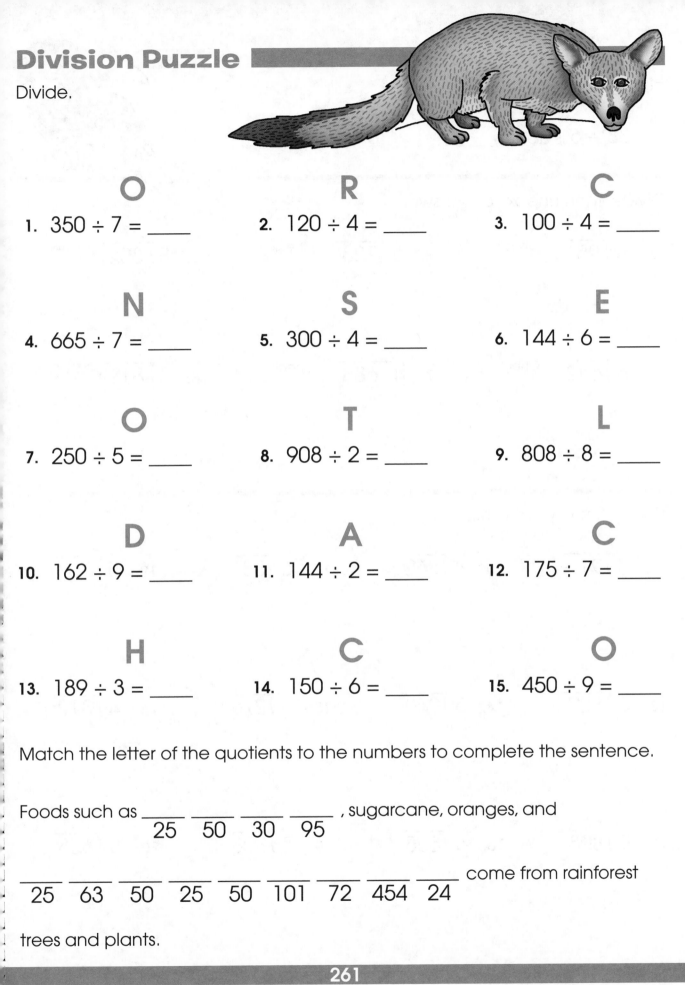

O

1. $350 \div 7 =$ ____

R

2. $120 \div 4 =$ ____

C

3. $100 \div 4 =$ ____

N

4. $665 \div 7 =$ ____

S

5. $300 \div 4 =$ ____

E

6. $144 \div 6 =$ ____

O

7. $250 \div 5 =$ ____

T

8. $908 \div 2 =$ ____

L

9. $808 \div 8 =$ ____

D

10. $162 \div 9 =$ ____

A

11. $144 \div 2 =$ ____

C

12. $175 \div 7 =$ ____

H

13. $189 \div 3 =$ ____

C

14. $150 \div 6 =$ ____

O

15. $450 \div 9 =$ ____

Match the letter of the quotients to the numbers to complete the sentence.

Foods such as ____ ____ ____ ____ , sugarcane, oranges, and
                  25   50   30   95

____ ____ ____ ____ ____ ____ ____ ____ ____ come from rainforest
25   63   50   25   50   101   72   454   24

trees and plants.

Reviewing Division Skills

What I Learned about Division

Estimate the quotient.

1. $38 \div 6$ is about ____.   2. $8\overline{)66}$ is about ____.

Divide. Then check your answer.

3. $4\overline{)95}$ Check:

4. $6\overline{)723}$ Check:

5. $8\overline{)302}$ Check:

6. $6\overline{)642}$ Check:

7. $4\overline{)688}$ Check:

8. $3\overline{)811}$ Check:

Divide. Show your work.

9. $7\overline{)91}$

10. $4\overline{)862}$

11. $6\overline{)58}$

12. $5\overline{)107}$

13. $6\overline{)820}$

14. $5\overline{)940}$

15. $8\overline{)275}$

16. $4\overline{)312}$

17. $9\overline{)803}$

18. $6\overline{)555}$

19. $7\overline{)808}$

20. $3\overline{)625}$

Circle the answer.

21. Which one of the five steps is missing in order to divide numbers?

Multiply Bring Down Divide Subtract

A. Add   **B.** Compare

C. Estimate   **D.** Remainder

22. How can you always check your answer to a division problem?

A. Multiply the quotient by the dividend, and then add the remainder.

B. Multiply the quotient and remainder by the divisor.

C. Multiply the quotient by the divisor.

D. Multiply the quotient by the divisor, and then add the remainder.

---

23. Estimate: $62 \div 8$ is about ____.

A. 6   **B.** 7   **C.** 8   **D.** 9

24. Estimate: $6\overline{)55}$ is about ____.

A. 7   **B.** 8   **C.** 9   **D.** 10

---

25. Divide: $916 \div 4 =$ ____

A. 219   **B.** 228 R2

C. 229   **D.** 229 R3

26. Divide: $488 \div 7 =$ ____

A. 68 R12   **B.** 69

C. 69 R5   **D.** 70 R8

---

27. Divide:
The remainder for $3\overline{)162}$ is ____.

A. 0   **B.** 3   **C.** 53   **D.** 54

28. Divide: $624 \div 3 =$ ____

A. 28   **B.** 201 R1   **C.** 208   **D.** 209

---

29. Which of these problems has a zero in the quotient?

A. $3\overline{)973}$ **B.** $3\overline{)627}$

C. $3\overline{)597}$ **D.** $3\overline{)651}$

30. Divide:
157 is the quotient for ____.

A. $4\overline{)730}$ **B.** $3\overline{)475}$

C. $5\overline{)885}$ **D.** $6\overline{)942}$

©School Zone Publishing Company 06320

Multiplication and Division Puzzle

Work the problems out on another piece of paper. Write the answers in the puzzle.

Across

1. 346 × 8

5. 4)‾148‾

7. 2 × 407

8. 900 ÷ 6

9. 6 × 0

10. 75 × 40

12. 9 × 407

13. 6)‾3,126‾

16. 800 × 3

18. 9 × 81

19. 107 × 8

Down

1. 9)‾252‾

2. 355 × 2

3. 8 × 8

4. 50 × ____ = 400

5. 7,006 × 5

6. 700 ÷ 1

8. 848 ÷ 8

10. 4 × 9

11. 3 × 509

14. 4)‾968‾

15. 654 ÷ 6

17. 8)‾368‾

1.	2.	3.	4.		5.	6.
7.				8.		
	9.		10.			
11.		12.				
13.	14.	15.				
16.						17.
18.			19.			

Divide or multiply to solve the problem.

1. On Joshua's trip to South America, his family stopped to visit a rainforest. Joshua counted 58 plants in 1 square foot of the rainforest. How many plants could there be in 75 square feet of the rainforest?

   _____

2. Joshua's family stopped to eat at a restaurant. All 6 members of his family ate the same thing. Each person's meal cost $7.65. What was the total amount of the bill?

   _____

3. Before Joshua visited South America, he read a book about rainforests that had 152 pages in it. If Joshua read 8 pages each day, how many days did it take him to read the book?

   _____

4. Joshua took 96 snapshots of the cities he visited on his trip to share with his friends. Each of his 6 friends received the same number of snapshots. How many snapshots did each friend get?

   _____

Solving Multiplication and Division Word Problems

Place Value through Thousands

Mexico City's elevation is 7,579 feet above sea level.

$\underline{7}$	$\underline{5}$	$\underline{7}$	$\underline{9}$
thousands	hundreds	tens	ones

word name: seven thousand, five hundred seventy-nine

Write the correct digit in each blank.

1. Mexico City has more than **350** neighborhood districts.

_____	_____	_____	_____
thousands	hundreds	tens	ones

2. The longest river, the Rio Bravo, is **1,880** miles.

_____	_____	_____	_____
thousands	hundreds	tens	ones

3. Mexico's Air Force has more than **5,500** people.

_____	_____	_____	_____
thousands	hundreds	tens	ones

Write the number in standard form.

4. 7,000 + 400 + 30 + 2

_____

> **expanded form**: 9,000 + 700 + 20 + 5
> **standard form**: 9,725

5. 6,000 + 300 + 40 + 1

_____

6. 1,000 + 90 + 5

_____

Place Value through Hundred Thousands

hundred-thousands
ten-thousands
thousands
hundreds
tens
ones

7 6 1 , 6 0 5

The area of all the land in Mexico is **761,605** square miles.
expanded form: 700,000 + 60,000 + 1,000 + 600 + 5
standard form: 761,605
word name: seven hundred sixty-one thousand, six hundred five

Write each number in standard form.

1. 50,000 + 7,000 + 200 + 60 + 9 _____

2. 300,00 + 5,000 + 800 + 6 _____

3. 700,000 + 40,000 + 50 + 3 _____

Write each number in expanded form.

4. 34,562 _____

5. 621,700 _____

6. 403,087 _____

Write the word name for each number.

7. 35,621 _____
_____

8. 246,809 _____
_____

©School Zone Publishing Company 06320

Place Value Through Hundred Thousands

Place Value through Hundred Millions

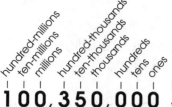

1 0 0 , 3 5 0 , 0 0 0

Mexico has more than **100,350,000** people.
word name: one hundred million, three hundred fifty thousand

Write each number in standard form.

1. nine million, one hundred three thousand, two hundred five

   _____

2. four hundred thirty-three million, six hundred forty-seven thousand, one hundred twelve

   _____

3. seventeen million, two hundred twenty-one thousand, fifty

   _____

Write the place value of the **7** in each number.

4. 379,882,154 _____

5. 17,205,148 _____

6. 2,057,268 _____

7. 508,672,304 _____

8. 540,916,278 _____

9. 789,544,912 _____

Place Value through Hundred Millions

©School Zone Publishing Company 06320

Compare and Order Numbers

Compare **3,783** and **3,698**.

Begin at the left. Find the first place where the digits are different. Then compare.

> **>** means greater than
> **<** means less than
> **=** means equal to
>
> The sign points to the number that is less.

3,783
3,698

7 hundreds > 6 hundreds   3,783 > 3,698

Compare the numbers. Write **<**, **>**, or **=** in the ◯.

1. 687 ◯ 593

2. 254 ◯ 221

3. 8 x 8 ◯ 6 x 10

4. 5,213 ◯ 8,436

5. 3,333 ◯ 3,491

6. 20 – 6 ◯ 2 x 7

7. 7,549 ◯ 9,264

8. 9,054 ◯ 9,268

9. 10 + 9 ◯ 5 x 5

Write the numbers in order from least to greatest.

10. 149   822   324   287

_____

11. 2,973   3,006   2,118   3,652

_____

12. 4,431   2,840   4,931   2,821

_____

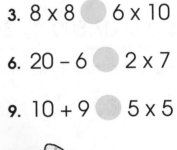

Solve.

13. Three girls were in a race. Juanita ran 135 yards, Maria ran 360 yards, and Lucia ran 310 yards. Mark the distances on the number line. Then write the names of the girls on the blanks.

100   200   300   400   500

_____   _____   _____

Compare and Order Numbers

Compare and Order Greater Numbers

Compare the numbers. Write <, >, or = in the ◯.

1. 49,653 ◯ 49,536

2. 756,281 ◯ 765,182

3. 8,300,475 ◯ 8,003,476

4. 27,853,654 ◯ 37,358,456

5. 50,000 ◯ five hundred million

6. 65,798 ◯ sixty-five thousand, eight hundred

7. 4,030,070 ◯ four million, thirty thousand, seventy

8. 32,007,800 ◯ 30,000,000 + 800 + 7

Order the numbers from least to greatest.

9. 20,000   22,000   20,200   20,202

_____

10. 565,565   556,556   556,565   565,556

_____

Order the numbers from greatest to least.

11. 30,300   30,030   33,003   33,030

_____

12. 4,570,800   4,507,080   4,705,800   4,578,000

_____

Solve.

13. What is the greatest six-digit number? _____

Compare and Order Numbers
©School Zone Publishing Company 06320

Round to the Nearest Ten or Hundred

To round numbers to the **nearest ten**, look at the **ones** place.

Round **583** to the nearest ten.
583 is between 580 and 590.

583   Look at the ones place. If the number is less than 5 round down.

round down
583 rounds to **580**.

To round numbers to the **nearest hundred**, look at the **tens** place.

Round **583** to the nearest hundred.
583 is between 500 and 600.

583   Look at the tens place. If the number is 5 or greater, round up.

round up
583 rounds to **600**.

Round each number to the nearest ten.

1. 43 _____

2. 85 _____

3. 62 _____

4. 386 _____

5. 251 _____

6. 805 _____

7. 1,283 _____

8. 4,065 _____

9. 8,763 _____

Round each number to the nearest hundred.

10. 378 _____

11. 542 _____

12. 439 _____

13. 1,894 _____

14. 2,538 _____

15. 7,509 _____

16. 109 _____

17. 85 _____

18. 47 _____

Round each amount of money to the nearest dollar.

19. $1.79 _____

20. $8.35 _____

21. $27.55 _____

Hint: Look at the number to the right of the number you are rounding to.

Round Whole Numbers

Round to the Nearest Thousand

To round numbers to the **nearest thousand**, look at the **hundreds** place.

Round **4,506** to the nearest thousand.
4,506 is between 4,000 and 5,000.

4,506   Look at the hundreds place.

↑

round up
4,506 rounds to **5,000**.

Round **37,195** to the nearest thousand.
37,195 is between 37,000 and 38,000.

37,195   Look at the hundreds place.

↑

round down
37,195 rounds to **37,000**.

Round each number to the nearest thousand.

1. 3,468 _____

2. 6,843 _____

3. 7,540 _____

4. 15,033 _____

5. 40,909 _____

6. 29,895 _____

7. 942 _____

8. 458 _____

9. 99 _____

Mexico has many volcanoes. Some have erupted in recent years while others lay dormant. Round the height of each volcano to the nearest thousand.

10. Pico de Orizaba 18,555 _____

11. Popocatépeti 17,390 _____

12. Colima 12,361 _____

13. El Chichón 7,300 _____

The area of all the land in Mexico is 761,605 square miles.
Round the number to the nearest place given below.

14. ten _____

15. hundred _____

16. thousand _____

17. ten thousand _____

18. hundred thousand _____

19. millions _____

Review Whole Numbers

Compare the numbers. Write <, >, or = in the ⬤.

1. 362 ⬤ 356

2. 6,137 ⬤ 2,814

3. 9 x 6 ⬤ 86

4. 6 x 6 ⬤ 9 x 4

Write the numbers in order from least to greatest.

5. 3,859   3,921   3,666   2,901   505   3,877

_____

Write the number in standard form.

6. one million, two hundred eleven thousand, five hundred one

_____

7. sixty-two thousand, eighty-nine

_____

Tell the place value of the **2** in each number.

8. 8**2**7 _____

9. 3**2**4,501 _____

Round to the nearest ten.

10. 46 _____

11. 132 _____

12. 91 _____

13. 98 _____

Round to the nearest hundred.

14. 620 _____

15. 1,890 _____

16. 87 _____

17. 7,888 _____

Round to the nearest thousand.

18. 54,890 _____

19. 809,114 _____

20. 905 _____

273

Partial Sum Addition

Add the **ones**.	Add the **tens**.	Add the **hundreds**.	Add the **partial sums**.
346	346	346	346
+ 582	+ 582	+ 582	+ 582
8	8	8	8
	120	120	120
		+ 800	+ 800
			928 ← sum
$6 + 2 = \mathbf{8}$	$40 + 80 = \mathbf{120}$	$300 + 500 = \mathbf{800}$	

Find the sum.

1. 68
   + 13

2. 23
   + 58

3. 35
   + 19

4. 47
   + 26

5. 654
   + 138

6. 321
   + 581

7. 841
   + 109

8. 924
   + 39

9. 3,407
   + 1,225

10. 6,295
   + 2,063

11. 2,457
   + 3,831

12. 8,536
   + 1,092

Write and solve an equation for each problem.

13. The boys' soccer team practiced for 45 minutes on Monday and 45 minutes on Wednesday. How many minutes did they practice in all?

14. There were 365 red apples and 283 green apples at the market. How many apples were there in all?

Partial Sum Addition   ©School Zone Publishing Company 06320

More Partial Sum Addition

Add the **ones**.	Add the **tens**.	Add the **hundreds**.	Add the **thousands**.
3,754 + 1,837 ‾‾‾‾‾ 11	3,754 + 1,837 ‾‾‾‾‾ 11 80	3,754 + 1,837 ‾‾‾‾‾ 11 80 1,500	3,754 + 1,837 ‾‾‾‾‾ 11 80 1,500 + 4,000 ‾‾‾‾‾ 5,591 ← sum

Find the sum.

1. 368
    + 593

2. 593
    + 668

3. 297
    + 493

4. 386
    + 857

5. 3,333
    +   777

6. 9,054
    +   857

7. 3,289
    + 1,931

8. 8,721
    + 1,189

Write and solve an equation for each problem.

9. Miguel is a mousetrap maker. Once, he made 563 mousetraps out of
   bubble gum. He made another 447 mousetraps out of doorknobs.
   How many mousetraps did he make in all?

10. Luis spends all day thinking. One day, he thought of 1,599 funny jokes
    to tell his friends. His friend Pedro thought of 2,735 very funny jokes to
    tell. How many jokes did their friends hear?

Partial Sum Addition

Add Three Numbers

When adding more than two numbers, look for sums of ten in each column to help you.

Add the **ones**.	Add the **tens**.	Add the **hundreds**.	Add the **thousands**.
51 3,436 + 359 —— 16	51 3,436 + 359 —— 16 130	51 3,436 + 359 —— 16 130 700	51 3,436 + 359 —— 16 130 700 + 3,000 —— 3,846 ← sum
Look for sums of 10. 1 + 9 = 10	Look for sums of 10. 5 + 5 = 10		

Find the sum.

1. 12
     6
  + 94

2. 70
    19
  + 31

3.   4
    59
  + 46

4. 325
    163
  + 785

5. 105
    347
  + 55

6. 392
    47
  + 741

7. 3,162
    6,392
  + 4,818

8. 1,322
    411
  +   78

Rewrite as a vertical problem. Find the sum.

9. 46 + 127 + 34

10. 502 + 88 + 9

11. 456 + 2,453 + 78

Write and solve an equation for the problem.

12. Melinda loves to read. First, she read a book about Mexico with 250 pages. Then, she read a joke book with 97 pages. Last, she read a poetry book with 453 pages. How many pages did she read?

Subtract with One Regrouping

Subtract the **ones**.	Subtract the **tens**. Regroup.	Subtract the **hundreds**.	Check:
856 − 582 ——— 4	$\overset{7\ 15}{8\cancel{5}6}$ − 582 ——— 74	$\overset{7\ 15}{8\cancel{5}6}$ − 582 ——— 274	582 + 274 ——— 6 150 + 700 ——— 856
6 − 2 = **4 ones**	5 − 8 = ? **Regroup** 8 hundreds 5 tens to 7 hundreds 15 tens. 15 − 8 = **7 tens**	7 − 5 = **2 hundreds** The difference is **274**.	

Find the difference. Check your answer.

1. 65
   − 48   Check: + _____

2. 92
   − 56   Check: + _____

3. 43
   − 37   Check: + _____

4. 845
   − 391   Check: + _____

5. 788
   − 259   Check: + _____

6. 555
   − 175   Check: + _____

7. 75
   − 49   Check: + _____

8. 91
   − 56   Check: + _____

9. 584
   − 352   Check: + _____

Write and solve an equation for each problem.

10. Laura bought 2 yards of ribbon. She cut off a piece of ribbon that is 58 inches long to wrap a package. How much ribbon does she have left? (1 yard = 36 inches)

_____

11. Juan's book about Mexico has 456 pages. He has already read 182 pages. How many more pages does he have to read?

_____

Subtract with Regrouping

Subtract Greater Numbers

Subtract the **ones**.	Subtract the **tens**.	Subtract the **hundreds**.

$$
\begin{array}{r}
\overset{2\;14}{2\,\cancel{3}\,\cancel{4}} \\
-\,1\,4\,8 \\
\hline
6
\end{array}
$$

$$
\begin{array}{r}
\overset{1\;12}{\underset{2\;14}{2\,\cancel{3}\,\cancel{4}}} \\
-\,1\,4\,8 \\
\hline
8\,6
\end{array}
$$

$$
\begin{array}{r}
\overset{1\;12}{\underset{2\;14}{2\,\cancel{3}\,\cancel{4}}} \\
-\,1\,4\,8 \\
\hline
8\,6
\end{array}
$$

$4 - 8 = ?$ **Regroup** 3 tens and 4 ones to 2 tens and 14 ones.

$2 - 4 = ?$ **Regroup** 2 hundreds and 2 tens to 1 hundred and 12 tens.

$1 - 1 = 0$, but do not write a leading zero in a whole number.

Find the difference.

1. $\begin{array}{r} 736 \\ -\;349 \\ \hline \end{array}$
2. $\begin{array}{r} 8{,}127 \\ -\;\;\;675 \\ \hline \end{array}$
3. $\begin{array}{r} 7{,}194 \\ -\;1{,}856 \\ \hline \end{array}$
4. $\begin{array}{r} 340 \\ -\;\;93 \\ \hline \end{array}$

5. $\begin{array}{r} 6{,}354 \\ -\;5{,}888 \\ \hline \end{array}$
6. $\begin{array}{r} 3{,}447 \\ -\;1{,}299 \\ \hline \end{array}$
7. $\begin{array}{r} 4{,}253 \\ -\;2{,}444 \\ \hline \end{array}$
8. $\begin{array}{r} 9{,}876 \\ -\;3{,}877 \\ \hline \end{array}$

9. $\begin{array}{r} 1{,}623 \\ -\;\;\;766 \\ \hline \end{array}$
10. $\begin{array}{r} 7{,}561 \\ -\;2{,}654 \\ \hline \end{array}$
11. $\begin{array}{r} 6{,}276 \\ -\;\;\;559 \\ \hline \end{array}$
12. $\begin{array}{r} 1{,}784 \\ -\;\;\;795 \\ \hline \end{array}$

Subtract with Regrouping

©School Zone Publishing Company 06320

Subtract with Zeros

Subtract the **ones**.	Regroup the hundreds to **show more tens**.	Regroup the tens to **show more ones**.	Finish the subtracting.
5,500 −2,376 ?	⁴10 5,5̶00 −2,376 ?	9 10 4 1̶0̶ 5,5̶0̶0̶ −2,376 4	9 10 4 1̶0̶ 5,5̶0̶0̶ −2,376 3,124
Since there are no tens to regroup, regroup the hundreds.	You still need more ones to subtract. Regroup the tens.	Now you can subtract the ones. 10 − 6 = **4**	

Regroup to show more ones.

1. 602 2. 400 3. 7,005 4. 4,000

Find the difference.

5. 204
− 117

6. 408
− 29

7. 800
− 529

8. 503
− 56

9. 6,700
− 5,379

10. 7,020
− 443

11. 5,002
− 661

12. 6,000
− 1,278

Write and solve an equation for the problem.

13. In 1521, Hernando Cortes conquered Mexico for the country of Spain. In the year 1810, Miguel Hidalgo y Costilla fought for Mexico's freedom from Spain. How many years did Spain rule Mexico before Mexico began to fight for its freedom?

©School Zone Publishing Company 06320

Subtract with Zeros

Add, Subtract, and Compare

To discover one of the best known civilizations in Mexico, solve each problem. Then fill in the blanks with the correct letters.

1. $442 \rightarrow$ _____

   $+\ 316 \rightarrow$ _____

   $\overline{?}$

   Round each number to the nearest ten. Estimate the sum.

   If your answer is greater than **750**, put an **A** in the blank.
   If your answer is less than **750**, put a **P** in the blank.

2. 648

   $+\ 237$

   Add to find the sum.

   If your answer is greater than **880**, put a **Z** in the blank.
   If your answer is less than **880**, put a **G** in the blank.

3. $5,639$

   $+\ 1,374$

   Add to find the sum.

   If your answer is greater than **7,100**, put an **S** in the blank.
   If your answer is less than **7,100**, put a **T** in the blank.

4. 392

   400

   68

   $+\ 715$

   Add to find the sum.

   If your answer is greater than **1,500**, put an **E** in the blank.
   If your answer is less than **1,500**, put an **O** in the blank.

5. 37

   Regroup the number to show more ones.

   If your answer is **3 tens** and **17 ones**, put a **B** in the blank.
   If your answer is **2 tens** and **17 ones**, put a **C** in the blank.

6. $4,205$

   $-\ 1,876$

   Subtract to find the difference.
   If your answer is greater than **2,500**, put a **D** in the blank.
   If your answer is less than **2,500**, put an **S** in the blank.

_____ _____ _____ _____ _____ _____
  1   2   3   4   5   6

Add, Subtract, and Compare Numbers

©School Zone Publishing Company 06320

Add, Subtract, and Review

Use the clues to fill in the puzzle.

Across

1. 50,000 + 300 + 70 + 5

5. 794 − 258

7. 403 − 319

8. 5,821 − _____ = 5,725

9. 1,375 to the nearest hundred

11. 9,000 − 1,281

13. 372 + _____ = 450

14. 1,000 − 729

15. sixty-one thousand, three hundred eight

Down

1. five thousand, seventeen

2. 375 to the nearest ten

3. 7,429 to the nearest hundred

4. 63 = _____ ten and 13 ones

5. 44,428 + 12,345

6. 483 + 37 + 109

8. 4,755 + 4,966

10. 400 + 6 + 80

12. 789 − 679

Review Whole Numbers

Multiply with Multiples of Ten

You can use mental math to multiply with tens and multiples of ten.
Recall the multiplication basic facts and how to multiply by tens.

Example 1:
Look at the pattern for multiplying by tens.

5 x 10 = 50
5 x 100 = 500
5 x 1,000 = 5,000

Notice that the product has the same number of zeros as the number of zeros in the factor with zeros.

Example 2:
What is 5 x 30?

5 x 30 = **5 x 3** x 10
basic fact
15 x 10 = 150

Now look at these:
5 x 300 = **5 x 3** x 100 = 1,500
50 x 30 = **5** x 10 x **3** x 10
15 x 100 = 1,500

Example 3:
What is 9 x 8 x 5?

Sometimes you can find two factors that have a product that is a multiple of ten.

9 x **8** x **5** =
9 x 40 =
36 x 10 = 360

Find the product.

1. 10 x 6 = _____

2. 49 x 100 = _____

3. 1,000 x 8 = _____

4. 10 x 10 = _____

5. 10 x 100 = _____

6. 100 x 100 = _____

7. 7 x 20 = _____

8. 300 x 6 = _____

9. 6 x 2,000 = _____

10. 80 x 5 = _____

11. 20 x 80 = _____

12. 70 x 70 = _____

13. 900 x 20 = _____

14. 500 x 60 = _____

15. 7,000 x 80 = _____

16. 6 x 10 x 10 = _____

17. 2 x 5 x 8 = _____

18. 4 x 7 x 5 = _____

19. 6 x 6 x 5 = _____

20. 8 x 9 x 5 = _____

21. 4 x 10 x 0 = _____

Multiply Multi-Digit Numbers

Multiply the **ones**.	Multiply the **tens**.	Multiply the **hundreds**.	Add.
$\begin{array}{r} 415 \\ \times \quad 3 \\ \hline 15 \end{array}$	$\begin{array}{r} 415 \\ \times \quad 3 \\ \hline 15 \\ 30 \end{array}$	$\begin{array}{r} 415 \\ \times \quad 3 \\ \hline 15 \\ 30 \\ 1,200 \end{array}$	$\begin{array}{r} 415 \\ \times \quad 3 \\ \hline 15 \\ 30 \\ +\ 1,200 \\ \hline 1,245 \end{array}$
$3 \times 5 = \mathbf{15}$	$3 \times 10 = \mathbf{30}$	$3 \times 400 = \mathbf{1,200}$	

Find the product.

1. $\begin{array}{r} 58 \\ \times\ 4 \\ \hline \end{array}$
2. $\begin{array}{r} 17 \\ \times\ 6 \\ \hline \end{array}$
3. $\begin{array}{r} 73 \\ \times\ 8 \\ \hline \end{array}$
4. $\begin{array}{r} 46 \\ \times\ 9 \\ \hline \end{array}$
5. $\begin{array}{r} 92 \\ \times\ 7 \\ \hline \end{array}$

6. $\begin{array}{r} 272 \\ \times\quad 3 \\ \hline \end{array}$
7. $\begin{array}{r} 971 \\ \times\quad 7 \\ \hline \end{array}$
8. $\begin{array}{r} 381 \\ \times\quad 2 \\ \hline \end{array}$
9. $\begin{array}{r} 812 \\ \times\quad 4 \\ \hline \end{array}$
10. $\begin{array}{r} 619 \\ \times\quad 8 \\ \hline \end{array}$

11. $\begin{array}{r} 1,522 \\ \times\quad 3 \\ \hline \end{array}$
12. $\begin{array}{r} 4,314 \\ \times\quad 2 \\ \hline \end{array}$
13. $\begin{array}{r} 9,171 \\ \times\quad 6 \\ \hline \end{array}$
14. $\begin{array}{r} 3,115 \\ \times\quad 8 \\ \hline \end{array}$
15. $\begin{array}{r} 4,123 \\ \times\quad 9 \\ \hline \end{array}$

Write and solve an equation for each problem.

16. There are 24 hours in a day. There are 7 days in one week. How many hours are in one week?

17. It is 472 miles between Houston, Texas and Mobile, Alabama. How many miles is a round trip?

_____   _____

Multiply Multi-Digit Numbers

Multiply Multi-Digit Numbers

Multiply the **ones**.	Multiply the **tens**.	Multiply the **hundreds**.	Add.
$$\begin{array}{r} 364 \\ \times\quad 4 \\ \hline 16 \end{array}$$	$$\begin{array}{r} 364 \\ \times\quad 4 \\ \hline 16 \\ 240 \end{array}$$	$$\begin{array}{r} 364 \\ \times\quad 4 \\ \hline 16 \\ 240 \\ 1{,}200 \end{array}$$	$$\begin{array}{r} 364 \\ \times\quad 4 \\ \hline 16 \\ 240 \\ +\ 1{,}200 \\ \hline 1{,}456 \end{array}$$
$4 \times 4 = \mathbf{16}$	$4 \times 60 = \mathbf{240}$	$4 \times 300 = \mathbf{1,200}$	

Find the product.

1. $$\begin{array}{r} 24 \\ \times\ 2 \\ \hline \end{array}$$

2. $$\begin{array}{r} 91 \\ \times\ 8 \\ \hline \end{array}$$

3. $$\begin{array}{r} 62 \\ \times\ 4 \\ \hline \end{array}$$

4. $$\begin{array}{r} 71 \\ \times\ 3 \\ \hline \end{array}$$

5. $$\begin{array}{r} 511 \\ \times\ 7 \\ \hline \end{array}$$

6. $$\begin{array}{r} 813 \\ \times\ 3 \\ \hline \end{array}$$

7. $$\begin{array}{r} 412 \\ \times\ 4 \\ \hline \end{array}$$

8. $$\begin{array}{r} 732 \\ \times\ 3 \\ \hline \end{array}$$

9. $$\begin{array}{r} 7{,}312 \\ \times\quad 2 \\ \hline \end{array}$$

10. $$\begin{array}{r} 5{,}132 \\ \times\quad 3 \\ \hline \end{array}$$

11. $$\begin{array}{r} 9{,}141 \\ \times\quad 2 \\ \hline \end{array}$$

12. $$\begin{array}{r} 6{,}222 \\ \times\quad 4 \\ \hline \end{array}$$

Write and solve an equation for each problem.

13. Enrico had 4 hoses. Each hose was 42 feet long. How long were they when he hooked them all together?

14. The average number of people living in one house in Mexico is 6. In a small village, there are about 410 houses. How many people are living in the small village?

Multiply with Zeros

Multiply the **ones**. Regroup as needed.	Multiply the **tens**. Regroup as needed.	Multiply the **hundreds**.
$50\overset{2}{4}$ $\times \quad 6$ $\overline{\qquad 4}$	$50\overset{2}{4}$ $\times \quad 6$ $\overline{\quad 24}$	$50\overset{2}{4}$ $\times \quad 6$ $\overline{3{,}024}$
6 x 4 ones = **24 ones** 24 ones = **2 tens and 4 ones**	6 x 0 tens = **0 tens** 0 tens + 2 tens = **2 tens**	6 x 5 hundreds = **30 hundreds**

Find the product.

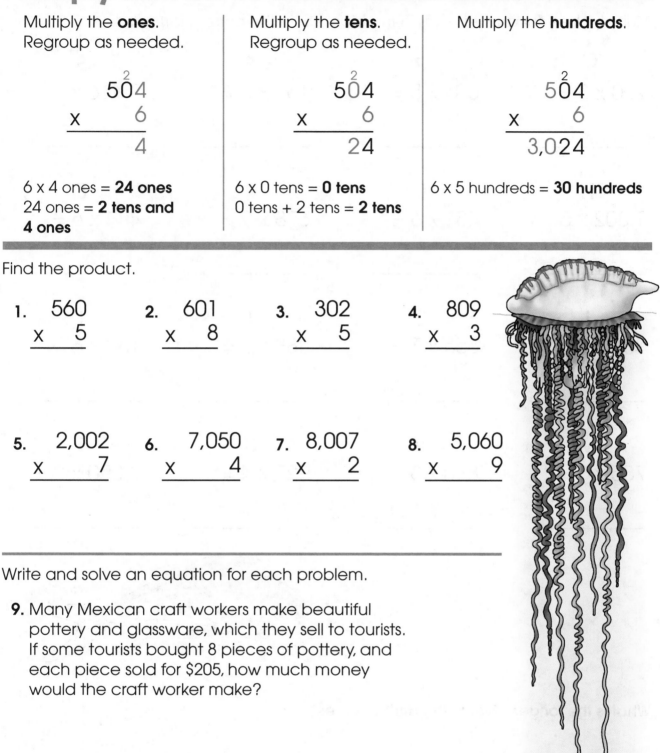

1. 560
    x   5

2. 601
    x   8

3. 302
    x   5

4. 809
    x   3

5. 2,002
    x   7

6. 7,050
    x   4

7. 8,007
    x   2

8. 5,060
    x   9

Write and solve an equation for each problem.

9. Many Mexican craft workers make beautiful pottery and glassware, which they sell to tourists. If some tourists bought 8 pieces of pottery, and each piece sold for $205, how much money would the craft worker make?

_____

10. The distance from Mexico City to Córdoba is about 170 miles. If a person made this trip 5 times, how many miles would he or she travel?

_____

Multiply with Zeros

Multiply. Use your answers to fill in the blanks with the correct letters.

O
220 x 3 =

R
604 x 5 =

E
165 x 5 =

S
1,416 x 4 =

_____

_____

_____

_____

H
1,302 x 5 =

R
431 x 6 =

R
678 x 9 =

E
444 x 6 =

_____

_____

_____

_____

I
460 x 7 =

S
555 x 7 =

T
888 x 6 =

I
132 x 6 =

_____

_____

_____

_____

M
755 x 5 =

V
840 x 3 =

U
920 x 4 =

I
7,090 x 2 =

_____

_____

_____

_____

What is the longest river in the United States?

____ ____ ____   ____ ____ ____ ____ ____ ____ ____ ____
5,328 6,510 825   3,775 792 5,664 3,885 660 3,680 2,586 3,220

____ ____ ____ ____ ____
6,102 14,180 2,520 2,664 3,020

Multiply by Two-Digit Numbers

Multiply the **ones** by the **ones digit** of the multiplier.	Multiply the **tens** by the **ones digit** of the multiplier.	Multiply the **ones** by the **tens digit** of the multiplier.	Multiply the **tens** by the **tens digit** of the multiplier. Then add.
56 x 23 ── 18	56 x 23 ── 18 150	56 x 23 ── 18 150 120	56 x 23 ── 18 150 120 + 1,000 ── 1,288
$3 \times 6 = $ **18**	$3 \times 50 = $ **150**	$20 \times 6 = $ **120**	$20 \times 50 = $ **1,000**

Find the product.

1. 26
    x 13

2. 95
    x 48

3. 71
    x 32

4. 84
    x 59

5. 332
    x 18

6. 816
    x 36

7. 194
    x 27

8. 776
    x 40

Multiply by Two-Digit Numbers

Multiply by Two-Digit Numbers

Find the product.

1. 38
   x 25

2. 43
   x 70

3. 78
   x 78

4. 90
   x 67

5. 246
   x 32

6. 456
   x 30

7. 509
   x 28

8. 430
   x 89

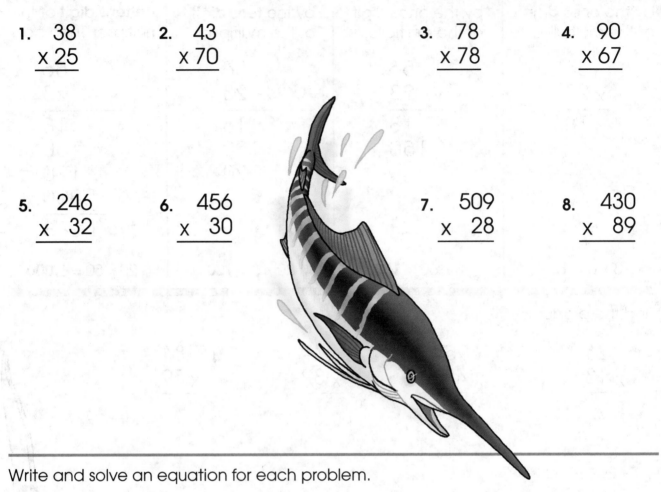

Write and solve an equation for each problem.

9. There are 32 seats in each row in a theater. If there are 24 rows of seats, how many seats are in the theater?

10. There are 12 inches in 1 foot. How many inches are in 35 feet?

11. There are 60 minutes in an hour. How many minutes are in a 24-hour day?

12. A farmer can store 20 dozen eggs on each shelf of a giant refrigerator. There are 3 shelves. How many eggs can be stored in the refrigerator?

Multiply by Two-Digit Numbers   ©School Zone Publishing Company 06320

Add, Subtract, and Multiply

Use the clues to fill in the puzzle.

Across

1. 8 x 67

4. 153 x 84

9. 150 x 5

10. 8,696 – 4,567

11. 299 + 202

12. 317 x 3

13. 3 x 202

14. _____ x 90 = 7,200

15. 4,876 + 9,321

Down

1. 238 + 337

2. 50 x 7

3. _____ x 20 = 12,020

5. 9,000 – 6,544

6. 747 + 47 + 17

7. 527 – 475

8. 59 x 50

14. 79 + 9

1.	2.	3.		4.	5.	6.	7.	8.
9.					10.			
11.				12.				
			13.				14.	
15.								

Review Whole Numbers

Division with Remainders

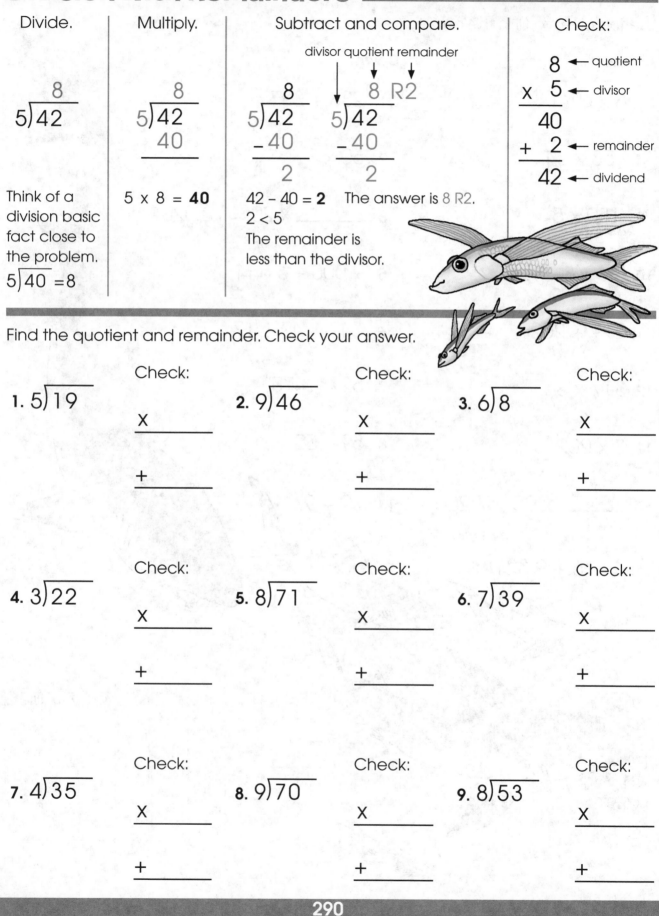

Divide.	Multiply.	Subtract and compare.	Check:

Divide.

$$5\overline{)42}\quad 8$$

Think of a division basic fact close to the problem.
$$5\overline{)40} = 8$$

Multiply.

$$5\overline{)42}\quad 8$$
$$40$$

$5 \times 8 = \mathbf{40}$

Subtract and compare.

divisor quotient remainder

$$5\overline{)42}\quad 8 \qquad 5\overline{)42}\quad 8\ R2$$
$$-40 \qquad\qquad -40$$
$$\ \ 2 \qquad\qquad\quad\ 2$$

$42 - 40 = \mathbf{2}$ The answer is 8 R2.
$2 < 5$
The remainder is less than the divisor.

Check:

$$\begin{array}{r} 8 \leftarrow \text{quotient} \\ \times\ 5 \leftarrow \text{divisor} \\ \hline 40 \\ +\ 2 \leftarrow \text{remainder} \\ \hline 42 \leftarrow \text{dividend} \end{array}$$

Find the quotient and remainder. Check your answer.

1. $5\overline{)19}$ Check:
$$\times \underline{\qquad}$$
$$+ \underline{\qquad}$$

2. $9\overline{)46}$ Check:
$$\times \underline{\qquad}$$
$$+ \underline{\qquad}$$

3. $6\overline{)8}$ Check:
$$\times \underline{\qquad}$$
$$+ \underline{\qquad}$$

4. $3\overline{)22}$ Check:
$$\times \underline{\qquad}$$
$$+ \underline{\qquad}$$

5. $8\overline{)71}$ Check:
$$\times \underline{\qquad}$$
$$+ \underline{\qquad}$$

6. $7\overline{)39}$ Check:
$$\times \underline{\qquad}$$
$$+ \underline{\qquad}$$

7. $4\overline{)35}$ Check:
$$\times \underline{\qquad}$$
$$+ \underline{\qquad}$$

8. $9\overline{)70}$ Check:
$$\times \underline{\qquad}$$
$$+ \underline{\qquad}$$

9. $8\overline{)53}$ Check:
$$\times \underline{\qquad}$$
$$+ \underline{\qquad}$$

Divide Numbers with Remainders

Two-Digit Quotients

Estimate.

$$\begin{array}{r} 20 \\ 4\overline{)95} \end{array}$$

Think:
$4\overline{)8} = 2$
So, $4\overline{)80} = 20$

Making an estimate can help you place the first digit in the quotient.

Divide the tens.

$$\begin{array}{r} 2 \\ 4\overline{)95} \\ -8 \\ \hline 1 \end{array}$$

Divide: $4\overline{)9}$
Multiply: $4 \times 2 = 8$
Subtract: $9 - 8 = 1$
Compare: $1 < 4$

Bring down the ones. Repeat the steps to finish the dividing.

$$\begin{array}{r} 23 \\ 4\overline{)95} \\ -8 \\ \hline 15 \\ -12 \\ \hline 3 \end{array}$$

Divide: $4\overline{)15}$
Multiply: $4 \times 3 = 12$
Subtract: $15 - 12 = 3$
Compare: $3 < 4$
The remainder is 3.
The answer is 23 R3.

Check:

$$\begin{array}{r} 23 \\ \times\ 4 \\ \hline 92 \\ +\ 3 \\ \hline 95 \end{array}$$

Remember these steps:
1. Divide
2. Multiply
3. Subtract
4. Compare
5. Bring down

Repeat the steps until there are no more digits to bring down.

Find the quotient. Check you answer. Hint: There may or may not be remainders.

1. $4\overline{)91}$ Check: X _____   + _____

2. $6\overline{)89}$ Check: X _____   + _____

3. $3\overline{)75}$ Check: X _____   + _____

4. $7\overline{)84}$ Check: X _____   + _____

5. $2\overline{)63}$ Check: X _____   + _____

6. $5\overline{)96}$ Check: X _____   + _____

Find the quotient.

7. $6\overline{)75}$ 8. $3\overline{)57}$ 9. $8\overline{)87}$ 10. $4\overline{)92}$ 11. $5\overline{)99}$

Two-Digit Quotients

Divide Three-Digit Numbers

When dividing a three-digit number by a one-digit number, the quotient may have two or three digits. Study these two examples.

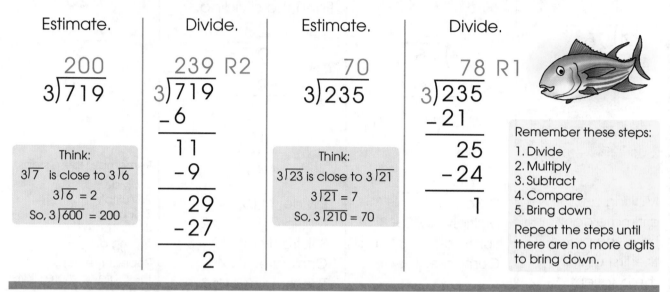

Estimate.

$$\overset{200}{3\overline{)719}}$$

Think:
$3\overline{)7}$ is close to $3\overline{)6}$
$3\overline{)6} = 2$
So, $3\overline{)600} = 200$

Divide.

$$\begin{array}{r} 239 \text{ R2} \\ 3\overline{)719} \\ -6 \\ \hline 11 \\ -9 \\ \hline 29 \\ -27 \\ \hline 2 \end{array}$$

Estimate.

$$\overset{70}{3\overline{)235}}$$

Think:
$3\overline{)23}$ is close to $3\overline{)21}$
$3\overline{)21} = 7$
So, $3\overline{)210} = 70$

Divide.

$$\begin{array}{r} 78 \text{ R1} \\ 3\overline{)235} \\ -21 \\ \hline 25 \\ -24 \\ \hline 1 \end{array}$$

Remember these steps:
1. Divide
2. Multiply
3. Subtract
4. Compare
5. Bring down

Repeat the steps until there are no more digits to bring down.

Estimate each quotient to the nearest ten or hundred.

1. $3\overline{)753}$

2. $5\overline{)173}$

3. $7\overline{)876}$

4. $8\overline{)333}$

5. $4\overline{)910}$

Find the quotient. Check your answer.

6. $3\overline{)753}$

7. $5\overline{)173}$

8. $7\overline{)876}$

9. $8\overline{)333}$

10. $4\overline{)910}$

11. $4\overline{)515}$

12. $3\overline{)264}$

13. $7\overline{)199}$

14. $5\overline{)590}$

15. $8\overline{)678}$

Zeros in the Quotient

Sometimes there are zeros in the quotient. Study these two examples.

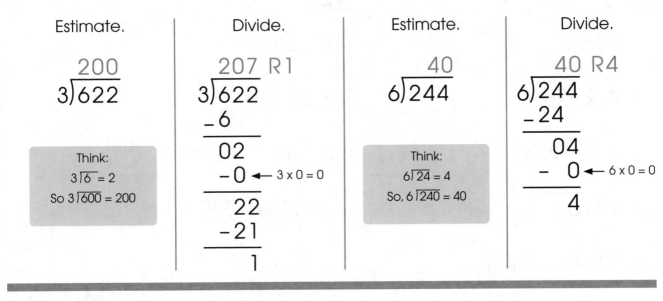

Estimate.	Divide.	Estimate.	Divide.

$$200$$
$$3\overline{)622}$$

Think:
$3\overline{)6} = 2$
So $3\overline{)600} = 200$

$$207 \text{ R1}$$
$$3\overline{)622}$$
$$-6$$
$$\overline{02}$$
$$-0 \leftarrow 3 \times 0 = 0$$
$$\overline{22}$$
$$-21$$
$$\overline{1}$$

$$40$$
$$6\overline{)244}$$

Think:
$6\overline{)24} = 4$
So, $6\overline{)240} = 40$

$$40 \text{ R4}$$
$$6\overline{)244}$$
$$-24$$
$$\overline{04}$$
$$-0 \leftarrow 6 \times 0 = 0$$
$$\overline{4}$$

Estimate to the nearest ten or hundred.

1. $3\overline{)616}$ 2. $6\overline{)122}$ 3. $5\overline{)545}$ 4. $7\overline{)211}$ 5. $3\overline{)962}$

Find the quotient. Check your answer.

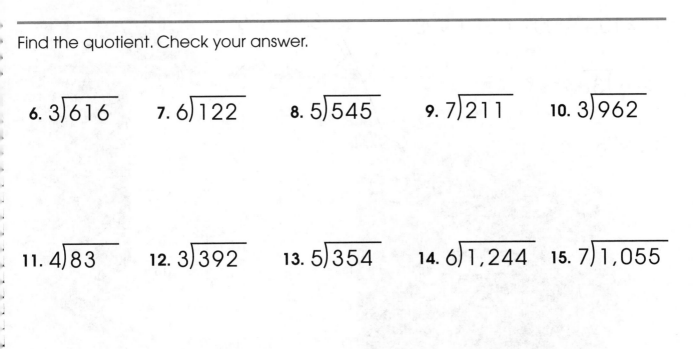

6. $3\overline{)616}$ 7. $6\overline{)122}$ 8. $5\overline{)545}$ 9. $7\overline{)211}$ 10. $3\overline{)962}$

11. $4\overline{)83}$ 12. $3\overline{)392}$ 13. $5\overline{)354}$ 14. $6\overline{)1,244}$ 15. $7\overline{)1,055}$

Divide with Zeros in the Quotient

Add, Subtract, Multiply, and Divide

Use the clues to fill in the puzzle.

Across

1. 43×9

4. $472 - 379$

6. $609 + 225$

7. $9\overline{)153}$

8. $13,003 - 3,425$

10. $\underline{\hspace{1cm}} \times 8 = 448$

11. $466 + 905 + 95$

14. $343 \div 7$

16. $410 + 1,009 + 51 + 998$

17. $8\overline{)384}$

18. $978 \div 6$

Down

1. 763×5

2. $6\overline{)498}$

3. $58 + 7 + 684$

4. $1,306 - 389$

5. 97×39

9. $973 - 467$

12. $576 \div 9$

13. 208×3

15. $888 + 75$

Review Whole Numbers

Understanding Fractions

Fractions can show parts of a whole, a set, or a line.
Study the examples below.

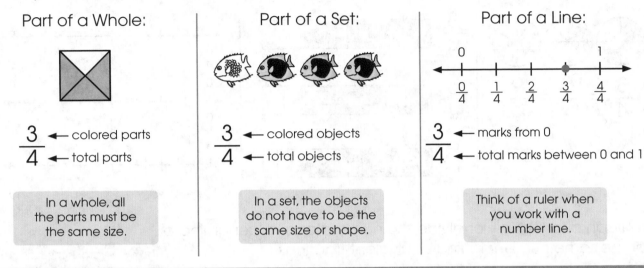

Part of a Whole:

$\frac{3}{4}$ ← colored parts
← total parts

In a whole, all the parts must be the same size.

Part of a Set:

$\frac{3}{4}$ ← colored objects
← total objects

In a set, the objects do not have to be the same size or shape.

Part of a Line:

0   1
$\frac{0}{4}$ $\frac{1}{4}$ $\frac{2}{4}$ $\frac{3}{4}$ $\frac{4}{4}$

$\frac{3}{4}$ ← marks from 0
← total marks between 0 and 1

Think of a ruler when you work with a number line.

Write a fraction for the colored part of the whole or set.

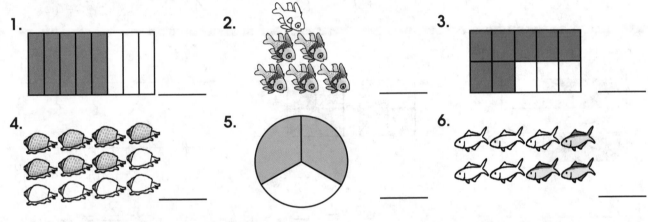

1. _____

2. _____

3. _____

4. _____

5. _____

6. _____

Write a fraction to indicate where the **red dot** is on each number line.

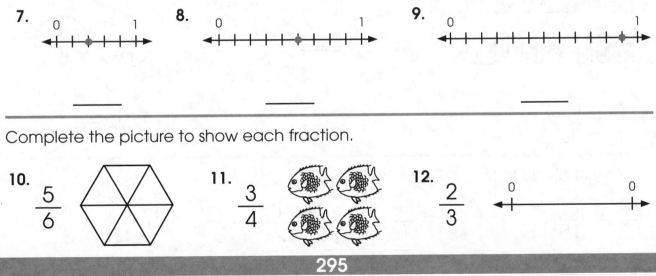

7. 0   1

_____

8. 0   1

_____

9. 0   1

_____

Complete the picture to show each fraction.

10. $\frac{5}{6}$

11. $\frac{3}{4}$

12. $\frac{2}{3}$ 0   0

©School Zone Publishing Company 06320

Understanding Fractions

Equivalent Fractions

Equivalent fractions are fractions that name the same amount.
Here are some different ways to show fractions equivalent to $\frac{3}{4}$.

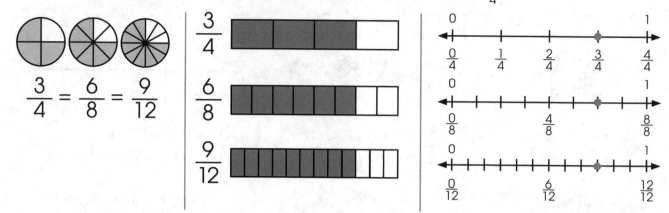

You can also multiply or divide the numerator and denominator
by the same number to find equivalent fractions.

$$\frac{3}{4} \times \frac{2}{2} = \frac{6}{8} \qquad \frac{3}{4} \times \frac{3}{3} = \frac{9}{12} \qquad \frac{6}{8} \div \frac{2}{2} = \frac{3}{4}$$

> The numerator is the part of the fraction that is above the line. The denominator is the part of the fraction that is below the line.

Write the missing numerator.

1. $\frac{2}{3} = \frac{}{6}$

2. $\frac{3}{4} = \frac{}{8}$

3. $\frac{2}{5} = \frac{}{10}$

4. $\frac{5}{6} = \frac{}{12}$

5. $\frac{2}{3} = \frac{}{9}$

6. $\frac{1}{6} = \frac{}{12}$

Multiply or divide to find the equivalent fraction.

7. $\frac{2}{3} = \frac{}{15}$

8. $\frac{3}{8} = \frac{}{16}$

9. $\frac{1}{2} = \frac{}{12}$

10. $\frac{8}{12} = \frac{}{3}$

Simplest Form Fractions

A fraction is in **simplest form** when both the numerator and denominator can only be divided by 1. You can use one or more steps to simplify a fraction.

Example 1: Simplify $\frac{8}{20}$

$$\frac{8}{20} = \frac{?}{?}$$

> Think: What is the greatest number that both 8 and 20 will divide into? It's 4.

$$\frac{8}{20} \div \frac{4}{4} = \frac{2}{5}$$

Check: Can you find a number that can still divide into both 2 and 5? **No!**

Example 2: Simplify $\frac{8}{20}$

Since both 8 and 20 are even, divide each number by 2.

$$\frac{8}{20} = \frac{?}{?}$$

Check: Can you find a number that can still divide into both 4 and 10? **Yes**.

$$\frac{8}{20} \div \frac{2}{2} = \frac{4}{10}$$

Since both 4 and 10 are even, divide each number by 2.

$$\frac{4}{10} \div \frac{2}{2} = \frac{2}{5}$$

Check: Can you find a number that can still divide into both 2 and 5? **No!**

If the fraction is in simplest form, write yes. If not, write the fraction in simplest form.

1. $\frac{2}{8}$ ____

2. $\frac{3}{5}$ ____

3. $\frac{6}{7}$ ____

4. $\frac{3}{9}$ ____

5. $\frac{5}{10}$ ____

6. $\frac{5}{12}$ ____

7. $\frac{9}{10}$ ____

8. $\frac{6}{15}$ ____

Write the fraction in simplest form.

9. $\frac{2}{4}$ ____

10. $\frac{6}{12}$ ____

11. $\frac{6}{8}$ ____

12. $\frac{3}{12}$ ____

13. $\frac{4}{10}$ ____

14. $\frac{6}{18}$ ____

15. $\frac{10}{20}$ ____

16. $\frac{12}{16}$ ____

17. $\frac{8}{12}$ ____

18. $\frac{12}{24}$ ____

19. $\frac{4}{4}$ ____

20. $\frac{0}{3}$ ____

Challenge: How can you tell when a fraction is equivalent to $\frac{1}{2}$?

Simplest Form Fractions

Compare Fractions

To compare fractions, you can look at pictures or objects or use equivalent fractions. Which is greater, $\frac{3}{4}$ or $\frac{5}{8}$?

Example 1:

You can see that $\frac{3}{4} > \frac{5}{8}$.

Example 2:

0 ————— 1

0 ————— 1

You can see that $\frac{3}{4}$ is further away from zero. So, $\frac{3}{4} > \frac{5}{8}$.

Example 3: Find equivalent fractions with a common denominator. Compare the numerators.

$$\frac{3}{4} = \frac{6}{8} \qquad \frac{5}{8} = \frac{5}{8}$$

$$\frac{6}{8} > \frac{5}{8}$$

SO, $\frac{3}{4} > \frac{5}{8}$

Compare the fractions. Write **<**, **>**, or **=** in the ◯.

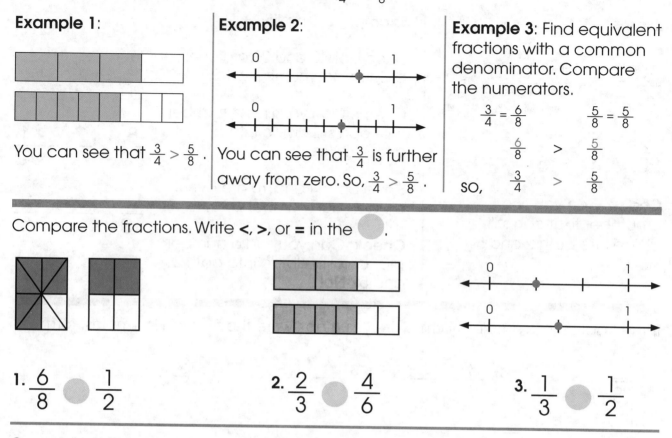

1. $\frac{6}{8}$ ◯ $\frac{1}{2}$

2. $\frac{2}{3}$ ◯ $\frac{4}{6}$

3. $\frac{1}{3}$ ◯ $\frac{1}{2}$

Complete the fraction pictures to show the fractions in each problem. Compare the fractions and then write **<**, **>**, or **=** in the ◯.

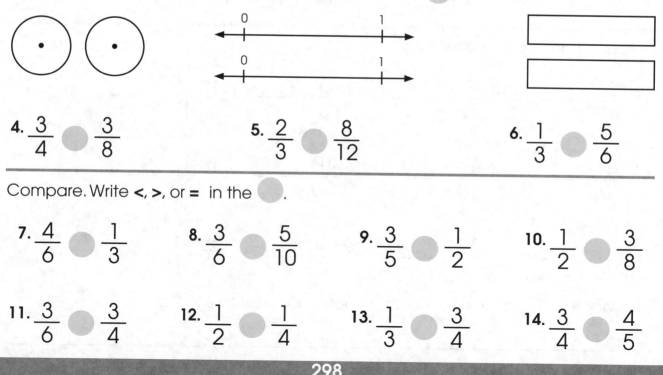

4. $\frac{3}{4}$ ◯ $\frac{3}{8}$

5. $\frac{2}{3}$ ◯ $\frac{8}{12}$

6. $\frac{1}{3}$ ◯ $\frac{5}{6}$

Compare. Write **<**, **>**, or **=** in the ◯.

7. $\frac{4}{6}$ ◯ $\frac{1}{3}$

8. $\frac{3}{6}$ ◯ $\frac{5}{10}$

9. $\frac{3}{5}$ ◯ $\frac{1}{2}$

10. $\frac{1}{2}$ ◯ $\frac{3}{8}$

11. $\frac{3}{6}$ ◯ $\frac{3}{4}$

12. $\frac{1}{2}$ ◯ $\frac{1}{4}$

13. $\frac{1}{3}$ ◯ $\frac{3}{4}$

14. $\frac{3}{4}$ ◯ $\frac{4}{5}$

Add and Subtract Like Fractions

When fractions have like (or common) denominators, you can add or subtract them.

- The denominator remains the same.
- Add or subtract the numerators.
- Write the sum or difference in simplest form.
- Fractions can be represented by number sentences.

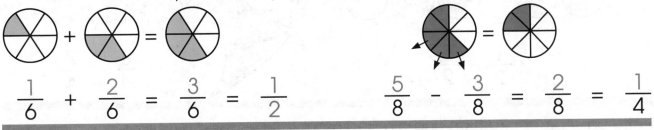

$$\frac{1}{6} + \frac{2}{6} = \frac{3}{6} = \frac{1}{2} \qquad\qquad \frac{5}{8} - \frac{3}{8} = \frac{2}{8} = \frac{1}{4}$$

Find the sum or difference. Color the circle on the right to show the answer. Write the answer in simplest form.

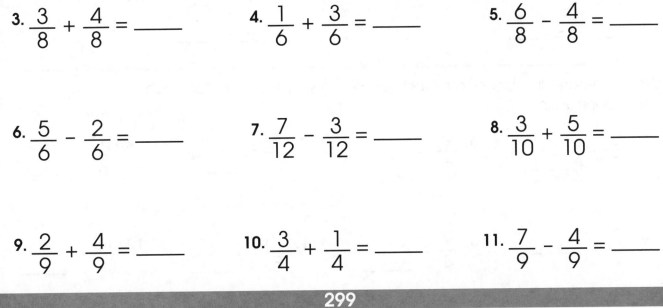

1. $\dfrac{3}{8} + \dfrac{1}{8} =$ _____ = _____

2. $\dfrac{4}{6} - \dfrac{2}{6} =$ _____ = _____

Find the sum or difference. Write the answer in simplest form.

3. $\dfrac{3}{8} + \dfrac{4}{8} =$ _____

4. $\dfrac{1}{6} + \dfrac{3}{6} =$ _____

5. $\dfrac{6}{8} - \dfrac{4}{8} =$ _____

6. $\dfrac{5}{6} - \dfrac{2}{6} =$ _____

7. $\dfrac{7}{12} - \dfrac{3}{12} =$ _____

8. $\dfrac{3}{10} + \dfrac{5}{10} =$ _____

9. $\dfrac{2}{9} + \dfrac{4}{9} =$ _____

10. $\dfrac{3}{4} + \dfrac{1}{4} =$ _____

11. $\dfrac{7}{9} - \dfrac{4}{9} =$ _____

Add and Subtract Like Fractions

Mixed Numbers

A **mixed number** consists of a whole number and a fraction.

An **improper fraction** consists of a numerator that is greater than or equal to the denominator.

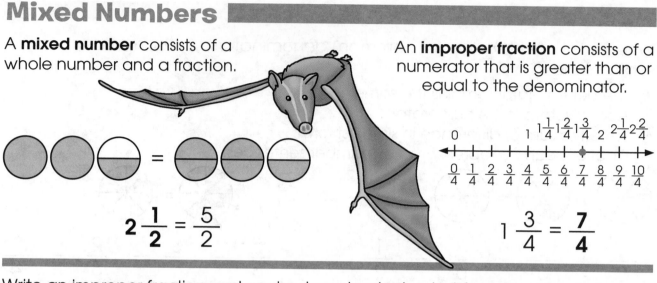

$$2\frac{1}{2} = \frac{5}{2}$$

$$1\frac{3}{4} = \frac{7}{4}$$

Write an improper fraction and a mixed number in simplest form for each picture.

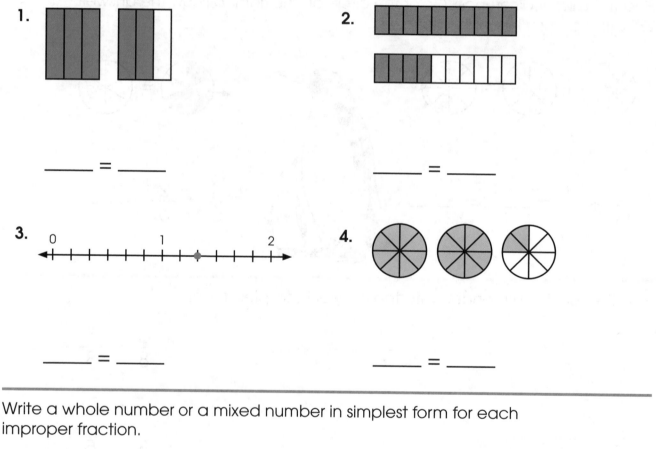

1. _____ = _____

2. _____ = _____

3. _____ = _____

4. _____ = _____

Write a whole number or a mixed number in simplest form for each improper fraction.

5. $\dfrac{5}{4} =$ _____

6. $\dfrac{9}{6} =$ _____

7. $\dfrac{6}{3} =$ _____

8. $\dfrac{10}{8} =$ _____

9. $\dfrac{7}{7} =$ _____

10. $\dfrac{9}{4} =$ _____

11. $\dfrac{16}{5} =$ _____

12. $\dfrac{10}{4} =$ _____

Add and Subtract Mixed Numbers

Mixed numbers with common denominators can be added and subtracted.

Write mixed numbers as improper fractions, then add or subtract.
Write the answer as a mixed number in simplest form.

$$1\frac{3}{4} + 2\frac{3}{4} = \frac{7}{4} + \frac{11}{4} = \frac{18}{4} = 4\frac{2}{4} = 4\frac{1}{2}$$

Use equivalent fractions to find common denominators. Then add or subtract.

$$3\frac{1}{3} - 1\frac{1}{6} = \frac{10}{3} - \frac{7}{6} = \frac{20}{6} - \frac{7}{6} = \frac{13}{6} = 2\frac{1}{6}$$

Find the sum or difference.
Write the answer as a mixed number in simplest form.

1. $1\frac{7}{8} - \frac{5}{8} = $ _____

2. $3\frac{1}{5} + 2\frac{3}{5} = $ _____

3. $2\frac{1}{3} + 3\frac{3}{9} = $ _____

4. $4\frac{3}{7} - 2\frac{5}{7} = $ _____

5. $3\frac{7}{8} + 2\frac{1}{4} = $ _____

6. $5\frac{1}{2} - 2\frac{3}{4} = $ _____

Add and Subtract Mixed Numbers

Solve Word Problems with Fractions

Find the sum or difference. Write the answers in simplest form.

1. Ben read $\frac{1}{2}$ of a book for a homework assignment. Later, he read another $\frac{1}{3}$ of the book. How much of the book has Ben read so far?

_____

2. The high school sold tickets to a talent show. They started with $5\frac{1}{3}$ rolls of tickets. They sold $3\frac{2}{3}$ of the rolls. How many rolls of tickets do they have left?

_____

3. Ms. Snow wants to make a quilt. She has some fabric that measures $\frac{3}{8}$ yard, $\frac{5}{8}$ yard, and $1\frac{7}{8}$ yards. How much fabric does she have in all?

_____

4. There were 10 pizzas at a party. The guests ate $7\frac{3}{8}$ of all the pizza. How much pizza was left?

_____

5. A piece of paper was $4\frac{1}{2}$ inches wide. It was trimmed $\frac{5}{8}$ of an inch. How wide is the paper now?

_____

6. Anna ran $1\frac{1}{3}$ miles yesterday and $1\frac{3}{4}$ miles today. How far did she run in the two days?

_____

7. A baker had $5\frac{1}{4}$ cups of flour. He used $3\frac{1}{2}$ cups of flour to make biscuits. How much flour does he have left?

_____

8. My aunt is knitting a scarf. The scarf was $2\frac{5}{6}$ feet long. Then she knit another $\frac{2}{3}$ foot. How long is the scarf now?

_____

Word Problems with Fractions   ©School Zone Publishing Company 06320

Multiply Fractions by Whole Numbers

Multiplication of a fraction by a whole number is repeated addition of the fraction.

$$4 \times \frac{1}{3} = \frac{1}{3} + \frac{1}{3} + \frac{1}{3} + \frac{1}{3} = \frac{4}{3}$$

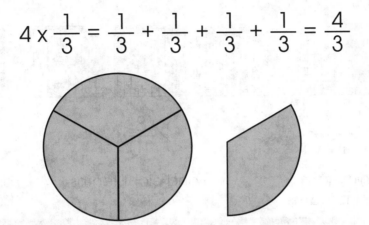

This is the same as multiplying the numerator of the fraction by the whole number.

$$6 \times \frac{3}{5} = \frac{18}{5}$$

Write each addition problem as a multiplication problem.
Find each sum and product. Write the answers in simplest form.

1. $\frac{1}{2} + \frac{1}{2} + \frac{1}{2} =$ _____

   _____ x _____ = _____

2. $\frac{3}{8} + \frac{3}{8} + \frac{3}{8} + \frac{3}{8} =$ _____

   _____ x _____ = _____

3. $\frac{1}{5} + \frac{1}{5} =$ _____

   _____ x _____ = _____

4. $\frac{6}{7} + \frac{6}{7} + \frac{6}{7} + \frac{6}{7} + \frac{6}{7} =$ _____

   _____ x _____ = _____

Write each multiplication problem as an addition problem.
Find each product and sum. Write the answers in simplest form.

5. $2 \times \frac{1}{9} =$ _____

   _____ + _____ = _____

6. $3 \times \frac{5}{4} =$ _____

   _____ + _____ + _____ = _____

Multiply Fractions

Fractions-Tenths and Hundredths

Study these examples to learn about fractions with 10 or 100 as the denominator.

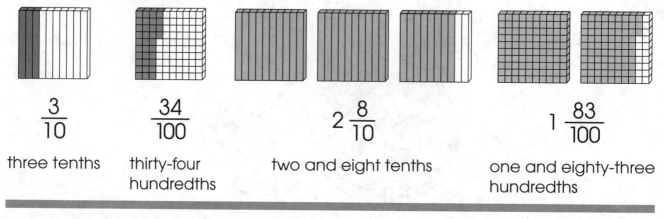

$\dfrac{3}{10}$

three tenths

$\dfrac{34}{100}$

thirty-four hundredths

$2\dfrac{8}{10}$

two and eight tenths

$1\dfrac{83}{100}$

one and eighty-three hundredths

Write the fraction or mixed number for the colored part of each picture. Then write the fraction word name.

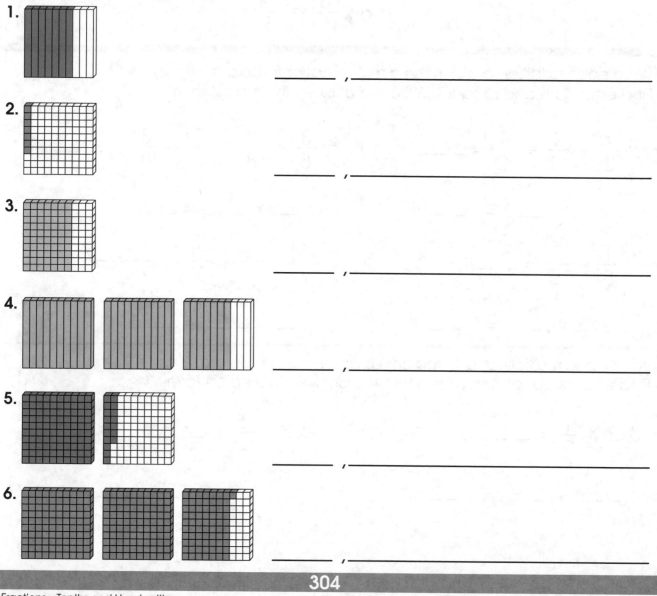

1. _____ , _____

2. _____ , _____

3. _____ , _____

4. _____ , _____

5. _____ , _____

6. _____ , _____

Decimal Place Value

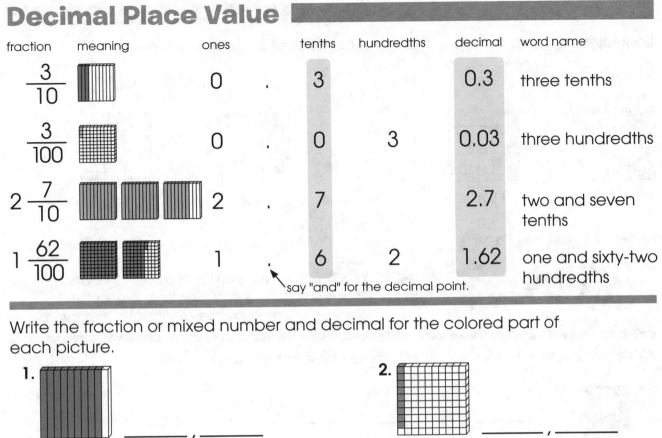

fraction	meaning	ones		tenths	hundredths	decimal	word name
$\frac{3}{10}$		0	.	3		0.3	three tenths
$\frac{3}{100}$		0	.	0	3	0.03	three hundredths
$2\frac{7}{10}$		2	.	7		2.7	two and seven tenths
$1\frac{62}{100}$		1	.	6	2	1.62	one and sixty-two hundredths

say "and" for the decimal point.

Write the fraction or mixed number and decimal for the colored part of each picture.

1. _____ , _____

2. _____ , _____

3. 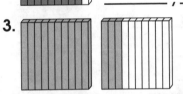 _____ , _____

4. _____ , _____

Write the decimal for each number name.

5. three and eight tenths _____

6. thirty-eight hundredths _____

7. five and seven hundredths _____

8. fifty-seven hundredths _____

Tell the place value of the **5** in each number.

9. 3.**5** _____

10. **5**.3 _____

11. 3.2**5** _____

12. **5**3.7 _____

Decimal Place Value

Equivalent Decimals

Equivalent decimals are decimals that name the same amount.

Equivalent decimals:

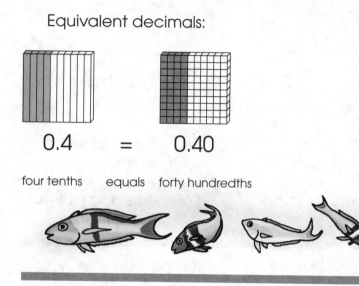

0.4   =   0.40

four tenths   equals   forty hundredths

Decimals **not** equivalent:

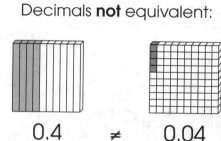

0.4   ≠   0.04

four tenths does not equal four hundredths

Always write a zero in the ones place in a decimal when the value of the decimal is less than 1.

Write two decimals and two word names for each picture.

1. _____ , _____

_____ , _____

2. _____ , _____

_____ , _____

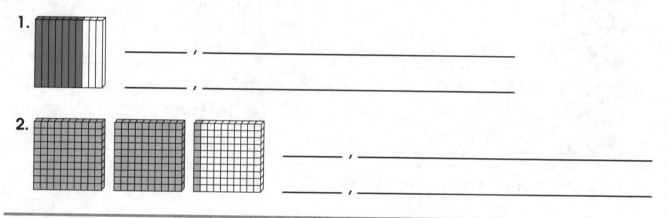

Rewrite each decimal in hundredths.

3. 0.9 = _____   **4.** 0.2 = _____   **5.** 3.6 = _____   **6.** 5.0 = _____

Rewrite each decimal in tenths. Be careful!

7. 1.40 = _____   **8.** 0.60 = _____   **9.** 7.30 = _____   **10.** 0.08 = _____

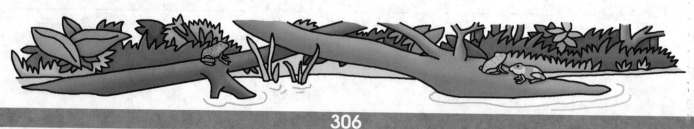

Find Equivalent Decimals

Compare and Order Decimals

Compare **2.38** and **2.8**.

Line up the decimal points.

↓

2.38
2.8

2.8 = 2.80
Write the numbers as equivalent decimals to the same place.

Begin at the left. Find the first place where the digits are different. Then compare.

2.38
2.80

↑
3 tenths < 8 tenths   2.38 < 2.8

> means greater than
< means less than
= means equal to

The sign points to the number that is less.

Compare the numbers. Write **<**, **>**, or **=** in the ⬤.

1. 0.7 ⬤ 0.07   2. 0.39 ⬤ 3.9   3. 3.15 ⬤ 3.5

4. 4.5 ⬤ 4.50   5. 4.5 ⬤ 4.05   6. 2.99 ⬤ 3

7. 3.01 ⬤ 301   8. 8.53 ⬤ 85.3   9. 6 ⬤ 6.00

Write the decimals in order from least to greatest.

10. 0.38 8.3 0.83 3.8

_____

11. 1.05 0.15 1.5 15

_____

12. 0.7 0.07 7 70.0

_____

13. 0.02 0.22 0.2 2.0

_____

14. 346.1 34.61 3,461 346.01

_____

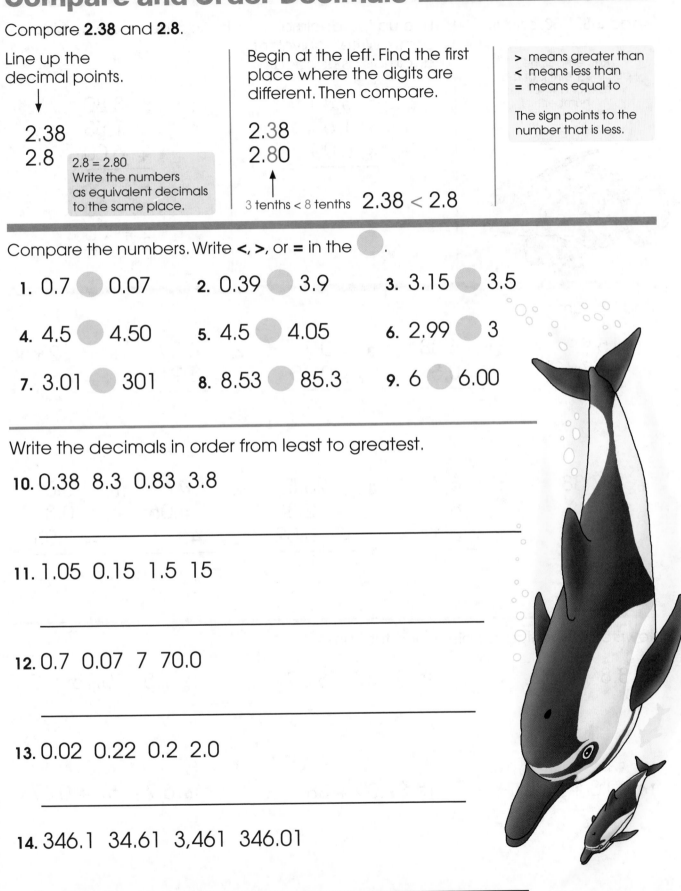

Compare and Order Decimals

Add Decimals

Add **3.8**, **1.53**, and **6**.

Remember the decimal point is at the end of a whole number.
6 = 6.0 or 6.00

Line up the decimal points. Write equivalent decimals as needed.

$$
\begin{array}{r}
3.80 \\
1.53 \\
+\ 6.00 \\
\hline
\end{array}
$$

Add like whole numbers.

$$
\begin{array}{r}
3.80 \\
1.53 \\
+\ 6.00 \\
\hline
3 \\
130 \\
+\ 1000 \\
\hline
11.33
\end{array}
$$

Find the sum.

1. $\begin{array}{r} 5.9 \\ +\ 3.7 \\ \hline \end{array}$

2. $\begin{array}{r} 6.38 \\ +\ 0.5 \\ \hline \end{array}$

3. $\begin{array}{r} 0.7 \\ +\ 0.65 \\ \hline \end{array}$

4. $\begin{array}{r} 4.09 \\ +\ 3.91 \\ \hline \end{array}$

5. $\begin{array}{r} \$23.65 \\ +\ \$9.71 \\ \hline \end{array}$

6. $\begin{array}{r} 7.38 \\ 4.6 \\ +\ 0.38 \\ \hline \end{array}$

7. $\begin{array}{r} 6.7 \\ 8 \\ +\ 0.49 \\ \hline \end{array}$

8. $\begin{array}{r} 23.5 \\ 2.35 \\ +\ 0.02 \\ \hline \end{array}$

9. $\begin{array}{r} 4.6 \\ 4.06 \\ +\ 46 \\ \hline \end{array}$

10. $\begin{array}{r} 3.0 \\ 0.3 \\ +\ 3.03 \\ \hline \end{array}$

Rewrite as a vertical problem. Find the sum.

11. $3.8 + 0.62$

12. $\$4.37 + \$1.99$

13. $1.5 + 0.15 + 5.1$

14. $40.8 + 4.08$

15. $\$7.09 + \$8$

16. $6.7 + 67 + 0.67$

Add Decimals

Subtract Decimals

Subtract: 5.3 – 2.18	Line up the decimal points. Write equivalent decimals as needed.	Subtract like whole numbers. Regroup as needed.	Check:
	$$\begin{array}{r} 5.30 \\ -\ 2.18 \\ \hline \end{array}$$	$$\begin{array}{r} \overset{2\ 10}{5.\cancel{3}0} \\ -\ 2.18 \\ \hline 3.12 \end{array}$$	$$\begin{array}{r} 3.12 \\ +\ 2.18 \\ \hline 10 \\ 20 \\ +\ 500 \\ \hline 5.30 \end{array}$$

Find the difference.

1. $$\begin{array}{r} 8.3 \\ -\ 1.5 \\ \hline \end{array}$$

2. $$\begin{array}{r} 4.58 \\ -\ 3.9 \\ \hline \end{array}$$

3. $$\begin{array}{r} 6.5 \\ -\ 0.79 \\ \hline \end{array}$$

4. $$\begin{array}{r} \$5.25 \\ -\ \$1.79 \\ \hline \end{array}$$

5. $$\begin{array}{r} \$8.50 \\ -\ \$3.99 \\ \hline \end{array}$$

Rewrite as a vertical problem. Find the difference.

6. 6.5 – 3.8

7. 9 – 3.7

8. $20 – $4.83

9. 7.05 – 1.9

10. 9.2 – 0.92

11. $15.26 – $3.27

Solve each problem.

12. Miss James has 59.3 acres of land. She brought 25 more acres. How much land does she have now?

13. Kevin bought a belt for $5.39. He paid for it with a $10 bill. How much change should he get?

Subtract Decimals

Fractions and Decimals

Circle the correct letter.

1. The word name for 6.7 is _____.

    A. sixty-seven tens

    B. sixty-seven hundredths

    C. six and seven hundredths

    D. six and seven tenths

2. Which set of decimals is in order from least to greatest?

    A. 0.57 5.7 5.07 50.7

    B. 0.57 5.07 5.7 50.7

    C. 5.7 5.07 0.57 50.7

    D. 50.7 5.7 5.07 0.57

3. The red dot is at _____.

    A. 0.1   B. $\dfrac{1}{8}$ C. $\dfrac{7}{8}$ D. $1\dfrac{1}{3}$

4. Which number sentence is not true?

    A. $\dfrac{1}{3} < \dfrac{3}{5}$ B. $\dfrac{3}{5} = \dfrac{2}{4}$

    C. $0.75 > 0.5$ D. $3.8 < 3.88$

5. $8.3 + 0.25 + 4 =$ _____

    A. 12.55

    B. 11.2

    C. 1.12

    D. 8.32

6. $5.3 - 1.79 =$ _____

    A. 3.24

    B. 3.51

    C. 12.6

    D. 7.37

7. $\dfrac{2}{3} + \dfrac{1}{4} =$ _____

    A. $\dfrac{3}{7}$ B. $\dfrac{1}{4}$

    C. $\dfrac{2}{12}$ D. $\dfrac{11}{12}$

8. $\dfrac{3}{4} - \dfrac{1}{8} =$ _____

    A. $\dfrac{1}{3}$ B. $\dfrac{2}{4}$

    C. $\dfrac{1}{4}$ D. $\dfrac{5}{8}$

Measurement Units

In the following table, each row displays equal amounts.

1 km (kilometer)	1000 m (meters)
1 m (meter)	100 cm (centimeters)
1 kg (kilogram)	1000 g (grams)
1 lb (pound)	16 oz (ounces)
1 L (liter)	1000 mL (milliliters)
1 hr (hour)	60 min (minutes)
1 min (minute)	60 sec (seconds)
1 yd (yard)	3 ft (feet)
1 ft (foot)	12 in (inches)

How long is a 6 ft rope in inches?

$$6 \text{ ft} = 6 \times 12 \text{ in} = 72 \text{ in}$$

Solve each problem.

1. A student spent 3 hours at a museum. How many minutes did the student spend at the museum?

   _____

2. A watermelon weighs 4 lbs. How much does the melon weigh in ounces?

   _____

3. Chelsea walked 1 km home from school. How far did she walk in centimeters?

   _____

4. How many milliliters of soda are in a 2 L bottle?

   _____

Measurement Units

More with Measurement Units

Robert is 5 feet (ft) 2 inches (in) tall. How tall is he in inches?

$$5 \text{ ft} = 5 \times 12 \text{ in} = 60 \text{ in}$$
$$60 \text{ in} + 2 \text{ in} = 62 \text{ in}$$

Solve each problem.

1. A school held a 5/4 km race. How far did the runners race in meters?

_____

2. How many inches are around a rectangle that is 4 feet long and 3 feet wide?

_____

3. Frida is 4 ft 10 in tall. How many inches tall is she?

_____

4. Billy is 4 feet tall. His older brother is 5 inches taller. His sister is 8 inches taller than his older brother. Is Billy's sister taller or shorter than 5 ft? How much taller or how much shorter?

_____

5. There are 100 pennies in 1 dollar. A certain postage stamp costs 83 pennies. How much does the postage stamp cost in dollars? Give your answer both in a fraction and a decimal.

_____

6. There are 25 pennies in 1 quarter. Loren paid 9 quarters for a greeting card. How much money did he spend in dollars? Give your answer as a decimal.

_____

7. This line segment represents 1 meter. What length does the dash, labeled $\frac{7}{10}$, represent in centimeters?

$$\frac{7}{10}$$

_____

Area and Perimeter

The **perimeter** is the distance around a figure. Perimeter is measured in linear units. The **area** is the number of square units needed to cover a figure. Area is measured in square units.

A rectangle has two pairs of equal sides.

3 cm

5 cm

This rectangle has a length of 5 cm and a width of 3 cm.

Its perimeter is 3 cm + 5 cm + 3 cm + 5 cm = 16 cm.

Its area is 5 cm x 3 cm = 15 cm².

The perimeter of any rectangle is P = 2*l* + 2*w*, where *l* is the length of the rectangle and *w* is the width of the rectangle.

The area of any rectangle is A = *l* x *w*, where *l* is the length of the rectangle and *w* is the width of the rectangle.

Find the perimeter and area of each rectangle.

1.

6 in

7 in

perimeter _____

area _____

2.

2 ft

10 ft

perimeter _____

area _____

Find the length of the room given the area and the width.

3. A room with an area of 110 ft² is 10 ft wide.

110 = *l* x 10

length _____

313

Line Plots

Jesse has a coin collection. The following line plot shows how many coins in the collection have a given diameter in inches. There is an X for each coin with the given diameter.

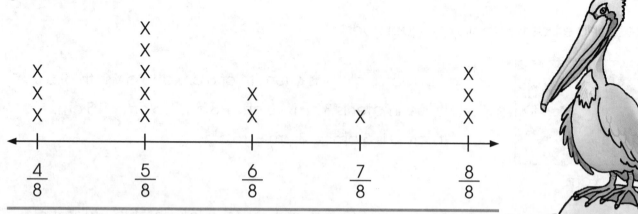

Solve each problem. All answers should be in inches.

1. What is the difference in diameter between the largest coins and the smallest coins, in simplest form? _____

2. Jesse takes 1 coin with a diameter of $\frac{5}{8}$ in and 1 coin with a diameter of $\frac{7}{8}$ in. What is the sum of the diameters of these two coins, in simplest form? _____

3. Jesse takes 1 coin with a diameter of $\frac{4}{8}$ in and 1 coin with a diameter of $\frac{6}{8}$ in. What is the sum of the diameters of these two coins, in simplest form? _____

4. Jesse takes 1 coin with a diameter of $\frac{4}{8}$ in and 1 coin with a diameter of $\frac{7}{8}$ in. What is the sum of the diameters of these two coins, in simplest form? _____

5. What is the sum of the diameters of all the coins? _____

Angles

An **angle** is formed by two rays or line segments sharing a common endpoint.

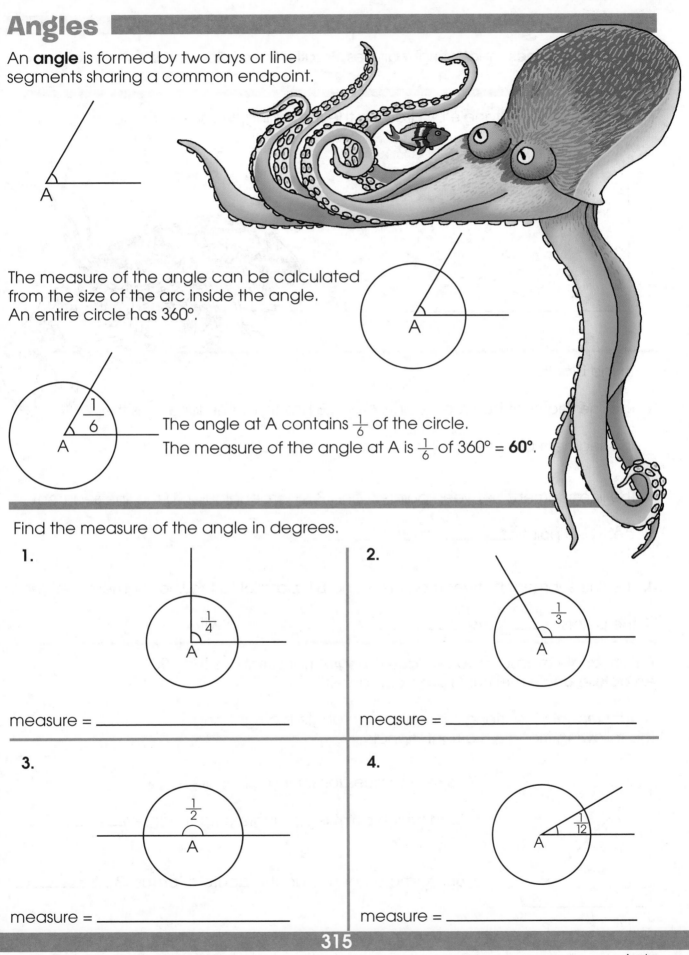

A

The measure of the angle can be calculated from the size of the arc inside the angle. An entire circle has 360°.

A

$\frac{1}{6}$

A

The angle at A contains $\frac{1}{6}$ of the circle.
The measure of the angle at A is $\frac{1}{6}$ of 360° = **60°**.

Find the measure of the angle in degrees.

1.

$\frac{1}{4}$

A

measure = _____

2.

$\frac{1}{3}$

A

measure = _____

3.

$\frac{1}{2}$

A

measure = _____

4.

$\frac{1}{12}$

A

measure = _____

315

Angles

Lines, Angles, and Shapes

Perpendicular lines meet at right angles. **Parallel lines** follow the same direction and never touch.

1. Complete the rectangle by drawing the remaining two sides.

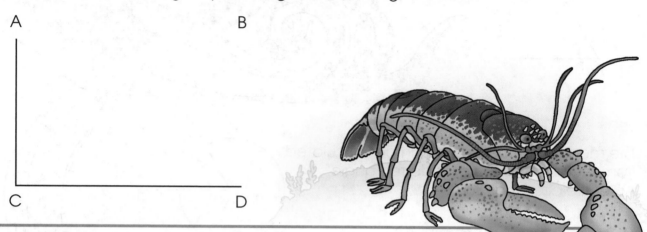

Fill in the blanks.

2. The line segment between points A and B has the same length as the

line segment between points _____ and _____.

3. The line segment between points A and B is perpendicular to the line segment

between points _____ and _____.

4. The line segment between points A and B is parallel to the line segment between

the points _____ and _____.

A **right angle** measures 90°. An **acute angle** measures less than 90°. An **obtuse angle** measures greater than 90°.

A **right triangle** is a triangle in which one angle is a right angle. The following triangle is a right triangle.

Answer the questions using this figure.

5. At which point is the angle a right angle? _____

6. Are the other two angles acute or obtuse? _____

Activities to Share

In 1989, the National Council of Teachers of Mathematics (NCTM) developed the Curriculum and Evaluation Standards for School Mathematics. These standards specify that the mathematics curriculum should emphasize problem solving, using reasoning skills, communicating about mathematics, and making connections among math topics. It also specifies that children should learn to value mathematics and become confident in their own abilities. The NCTM advises that children have hands-on and varied experiences; use manipulatives, calculators, and computers; and work in pairs or cooperative groups. The NCTM wants children to "do" math, "make sense" of math, and "connect" math to real life to develop the skills necessary to function in today's society.

At home, you can help your child accomplish the NCTM goals. Here are some ways to follow up the math activities in this book and nurture a curiosity for mathematical ideas:

Follow Up the Lessons. Follow up the math lessons in this book by asking similar questions or thinking of similar problems. Urge your child to talk about mathematics to develop communication skills. Also ask how math lessons in school are similar to the activities you share at home.

Keep a Math Journal. Have your child record math vocabulary words as they appear in the lessons. Review these words from time to time. Have him or her record interesting problems and puzzles, as well as ways math is used at home, in stores, and in the neighborhood. Take the journal on trips so your child can make entries about numbers on signs or buildings, record license plate numbers, write down times and temperatures, make a list of words that can be made from the letters in the word *mathematics*, or figure out how many ways a number can be written (e.g., 10: $4 + 6$, $3 + 3 + 2 + 2$, $2 \times 3 + 4$). Many of the Go for It! extension activities can be written in the math journal.

Do Math Every Day. Nurture your child's curiosity by asking a math question every day. Ask your child to help you figure out an answer to a real-life problem, such as finding the best buy or measuring something. Ask him or her about shapes in nature and man-made things, such as boxes or buildings. Plan periodic "scavenger hunts" to look for mathematics in the home, at an event, or in the park. Involve other members of the family, friends, or neighbors occasionally to work cooperatively towards a solution.

Follow a Recipe. This is an enjoyable way for your child to practice using fractions. Challenge your child to double or halve a recipe. Use measuring cups and spoons. Help your child learn how many ounces are in a cup, how many cups are in a quart, and how many quarts are in a gallon.

Activities to Share

Activities to Share

By third grade, most children are reading independently, but that's no reason to stop reading aloud to your child. Reading and talking about books you read together are wonderful ways to develop your child's language arts skills—reading, writing, listening, and speaking. Show your child you value reading by taking time to read yourself. Talk about what you're reading, too.

Be on the lookout for opportunities in your daily routine to read and write with your child. Write shopping lists together. At the grocery store, read signs and food labels. Ask your child to read signs and billboards. As you work in the kitchen, encourage your child to read recipes with you, and when assembling a toy or using an appliance for the first time, have your child help you read and follow the directions.

Here are some additional language arts activities for you and your child:

Word Chains and Circles Give your child a word and then have him or her change the word into a different word by changing a single letter. For example: *cane, cone; done, dome; dime, dire; tire, tore.* Encourage your child to make a long chain.

Compound Word Chains Start your child out with a compound word. Then challenge your child to make a chain of compound words by changing one word of the compound at a time. For example: *honeybee, beekeeper, housekeeper, treehouse, treetop, etc.*

Draw the Idioms Explain that English has many expressions that mean something very different from the meanings of the individual words. Give examples, such as *He was flat broke, She threw caution to the wind,* or *He is beside himself with anger.* Think of some familiar idioms together and encourage your child to draw the literal meanings of the expressions.

Postcards Postcards aren't just for vacations. Buy postcards or have your child make some of heavy postcard stock cut to standard size. Show your child where to write the salutation, date, address, body, closing, and signature. Encourage your child to write to relatives and friends close to home or far away. Everyone loves to get postcards. Encourage grandparents and other relatives to send postcards to your child. Letters and e-mail are fun to send and receive, too.

Story in a Box Fill a shoebox with a number of small, interesting items, such as figurines, tickets, natural objects, and so on. Have your child reach in and pull out three items. Ask your child to study the items and write a story that includes all three.

Activities to Share

The social studies range from geography to history, from economics to citizenship and government. Generally speaking, they are the study of how people relate to their environment and to one another.

You can make **geography** and **regional studies** meaningful to your child by relating them to your own home and community. Talk about your town and the types of houses people live in there. If you live in a region where the winters are cold, point out how the homes are built to be warm in the winter. If you live in a warm climate, explain to your child that your home has features that help it stay cool. Ask your child to imagine what it would be like to live in a different climate.

You have many opportunities to teach your child **map skills**. Together, you can draw a map of your house showing your escape plan in case of fire or another emergency. You can also involve your child in planning a route for a trip. Study a map together and discuss the various symbols. Show your child the route you intend to take.

Being aware of how we use and protect **natural resources** is becoming increasingly important as the population grows and resources become more scarce. If you have a good-sized yard, you and your child can make your own small "national park." Set aside an area that you will allow to grow naturally. If you live in the plains, your national park may become a prairie. If you live in a desert climate, very little may grow there. Observe your national park to see if any animals move in. If they do, observe them carefully so you don't disturb them.

Many youngsters are fascinated with the culture and history of **Native Americans**. You and your child will enjoy making—and eating—this Native American fried bread.

Ingredients:

2 1/2 cups flour	1 tsp. salt	3/4 cup warm water
1 1/2 tbs. baking powder	1 tbs. dried skim milk	1 tbs. vegetable oil

Mix the flour, baking powder, and salt in a large bowl. Mix the powdered milk, water, and vegetable oil in a small bowl. Mix the liquid with the dry ingredients and stir until the dough is smooth. Knead the dough for 30 seconds. Cover it with a cloth and let it sit for 10 minutes. Divide the dough in half and keep dividing each piece in half until you have 8 pieces. Roll each piece of dough into a circle 8 to 10 inches across. In a large frying pan, heat about 1 inch of vegetable oil. Fry each circle of dough until golden brown. Drain on paper towels. Serve the bread hot.

©School Zone Publishing Company 06320

Activities to Share

You and your child will enjoy these hands-on science activities. You will find that science skills, such as predicting, observing, measuring, classifying, analyzing, and evaluating, come naturally as your child's innate curiosity about the world and how it works is engaged.

The **physical science** concept of buoyancy taught in this book is easy to demonstrate at home. Float margarine or yogurt containers in a container of water. Add objects to them until they sink and then weigh the objects. Explore reasons why it took different amounts of weight to sink different containers. Another way to demonstrate this concept is by filling a container with water to the very top. Place the container in another, empty, container. Put a solid object in the first container so that some of the water overflows. Measure the volume of water that is displaced by the object. Explain that the weight of this volume of water equals the buoyancy of the water.

Extend the **natural science** concepts in this book by observing nature with your child. With your child, examine a flower's parts. Using the diagram in the book, identify the parts. Look at flowers gone to seed and flowers that have changed into fruit. Explain that fruits are one way that plants spread their seeds so that new plants can grow. Find out together the role that insects play in the development of seeds.

Earth and space concepts can be as close as your backyard. Your child learned about satellites and other space devices in this book. If you live in an area without too much light, you can see satellites almost any night. On a dark, clear night, look for starlike points of light that move very slowly in a straight line across the sky. If they look too small to be airplanes, they are likely to be satellites.

Explain that soil is ground-up rocks and minerals mixed with decayed plant material. Find out what kind of soil is most common in the area where you live. If you have a garden, show your child how you enrich the soil. Encourage your child to help you with planting, weeding, and other gardening tasks.

It is especially important to put the concept of **nutrition** into practice in everyday life. Help your child plan a meal. Make a chart with spaces for protein, fiber, carbohydrates, and fat. Allow your child to fill out the chart with a favorite food from each category. As long as the choices create a balanced meal, let your child choose a family dinner.

Big Third & Fourth Grade Workbook **06320**